Unwin Critical Library
GENERAL EDITOR : CLAUDE RAWSON

THE AMBASSADORS

The Ambassadors

ALAN W. BELLRINGER

Senior Lecturer in English,
University College of North Wales, Bangor

London
GEORGE ALLEN & UNWIN
Boston   Sydney

George Allen & Unwin (Publishers) Ltd,
40 Museum Street, London WC1A 1LU, UK

George Allen & Unwin (Publishers) Ltd,
Park Lane, Hemel Hempstead, Herts HP2 4TE, UK

Allen & Unwin, Inc.,
9 Winchester Terrace, Winchester, Mass. 01890, USA

George Allen & Unwin Australia Pty Ltd,
8 Napier Street, North Sydney, NSW 2060, Australia

First published in 1984.

British Library Cataloguing in Publication Data

Bellringer, Alan W.
   The ambassadors.—(Unwin critical library)
1. James, Henry, *1843–1916*. Ambassadors, The
I. Title
813'.4   PS2116.A53
ISBN 0–04–800026–4

Library of Congress Cataloging in Publication Data

Bellringer, Alan W.
   The ambassadors.
(Unwin critical library)
Bibliography: p.
Includes index.
1. James, Henry, 1843–1916. The ambassadors.
I. Title.   II. Series.
PS2116.A53B42 1984   813'.4   84–381
ISBN 0–04–800026–4

Set in 10 on 11 point Plantin by Phoenix Photosetting, Chatham and
printed in Great Britain
by
Biddles Ltd, Guildford, Surrey

ACKNOWLEDGEMENTS

I am grateful to Claude Rawson, the General Editor of this series, for advice, correction and encouragement during my writing of this book. I acknowledge also the assistance of the British Academy in awarding me a research grant from the Small Grants Research Fund in the Humanities to enable me to trace Strether's footsteps in Paris. I am indebted to my colleagues in the Bangor English Department and to Professor Alan Büsst of the French Department for their intellectual and psychological support, and to my wife, Wendie, to whom this book is dedicated, for constant thoughtfulness and wit-sharpening. I am grateful to Joyce L. Williams and Ann McCallum for secretarial assistance.

ACKNOWLEDGMENTS

GENERAL EDITOR'S PREFACE

Each volume in this series is devoted to a single major text. It is intended for serious students and teachers of literature, and for knowledgeable non-academic readers. It aims to provide a scholarly introduction and a stimulus to critical thought and discussion.

Individual volumes will naturally differ from one another in arrangement and emphasis, but each will normally begin with information on a work's literary and intellectual background, and other guidance designed to help the reader to an informed understanding. This is followed by an extended critical discussion of the work itself, and each contributor in the series has been encouraged to present in these sections his own reading of the work, whether or not this is controversial, rather than to attempt a mere consensus. Some volumes, including those on *Paradise Lost* and *Ulysses*, vary somewhat from the more usual pattern by entering into substantive critical discussion at the outset, and allowing the necessary background material to emerge at the points where it is felt to arise from the argument in the most useful and relevant way. Each volume also contains a historical survey of the work's critical reputation, including an account of the principal lines of approach and areas of controversy, and a selective (but detailed) bibliography.

The hope is that the volumes in this series will be among those which a university teacher would normally recommend for any serious study of a particular text, and that they will also be among the essential secondary texts to be consulted in some scholarly investigations. But the experienced and informed non-academic reader has also been in our minds, and one of our aims has been to provide him with reliable and stimulating works of reference and guidance, embodying the present state of knowledge and opinion in a conveniently accessible form.

C.J.R.
University of Warwick,
December 1979

PREFACE

Henry James's stature as a classic novelist writing in English is, a hundred years after the epoch in which he flourished, though not seriously in doubt, vulnerable to impatient judgements. One problem is that James seems to escape the usual advantages of time and place. As an American who preferred England he lacks the rooted native pride or regionalism which gives so much fiction its strength of character. Again, as a technical innovator breaking new ground James is not a typical representative of his age, the mid- and late-Victorian and the Edwardian periods. Always avant-garde, writing the novels of the future, James narrowed the audience of good fiction and dangerously raised the stakes. James's interest in personal relationships rather than in personalities, in consciousness rather than in action, in situation rather than in event, in openmindedness rather than in 'causes' makes his work altogether too subtle, complex and indirect for the devotee of the quick, comfortable 'read'. At the same time his insistence on intelligence and a civilised tone restricts the social milieu of his characters generally to people of ample income and their dependents. James's apparent view that all but the culturally refined and morally sensitive echelon of society is essentially boring undoubtedly drains his fiction of half the life, humour, pathos, violence and robustness which had kept the novel, up to his day, a popular art-form. Lacking, then, in local colour, period charm, simplicity of feeling and breadth of human knowledge, why do his novels fascinate so? The answer lies partly in the changing conditions in which literature has been produced and studied since James's death, the increasing compartmentalising and professionalising of writing into 'English'. James is very much the specialist's novelist. He appeals to most of those who with varying degrees of guilt and pride have made literature their career or part of their career. His subject-matter – the comparison of cultures, the impingement of money and power on art and taste, the preservation of restraint and reasonableness in a post-religious era – is largely their subject-matter still, too. James's respect for science, yet fastidious diffidence before its methods, his suspicion of politics, detachment from nationalism, love of art, indifference to religion, fear of sex, refined scrupulosity of conscience, commitment to friendship, cultivation of the genial intellectual tone are traits which, give or take one or two, many literary and academic intellectuals share or like, or like to dislike. But, although these values are mediated with varying degrees of effectiveness in James's novels, tales and essays and in the associated biographical texts, the ultimate secret of James's high reputation is linguistic. James's language is dense with felicitous irony, allusion, metaphor, playfulness and endless suspense of meaning. Once having determined not to be fatigued, his readers are caught in an ongoing pleasure. James is one of those writers who grow on you, of whom the third reading, or the fourth, if you live long enough, yields more fruit even than you expected, and you expected a lot.

A glance at the voluminous bibliographies of writings about James will confirm that, despite various memorable pleas for this or that work, his wider reputation rests on three main works: *The Portrait of a Lady*, 'The Turn of the Screw' and *The Ambassadors*. Critical discussion of these three texts is phenomenally prolific. The first, though a beautiful, deeply amusing and also chilling story, was largely written to a formula, I feel, and does not raise the particular Jamesian critical problems in their full complexity. The novella is a masterpiece of terror, the very ambivalent seriousness of which accounts for its fame or, rather, notoriety. It is the third of these works, *The Ambassadors*, the first-written of James's three last completed long novels, which surely selects itself as the crucial Jamesian 'case', for consideration as the key-specimen of his achievement. Written when he was at the height of his powers, when he had perfected his point-of-view method and found a subject which was, we can say, right up his street, *The Ambassadors* astonished even James himself by its artistry. In spite of the inevitable knocks it has had, it holds its own today, as I hope to show, for its engagement with lively issues and its incredible poise.

CONTENTS

TEXT AND REFERENCES

The text of Henry James's *The Ambassadors* quoted in this work is that of the first English book edition, published by Methuen in September 1903. The chapters are numbered in roman numerals (e.g. chapter XXX).

Full details of all works cited will be found in the Bibliography. The principal references are abbreviated as follows:

Blackmur   R. P. Blackmur, *The Art of the Novel: Critical Prefaces by Henry James* (New York: Scribner, 1934).

Cargill   O. Cargill, *The Novels of Henry James* (New York: Macmillan, 1961).

Edel 1   Leon Edel, *Henry James: The Untried Years, 1843–1870* (London: Hart-Davis, 1953).

Edel 2   Leon Edel, *Henry James: The Conquest of London, 1870–1883* (London: Hart-Davis, 1962).

Edel 3   Leon Edel, *Henry James: The Middle Years, 1884–1894* (London: Hart-Davis, 1963).

Edel 4   Leon Edel, *Henry James: The Treacherous Years, 1895–1900* (London: Hart-Davis, 1969).

Edel 5   Leon Edel, *Henry James: The Master, 1901–1916* (London: Hart-Davis, 1972).

Letters   *Henry James Letters*, ed. Leon Edel, 3 vols (London: Macmillan, 1975).

Lubbock   *The Letters of Henry James*, ed. Percy Lubbock, 2 vols (London: Macmillan, 1920).

Notebooks   *The Notebooks of Henry James*, ed. F. O. Matthiessen and K. B. Murdock (New York: Oxford Univeristy Press, 1947).

Super   *The Complete Prose Works of Matthew Arnold*, ed. R. H. Super, 11 vols (Ann Arbor, Mich.: University of Michigan Press, 1960–76).

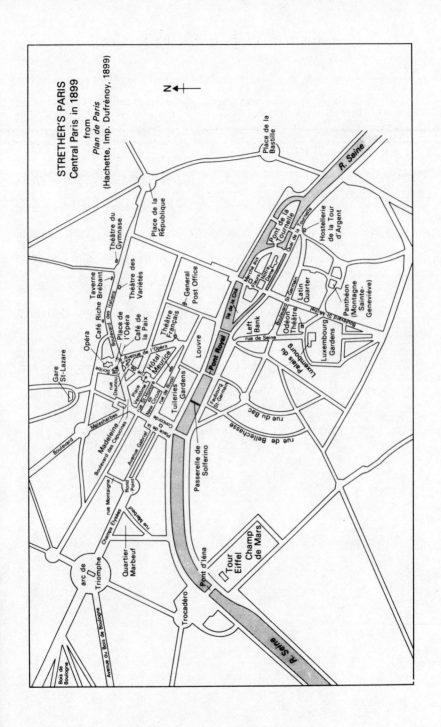

STRETHER'S PARIS
Central Paris in 1899
from
Plan de Paris
(Hachette, Imp. Dufrénoy, 1899)

N

R. Seine

Place de la Bastille

Place de la République

Théâtre du Gymnase

Taverne
Café Riche Brébant
Théâtre des Variétés

Boulevard des Italiens
Opéra

Place de l'Opéra
Café de la Paix

Théâtre Français

Général Post Office

Ile de la Cité

Marché aux Fleurs
Notre Dame

Pont de la Tournelle

Quai de la Tournelle

Hostellerie de la Tour d'Argent

Boulevard St-Germain

Latin Quarter

Panthéon (Montagne Sainte-Geneviève)

Boulevard St-Michel

Gare St-Lazare

rue Scribe
rue Auber

Avenue de l'Opéra
rue Daunou

Hôtel Maurice

Odéon Théâtre

Left Bank

rue de Seine

Luxembourg Gardens

Faubourg St-Germain

Malesherbes

Boulevard des Capucines

Place Vendôme
rue St Honoré
New Circus
rue de Rivoli

Louvre

Tuileries Gardens

Pont Royal

rue du Bac

rue de Bellechasse

Boulevard de la Madeleine

Avenue Gabriel

Place de la Concorde

Passerelle de Solferino

rue Montaigne

Rond Point

Champs Elysées

rue Marbeuf

arc de Triomphe

Quartier Marbeuf

Pont d'Iéna

Tour Eiffel

Champ de Mars

Trocadéro

R. Seine

Bois de Boulogne

Avenue du Bois de Boulogne

For Wendie

CHAPTER 1

Biographical Setting

In 1903, when *The Ambassadors* was published, Henry James was a man of 60, an American citizen who had been resident for the previous twenty-seven years in England. It was his seventeenth novel to be published, but his sixteenth to be written. Its composition, begun in the summer of 1900 after the completion of *The Sacred Fount*, spanned the turn of the century and was finished by mid-1901, when James went on directly to work on *The Wings of the Dove* (1902). The Boer War was being fought at that time. James hated the war and felt that it had sickened and 'finished' Queen Victoria, whose death, early in 1901, he thought would 'let loose incalculable forces for possible ill' (J. Hasler, *Switzerland in the Life and Work of Henry James* (1966), p. 143). *The Ambassadors* was composed orally by James; he dictated it directly to his typists, the bulk of it to a Scottish stenographer, William Macalpine, and the last chapters, from April 1901, to his new typist, Mary Weld. The text was typed with wide-spaced lines so that subsequent revisions could be made; the 'resultant script was then re-typed' (H. Montgomery Hyde, *Henry James at Home* (1969), p. 146). The work was done partly in the Reform Club, London, and partly in the Green Room and the Garden Room at Lamb House, Rye, James's home since 1898. A 'troublesome eczema' bothered him during the producing of *The Ambassadors* text. However, he devoted a considerable amount of his spare time thereabouts to the pleasant company of his 14-year-old niece, Peggy, then staying with a family in Harrow; he took her to the cinema, then in its earliest phase, to *Twelfth Night* at the theatre and to museums, spent Christmas with her at Rye, encouraged her to read Scott's novels, corrected her American speech and accompanied her on walks with his dog (Edel 5, pp. 83–92). There may be some reflection of Peggy's potential in the portrait of Mamie Pocock in *The Ambassadors*. Peggy's father, William James, and her mother and brother, visited Henry James at Rye for several weeks in the spring of 1901, William having to deliver his lectures on *The Varieties of Religious Experience* in Edinburgh. Such was the immediate background of experience to the novel.

The Ambassadors uses an English background very lightly, however, and only at the beginning; it has no British characters. It relies on James's knowledge of America and France for most of its contents, without being closely autobiographical at all. Henry James wrote fiction from the stance of the intelligent and informed imagination: the records of his life have only an indirect bearing on his novels. Henry James was a New Yorker, the second son of a financially independent, very unorthodox intellectual, and had by 1900 spent more than half his life out of the United States. He was born on 15 April 1843, at 21 Washington Place, between Broadway and Washington Square. At the age of six months he was taken to live in a cottage near Windsor Castle in England and in the following year to Paris, where he was to locate his earliest memory: it was of the Place Vendôme and its column erected in honour of Napoleonic victories, 'a tall and glorious column'. This 'admirable aspect' impressed itself upon the infant James through 'the clear window of the vehicle as we passed' (*A Small Boy and Others* (1913), pp. 57–8). From 1845 to 1847 the James family lived in Albany, in New York State, a town a hundred miles north of New York; near the homes of his paternal grandmother and uncle. The James family then returned to New York, settling near Union Square. It was here that Henry James was a small boy, met Emerson and Thackeray, read *Punch*, heard *David Copperfield* read aloud and saw plays by Shakespeare and Boucicault (Edel 1, pp. 90–103). He was educated by a large number of teachers at a succession of schools. His father, opposed to pedantry and dogma, experimented freely with his sons' education, so that, as James later wrote, 'The literal played in our education as small a part as it perhaps ever played in any', but the 'presence of paradox was so bright among us' (*A Small Boy and Others* (1913), p. 227). He was never permanently attached to any school or college.

The James family spent three years from 1855 to 1858 abroad. Henry James attended a language school in Geneva, resided in St John's Wood in London, where he had lessons from a Scottish tutor and a French governess, and then went to a Fourierist school in Paris. Later he was enrolled at the Collège Impérial in Boulogne, where he met the young B. C. Coquelin, who was later to act in *Cyrano de Bergerac*. While he was in Paris at the age of 13, as James relates in his autobiography, he paced the city streets for impressions, enjoying particularly the quays of the Left Bank with their book-shops and print-shops, the gardens and art galleries of the Luxembourg Palace, the style of the old buildings, and the overwhelming artistic heritage of the Louvre; he felt he had 'looked at France and looked at Europe, looked even at America as Europe itself might be conceived so to look, looked at history, as a still-felt past and a complacently personal future, at society, manners, types, characters, possibilities and prodigies and mysteries of fifty sorts' (*A Small Boy and Others* (1913), p. 366). Such impressions, relating clearly to the international theme of *The Ambassadors*, seemed to James a fortunate 'order' of education, and were often renewed. Next, for over a year James lived with his family in Newport, Rhode Island, where he read Latin at the Berkeley Institute (Edel 1, p. 146) and Ruskin privately. But in late 1859 they again travelled to Europe. James was enrolled at the Institution Rochette in Geneva, where he studied mathematics and languages, and he subsequently studied Latin and read Schiller privately in Bonn. From 1860 to 1864 the family lived in Newport again. James took no part in the American Civil War, owing to a back injury. He studied law at Harvard from September 1862 for a year. From 1864 to 1866 the James family lived at 13 Ashburton Place, Boston. James began contributing reviews and short stories to literary periodicals from 1864 onwards. From August to December of that year he stayed at Northampton, Massachusetts, a health resort, which he connected with Balzac's provincial scenes and characters (Edel 1, p. 209) and which may serve in part as the model for Woollett in *The Ambassadors*. In the autumn of 1866 the James family moved to 20 Quincy Street, Cambridge, Massachusetts, which was to be permanently 'home' for James from then onwards. Over the next three years he wrote up to a dozen short stories on American themes, encouraged by William Dean Howells, the assistant editor of the *Atlantic Monthly*. Howells became himself the most distinguished realist American novelist of his generation, though he preserved a more restrictive attitude to sex in fiction than James did. It was Howells's later speech about what he had missed in life which formed the original root of *The Ambassadors*.

In 1869 and 1870, James returned to Europe, but this time alone. He met leading literary figures in London and toured from Malvern to Oxford. He revisited Switzerland, and then saw the principal cities of Italy. On his way back to England he stayed briefly in Paris, visiting the Louvre, the Gymnase and the Théâtre Français, where he saw Coquelin in Molière. Returning to New England, he wrote his first novel, *Watch and Ward* (serialised, 1871), and served as an art reviewer for the *Atlantic Monthly*, noticing among others the exhibition of French paintings at a gallery in Tremont Street, Boston, the place recalled by Strether in chapter XXX of *The Ambassadors* in the passage about the Lambinet landscape. In May 1872, James again sailed for Europe, this time commissioned to write travel articles for the *Nation*. He stopped first in Chester at the Queen Hotel, an establishment like the one featured at the beginning of *The Ambassadors*. He was accompanied by his aunt and sister, the latter of whom he sketched sitting looking out into the garden through an ivy-framed 'casement' (*Letters*, Vol. 1, p. 285). They travelled through Switzerland, Italy, Austria and Germany. Henry James saw his relatives to their boat at Liverpool and then returned alone to Paris, mixing mainly with American visitors such as J. R. Lowell, G. E. Norton and Emerson. The year 1873 was spent mainly in Italy, among artists and friends, but he spent the summer in Switzerland and Germany. He wrote tales and essays, and in 1874 began *Roderick Hudson* while living in Florence. Later the same year he returned to America to complete the novel. He spent the first six months of 1875 in New York, living by reviewing, and was eventually engaged by the *New York Tribune* to be its correspondent in Paris, where he arrived on 11 November.

In 1875, James hoped to settle in Paris, but at the end of 1876 he sailed for Britain for good. 'I saw that I should be an eternal outsider,' he said of his year in France (Edel 2, p. 270). He took an apartment in the rue de Luxembourg. He cultivated the acquaintance of Turgenev and met Flaubert, Zola, Daudet and Maupassant, but became disillusioned with what he considered the narrowness of the French literary mind. He enjoyed reading George Eliot's *Daniel Deronda* 'in this beastly Paris, and realizing the superiority of English culture and the English mind to the French' (letter to Alice James, 22 February 1876: *Letters*, Vol. 2, p. 30). He met American expatriates like Henrietta Reubell, who is a possible model for Miss Barrace in *The Ambassadors* (she kept 'a saloon for gifted infants': *Letters*, Vol. 3, p. 435), and reviewed an Impressionist exhibition unenthusiastically. He was writing the instalments of *The American* for serialisation in the *Atlantic Monthly*. He told his brother that his life in Paris consisted mainly of a 'good deal of Boulevard and third rate Americanism'. He had 'got nothing important out of Paris', nor was likely to (letter of 29 July 1876: *Letters*, Vol. 2, p. 59). However, his visual impressions of France remained deeply scored on his imagination.

From 1876 onwards James settled in London, in Bolton Street, Piccadilly, achieving celebrity with 'Daisy Miller', *The Europeans*, *Washington Square* and *The Portrait of a Lady*. He revisited Paris and Rome in the autumn of 1877, Paris again in 1879, and Italy in 1880 and 1881. He stayed twelve days in Paris in February 1881, put off by the low style of culture of his compatriots there, 'whose horizon is bounded on one side by the *Figaro* and on the other by the Théâtre Français'. But he believed that a deeper Parisian life existed, from which 'one could extract an intellectual subsistence' (letter of 24 February 1881: *Letters*, Vol. 2, p. 344). Late in 1881, after six years of absence, he returned to the United States. He visited Washington and admired 'happy specimens of the *finished* American girl' (letter of 23 January 1882: *Letters*, Vol. 2, p. 373), but regarded the city as 'too rustic and familiar' for residence. Early in 1882 his mother died. James took rooms in Boston, but longed to return to London. He attended Emerson's funeral in Concord. He wrote in his journal that this visit to

America had been like 'a very painful dream', yet he looked back on it with 'a great deal of tenderness'. Boston meant 'absolutely nothing to me – I don't even dislike it. I like it, on the contrary; I only dislike to live there' (Edel 2, p. 475). On his return to Europe he made his 'little tour' of France, which he used as the basis of a travel-book. But in December 1882 he got word of his father's last illness and arrived in New York too late for the funeral. He remained in America for several months, attending to family affairs, and then departed, not to return for twenty-one years.

Of these years in England, the seventeen before he began writing *The Ambassadors* brought him many disappointments. The satirical *The Bostonians* (1885–6) lessened his popularity in America; *The Princess Casamassima* (1886), a novel which contains no American characters, seemed unconvincing to a considerable degree and *The Tragic Muse* (1890) diffuse. James felt that the demand for his work had been reduced to nil. In 1886 he had moved into an apartment in 34 De Vere Gardens in Kensington. He turned increasingly to the stage; a dramatisation of *The American* had some success in 1891, but the fresh, original play *Guy Domville* (1895) was a fiasco, James being personally booed by the audience at the St James's Theatre when he came on to the stage to take a bow. However, a series of novella-length tales and short novels, in which the use of an unreliable narrator or questionable figure from whose point of view the story is told gives rise to intriguing ambiguity, restored interest in his work. 'The Aspern Papers' (1888), *The Spoils of Poynton* (1896), *What Maisie Knew* (1897), 'The Turn of the Screw' (1898), *The Sacred Fount* (1901) and 'The Beast in the Jungle' (1903) all belong to this group. *The Awkward Age*, a novel mostly in dialogue, appeared in 1899. Most of his trips abroad during this period were to Italy, where he stayed with American expatriate friends, especially in Florence and Venice. He spent a month in Paris in 1884, renewing his acquaintance with Edmond de Goncourt, Daudet and Zola; he praised the precision and artistry of French prose, but still felt that the French writers, leading bohemian lives, concentrated on too restricted a field, the warts of man in Paris (Edel 3, p. 39). He was there again in the autumn of 1885, in December 1888, when he visited the actress Julia Bartet in her *loge* at the Thèâtre Français (Paris then struck him as 'bright, charming, civilized, even interesting', whereas London when he came back 'looked like a big black inferno of fog, mud, drunkenness and pauperism': *Letters*, Vol. 3, p. 252), and in late 1889, when he visited the Exhibition and also translated Daudet's *Port-Tarascon* into English. He returned in the spring of 1893, when he possibly met Proust in Daudet's dining-room in the rue de Bellechasse (Edel 3, p. 275) and certainly visited the Whistlers in their garden-house in the rue du Bac, a scene he was to adapt as the setting cf

Gloriani's garden in *The Ambassadors*. He refers to 'some babyish little Decadents' whom he met around that time (*Letters*, Vol. 3, p. 430). James's final visit to France before writing *The Ambassadors* was in the spring of 1899. He disliked the reactionary aspects of the Dreyfus affair then raging and criticised the new element of 'chronic *expositionism*' in the capital (Edel 4, p. 262), but still admired the beauty of its light and perspectives. He entertained two young American cousins of his, Rosina and Leslie Emmet, in the restaurants and theatres there and re-visited Henrietta Reubell. He felt at one point during this trip that France was a country *en décadence*.

James said that *The Ambassadors* was the most rounded and 'most proportioned of his productions' (Blackmur, p. 52); form and meaning are closely intertwined in James, so that it would be wrong to expect any passing judgement or stated affinity to have influenced the novel strongly. The fact that James had been away from America for so long and had had all his recent experience of Americans when they were living or travelling in Europe is a factor which affects the indirect presentation of American themes in the novel, of course. He admitted in 1890: 'It has been growing distincter that America fades from me' (*Letters*, Vol. 3, p. 284).

James's revised views of his native land, acquired during a long visit in 1904 and 1905, were to be expressed in *The American Scene* (1907). He had by then published his last main novel, *The Golden Bowl* (1905). His subsequent writing career was dominated by non-fictional enterprises such as the critical prefaces to his novels and his autobiography. This last was left incomplete at his death in 1916, as were two late novels, *The Ivory Tower* and *The Sense of the Past*.

CHAPTER 2

The Subject

THE INTERNATIONAL THEME: THE VIEW OF AMERICA

The independence of the United States gave a twist to its already long and complex relationship with the nations of Europe which made balanced mutual comprehension probably more difficult than ever. The interaction of ideas and attitudes was dominated, as it still is, by the 'special relationship' with the ex-colonising power, Britain. Indeed, the evocation of a European dimension to the relationship is an aspect of the American insistence on independence from Britain – a fact which is more immediately obvious in the political than in the cultural sphere. Europe, in this sense, cohered only from the American point of view. James's idea of Europe involves the same assumption. The point is clearer if we compare the Anglo-American connection with a more relaxed one (though physically more remote and historically more recent), that between Britain and Australia, which has tended to exclude, not include, Europe.

Though the federal constitution of the United States of America was conceived and expressed largely in terms of Enlightenment cosmopolitanism, the new republic, adversely affected psychologically by two wars with Britain, achieved its identity in the nineteenth-century world of Romantic nationalism, where it rapidly became yet another great power, as it was in James's day. The widely voiced American need for national distinctiveness was, however, frustrated by the absence of a distinctive national language or a separate religion. Nineteenth-century American literature inevitably developed as a branch of English literature, and its popular Protestant ethical basis was one recognisable as totally familiar in Britain. Its great writers, like Hawthorne and Melville, valued the English inheritance, and there was apprehension of its dilution in a changing new world. A somewhat nervous cultural situation persisted in America; two phenomena emerged as intelligible reactions to this uncomfortable state of dependence within independence. First, American self-consciousness became a major topic of American writing and the reports of European (mainly British) writers on their visits to the United States were incorporated as a genre within American literature itself. Second, in order to see America whole and fresh, many American writers went into exile, particularly to Paris. Travel across the Atlantic in both directions seemed to be necessary for stimulation and self-discovery.

The outstanding feature of American experience in the nineteenth century which contrasted with this intercontinental traffic was the movement of the frontier westwards. The expansion across the continent was not formally complete until Arizona and New Mexico attained full statehood in 1912. This development, symbolically contrary to the return to Europe of those who wanted to define American civilisation, produced an East–West cultural conflict within the United States itself which was second only in importance to another great division, the North–South conflict, which had produced the Civil War over slavery. James lived through the Civil War, and in Basil Ransom in *The Bostonians* (1885) he treated the figure of the Southern gentleman (making his way in the North in the legal profession after the war) with respect. But he regarded the pioneering character of the Westerner with far less sympathy. Indeed, the words 'West' and 'Western' acquire a piquant ambiguity in James, covering as they do both the whole American world itself, as seen from the perspective of Europe, and also the unsettled Western portion of the country as seen from its Eastern seaboard. The 'breath of some vague western whiff' with which Mamie Pocock is compared in chapter XXIV of *The Ambassadors* for her effect upon Strether of making him both 'homesick and freshly restless' has just this ambivalence. Strether feels homesick for the New England world, but the disturbing intimation of an 'unmapped hinterland' (ch. V) is also present.

The challenge of the West had an unsettling effect generally: it not only encouraged characteristics like aggressive confidence and violent non-egalitarian individualism, but was also felt to contribute largely to the impression of mobility, hurry and restlessness which American society made upon observers from Europe. The American use of wood in architecture and for pavements was seen as a sign of this transience and inquietude, as were the habits of eating hastily, spitting, chewing tobacco and gum, and sitting in rocking-chairs. These themes are prominent in the satirical American episodes in Dickens's influential *Martin Chuzzlewit* (London, 1843), where the hero, believing he would be needed as an architect in a land where men were constantly moving 'further off' and changing their residences (ch. 15), ends up there as a victim of swindling. Personal financial instability proved the most significant instance of American unsettledness. The sheer speed with which fortunes were made and lost in America seemed the most alarming of all those factors which were thought to make that country different from Europe. Commerce seemed more openly associated with unscrupulousness and violence there than in Europe. Dickens's Martin Chuzzlewit is assured at first that intelligence and virtue, which form the only aristocracy of the new republic, have as 'their necessary consequence . . . Dollars, sir,' but he rapidly discovers that men would do anything for dollars, even 'Make commerce one huge lie and mighty theft' (ch. 16). The word 'dollars' was apparently always on American lips. Nineteenth-century America was primarily a world of economic expansion and technical advancement. James's own grandfather had benefited immensely from the opportunities it offered him to lay the family fortunes once and for all. James's novels are full of self-made Americans and their heirs from places like the 'New York of the billionaires' (*The Ambassadors*, ch. X), some of them perfectly respectable, like Christopher Newman of *The American* (1877), who, despite some failed enterprises, had 'made money largely' in the West (ch. 2) and had acquired the ease and superiority of being a commercial power, others equally reprehensible, like Abel Gaw of *The Ivory Tower* (1917), who paid with a dried-up life for the 'mostly very awful' things he did to acquire 20 million dollars (bk 2, pt 3). James dissociated himself from such men, whether settled or unsettled. In his autobiography James defined the New England milieu of his boyhood as:

> a social order (so far as it *was* an order) that found its main ideal in a 'strict attention to business', that is to buying and selling over a counter or a desk, and in such an intensity of the traffic as made, on the part of all involved, for close localisation. (*Notes of a Son and Brother* (1914), p. 110)

He added that he had not, even in his seventies, outlived the particular satisfaction of 'thus being in New England without being of it'. He valued the detachment and mobility which financial independence afforded him. The James family's pecuniary inheritance enabled him to avoid being tied down to any one place of business, which the more settled commercialism of New England required. This was a fact which he deeply appreciated, though he protested that personally he was abnormal in not being 'a man of business or acquainted with the rudiments of any business transaction whatever', having always had 'a constitutional incapacity for everything of the sort and an insurmountable aversion to it' (letter to Mrs R. L. Stevenson, 26 December 1894: *Letters*, Vol. 3, p. 499). This psychological disconnection from American business life, not perhaps entirely convincing in James himself, as a glance at his dealings with his publishers and brothers will confirm, is undoubtedly a feature of Strether in *The Ambassadors*. Strether does not 'touch the business' of the Newsomes and he refuses to describe the business exploits of Chad's grandfather or father, men

who did shamelessly, 'as everyone does' today (ch. IV). It is interesting
that the one 'leading' businessman in the novel, Jim Pocock, is discerned by Strether as being cut off not only from the world of civilised
taste but also from the strict, moral censoriousness of the Newsome
women. He is 'out of the question' as far as both rival traditions are
concerned and, devoted merely to business and pleasure, lacks identity
and fails as a type (ch. XX). This failure is, according to Strether, the
normal thing among American men.

What James is getting at here is a certain grey uniformity of character
among Americans, associated with egalitarianism. There was a sameness
about American acquisitions and manners which many early visitors to
the republic remarked and which perhaps persisted more markedly in
New England than elsewhere in James's time. As early as 1782, J. H. St
J. de Crèvecoeur reported: 'A pleasing uniformity of decent competence appears throughout our habitations' (*Letters from an American
Farmer*, ed. A. E. Stone (1981), p. 67). The lack of differentiation
among American cities, the flatness and large-scale similarity of much of
the landscape, the sameness of political and social life in all the localities,
a regionalism that was only minimally various, the assimilation of immi-
grant minorities to a thin, rootless Anglo-Saxonism, all constituted a
kind of national monotony which at its best had the advantage of Puritan
plainness and simplicity, at its worst degenerated into dullness, the cause
of boredom and disappointment. Any such adverse comments, however,
usually accompanied admiration for the comparative fairness of
American justice and the ameliorating potential of democratic practices,
as in Harriet Martineau's *Society in America* (1839). She found that in the
free states labour was 'more really and heartily honoured than, perhaps,
in any other part of the civilised world' (Vol. 2, p. 302) and merchants
pursued wealth not necessarily for its own sake but benevolently 'to
provide for the improved civilisation of the whole of society' (Vol. 2,
p. 363). Enlightened practices with regard to the treatment of criminals
and women's property rights also elicited her commendation. She
noted with displeasure, however, the whine and twang in American
women's voices and the 'dull and prosy' conversation of the men
(Vol. 3, p. 71). Anthony Trollope, too, in *North America* (1862), while
noting the faults of rowdyism in religion and the 'empire of King Mud'
in America, approved the educational opportunities available in the
United States and the lack of condescension and deference between the
better-off and the poorer people: 'In America men stand upon a
common platform, but the platform is raised above the ground' and,
'though it does not approach in height the top of our staircase', the
average height is greater, Trollope concluded (Vol. 2, ch. 4). Again,
Matthew Arnold, while finding America culturally uninteresting and
dominated by middle-class vulgarity, agreed that equality gave a more

genial tone to social intercourse there and welcomed the absence of invidious social discriminations (see Allan Nevins, *American Social History as Recorded by British Travellers* (1923), pp. 6, 430, 438). Henry James's basic commitment to American democratic values is clear throughout his career. The seriousness of this commitment is perhaps most evident in that stunningly modest statement of Mr Wentworth in *The Europeans* (1878): 'We are all princes here' (ch. 4). For all the amusing quality of New England straitlacedness, the republican virtue of American society is superior to anything in Europe.

Yet James also felt that the innocent phase of American experience was past. He believed, for example, that Hawthorne was an American writer of an earlier and simpler type than himself with an 'uncritical' faith that Providence looked over the American state so that there were 'no rocks ahead' (*Hawthorne* (1879), p. 142). In fact many of Strether's comments upon the provincial tone of Woollett and the life of missed opportunities which he had led there are anticipated in James's critical account of New England culture in his *Hawthorne*. For instance, there are his remarks on the thinness and impalpability of the deposit which History has left upon the United States, that 'large juvenility' which is stamped upon the face of things there (pp. 12–13) and the absence of groups of people proposing to themselves 'to enjoy life'; for American life, James stated, had simply 'begun to be', but was still at an immeasurable distance from having 'begun to enjoy' (p. 29). Better known is the passage on 'the coldness, the thinness, the blankness' of American social life and that 'terrible denudation', its lack of manners and types (pp. 43–4). It was this absence of social types, James contended, which accounted for the self-consciousness and uncertain standards with which individuals judged one another in America, their 'rather chilly and isolated sense of moral responsibility' without accepted standards, and the 'somewhat agitated conscience' which was so typical there (pp. 50–1). James applies the idea of unsettledness to American ideas, it will be noted. James's complex response to the unsettled economic and intellectual state of his native land is embodied most successfully in *The Bostonians* (1885). There is a particularly telling descriptive passage in chapter 20, in which the innocent Verena Tarrant, the 'flower of the great Democracy', trained to be a kind of ventriloquist's dummy mouthing all the 'third-rate palaver' about progressive causes which the gullible public would swallow in 'unlimited draughts' (chs 14 and 33), looks out of the window of her friend's affluent drawing-room in Charles Street, Boston, at the view:

the general hard, cold void of the prospect; the extrusion, at Charlestown, at Cambridge, of a few chimneys and steeples, straight, sordid tubes of factories and engine-shops, or spare, heavenward finger cf the New England meeting-house. There was something inexorable in the poverty of the scene, shameful in the meanness of its details, which gave a collective impression of boards and tin and frozen earth, sheds and rotting piles, railway-lines striding flat across a thoroughfare of puddles, and tracks of the humbler, the universal horse-car, traversing obliquely this path of danger; loose fences, vacant lots, mounds of refuse, yards bestrewn with iron pipes, telegraph poles, and bare wooden backs of places. Verena thought such a view lovely, and she was by no means without excuse when, as the afternoon closed, the ugly picture was tinted with a clear, cold rosiness.

Such richly symbolic specificity is lacking in *The Ambassadors*, where the American scene is rather implied than described, though James may indeed assume some knowledge of his previous works in the reader and may want, quite properly, to avoid repeating himself too obviously. Sarah Pocock and her mother represent a more confident and commonplace strain of the New England 'chilly and isolated sense of moral responsibility' than the tense feminist Olive Chancellor of *The Bostonians* does, but they have their own uncertainty of standards, as we see when, with Waymarsh, the Pococks are happy in Paris, 'rushing about', overspending on food and taking in the circus (ch. XXIII), while neither Sarah nor her mother really appreciates how 'bad' Jim Pocock is. Chad Newsome is, of course, a study in the uncertainty of standards.

Mamie Pocock is a variation of the Verena Tarrant type, but better educated and with more social advantages, though not quite as much beauty. She represents a favourite Jamesian theme, the American girl, more emancipated than her European counterpart, less in need of chaperoning and yet more innocent for all her greater experience, not less innocent. In *The Bostonians* we learn that 'the consummate innocence' of the American girl had 'survived the abolition of walls and locks' (ch. 15), since in 'the pure code of New England' a friendship between a young woman and a young man was 'a common social tie' (ch. 20). Similarly Mamie Pocock and Chad Newsome spend their evenings together splendidly without flirting (*The Ambassadors*, ch. XXIII). In earlier Jamesian heroines like Daisy Miller and Isabel Archer the New England qualities of moral autonomy and cultural curiosity are conjoined with failures of perception as to the nature of evil in others as well as to the significance of European social forms so as to produce a tragi-comedy of deception. Mamie Pocock is, however, very intelligent in her personal perceptions.

James believed that the heroic age of the New England conscience, the age of abolitionists and transcendentalists, with its struggles against slavery and intemperance and its eccentric efforts to establish a more 'natural' way of life, was over. In the late nineteenth century the effort was, rather, to acquire the virtues of civilisation and self-criticism and rediscover the strengths of social traditions through European contacts, travel, international friendship and marriage, and humane study. James's satirical treatment of the blindnesses of earlier idealism is generally sympathetically mild, as in the presentation of Miss Birdseye in *The Bostonians*. Certain defects of democratic arrogance persisting into the new age are treated more sharply, however. Especially, popular journalism, which is regarded as the typical literary form of an un-tutored democracy, receives the sharp edge of James's wit, as it had of Dickens's before him. The scandalous and defamatory quality of American journalism particularly offended Dickens; his account of the 'New York Sewer' and the 'Rowdy Journal', with their resort to bribery, and of the hypocritical 'war correspondent', Jefferson Brick, who claims to place his hyperbolical rhetoric at the service of 'civilisation and purity' (*Martin Chuzzlewit*, ch. 16), is pugnaciously satiric. James, though in *The Portrait of a Lady* he treats the radical lady journalist Henrietta Stackpole with milder irony than anything that we find on the topic in Dickens (she becomes in the end more tolerant of European privileges than before and marries a typical upper-class Englishman), was equally critical of gossip columnists. Matthias Pardon in *The Bostonians* is such a type, indelicate and jocular, and thoroughly modern; for him the 'distinction between the person and the artist had ceased to exist' (ch. 16). Mr Flack in *The Reverberator* (1888) is even more unscrupulous, yet the members of the Dosson family, whom he exploits professionally, have no means of judging him on his conduct. Beset by 'a sense of an absence of precedents', Mr Dosson and his daughter Francie evince only a 'pleasant cheerful helplessness' which precludes discussion of the irresponsibility of sensational journalism. The contents of American newspapers are for them 'a part of the general fatality of things, of the current freshness of the universe', like the weather (ch. 12) – one of James's firmest placing authorial comments upon American unconventionality and candour. In *The Ambassadors* the menace of journalism is not an explicit theme. But the account of Way-marsh's fondness for the reception room of the American bank in the rue Scribe, where he spends 'a succession of hours' with the American papers, cannot be fully appreciated without reference to James's view of the American press: Waymarsh's impulsive need to know 'what was going on' and his reliance on the room in the bank as a trap 'for the arrest of wandering western airs' (ch. V) are especially ironic.

Prominent in *The Ambassadors* is the related theme of advertising, for which America was held to have an unprecedented and unfortunate flair. One of the first things to strike Dickens's hero in *Martin Chuzzlewit* in New York was the density of the advertising on the storehouses and office-buildings, 'ornamented with more black boards and white letters, and more white boards and black letters, than Martin had ever seen before, in fifty times the space' (ch. 16). James regarded the cultivation of publicity as an integral part of the will-to-power and, at the same time, of the excessive eccentricity of American religious movements and political campaigns. In *The Bostonians* the mesmeric healer Selah Tarrant depends on copious advertising for his success. Known as 'the irrepressible Tarrant', he waits in hotel vestibules, where men write letters 'at a table inlaid with advertisements', and hangs about the '*penetralia* of the daily press', for 'human existence to him, indeed, was a huge publicity', the vision of which 'haunted his dreams' (ch. 13). Compared with such a grotesque monster, Chad Newsome is potentially a much smoother operator, bent on studying advertising 'scientifically worked' in 'our roaring age' (*The Ambassadors*, ch. XXXV). Strether's and Miss Gostrey's deliberate abstention from naming the object manufactured by the Newsome firm is a gesture of dissociation, not only from sales promotion as an art, but from what they see as the whole overvalued, overemphasised commercialism of the United States.

In *The Ambassadors*, then, James treats his theme of American experience viewed from a European perspective at what is a very late stage in its development. He has the whole nineteenth century of American and English literature behind him and the presence beside him among his own acquaintance of many American individuals of sophisticated culture and acute critical power. Inevitably his own personal example as an Anglo-American man of letters influences the novel and pervades and strengthens all the value judgements made within it. Indeed, the style is an element in the theme. Without the obtrusion of any autobiographical element, *The Ambassadors*, again inevitably, still exhibits a control of the English language which is distinctively Jamesian. James manipulates American idioms for the sake of both amusement and originality within a prose of literary decorum which comes down to him basically from Scott, though through many channels on both sides of the Atlantic. The Anglo-American style of the work is, therefore, not only a means to expose the theme, but also provides incontrovertible evidence of its potency.

THE INTERNATIONAL THEME: FRANCE REVISITED

The assistance given by France to the United States of America in gaining independence, and the subsequent American influence on revolutionary, democratic and liberal movements in France, made for a lively intellectual Franco-American relationship during the nineteenth century. The general idealising admiration of America among liberal French writers was matched by sceptical criticism in French conservative circles, aristocratic, clericist and petty-bourgeois. Personal ties between the two populations, however, were comparatively few. France's adherence to the classical tradition of European culture gave her a fascinating prestige and a strangeness in American eyes. For their part, the French kept up the sense of dissimilarity. Following Tocqueville's *De la démocratie en Amérique* (1835–40), they studied American politics and culture as products of specifically American conditions which they judged to be very different from their own or Great Britain's. American leaders of opinion, desiring French approval, often discovered instead warm affection combined with analytic coolness, at times prejudiced and derisory, though by the 1880s, as Sigmund Skard points out in *American Studies in Europe* (1958), French reformers believed that the future lay with the Anglo-Saxon nations (p. 144). Also France became the focal point of American expatriate artists and writers, a tendency which reached a climax in the 1920s. Van Wyck Brooks points to the number of important American books written in Paris from the times of Franklin, Jefferson and Irving to those of Henry Adams, Hemingway and Fitzgerald: 'Writing in Paris is one of the oldest American customs' (*The World of Washington Irving* (1945), p. 256 n, quoted in Malcolm Bradbury's 'The expatriate tradition in American writing', in *The Yearbook of English Studies*, vol. 8 (1978), p. 19). Most American novelists have set at least one novel abroad, in Europe, in which they have looked homeward from that foreign, often French, viewpoint. Of these writers, James is one who actually planned to settle permanently in Paris: he wrote there, during 1875 and 1876, *The American*, which is his main full-length work on Franco-American themes apart from *The Ambassadors*. He kept in touch with French cultural developments during the rest of his life in England. He retained a remarkable competence in both speaking and writing the French language, and was visited in Britain by French friends. The francophile tone of James's prose is readily marked. His penchant for Gallicisms goes beyond the accepted borrowings: he sprinkles his pages with italicised French words and phrases which are usually highly idiomatic and often hard to translate.

James's lifelong engagement with French society, literature and art results in his expressing many attitudes to France, often deeply admiring ones, but also deploring. He was, basically, always a friend of the French, but felt that as an American he could give as well as he got. Several of the leading characters in his fictions are francophile Americans like himself who come to some readjustment of attitude when faced with aspects of French behaviour which seem morally insensitive. The heroine of 'Madame de Mauves' (1874), for instance, is an American who finds the philandering of her French husband hard to take. She had once thought that all the prose of life was in America and the poetry in France, 'which was very foolish': now she wishes she were just the daughter of some New England minister. The lesson of the tale is simply what the evening look of Paris tells you: 'this is no world for you unless you have your pockets lined and your scruples drugged'. In the earlier James, Paris is often treated as a centre of corruption, both sexual and materialistic, as well as an exemplar of visual good taste and of the cultural enrichment which derives from long historical experience.

James's personal observations confirm this ambiguous attitude. The 'best of one's education' proceeded, he believed, with the aid of a French periodical, the *Revue des deux mondes*, an indispensable guide to the current civilised scene (*Notes of a Son and Brother* (1914), p. 80). Yet he felt that French novelists for their part scarcely did justice to the 'life' which France herself exhibited in abundance. They were guilty of a moral levity and a psychological shallowness, when compared with the English novelists. Despite the precision of their prose and their skill in picturesque evocation, they indulged in gross sensuality or perverse aestheticism. Although French readers were the most sophisticated in the world, in James's view, and French critics the most professional, yet the French novel was in decline. Even Flaubert, a perfectionist in form and a most powerful realist, produced a style rich in similes, which could render only the visible, not the moral; 'he had no faith in the power of the moral to offer a surface' ('Gustave Flaubert' (1893), in *Henry James: Selected Literary Criticism*, ed. M. Shapira (1963), p. 188). The trouble was largely connected with the French tolerance of adultery. That figure which is found so frequently in French novels, 'du jeune homme sensible et distingué qui débute dans l'adultère', was a profoundly antipathetic one not only to James, but also, as he considered, to Anglo-Saxons generally (letter of 23 February 1888: *Letters*, Vol. 3, p. 221). England and America had a special relationship in their distaste for adulterers. Indeed, any insistence upon the differences between life in England and life in America seemed 'more and more idle and pedantic' to James: 'THERE is the *real* difference – a gulf, from the English (or the American) to the Frenchman, and vice versa (still more); and not from the Englishman to the American' (letter of 29 October 1888: *Letters*, Vol 3, pp. 244–5). The main international theme for James was this difference, especially as manifested in attitudes to marriage.

Observation of French customs regarding the upbringing and disposal of women had long been a Jamesian pre-occupation. In the series of sketches on France which he had contributed regularly to the American press in the 1870s there is one in which he generalises on the training of the French *jeune fille* for a position in marriage which was, 'not simply (as is mostly the case with us) a sentimental, but really an official position'; he had to admit, however, that most French marriages were arranged successfully ('From Normandy to the Pyrenees', in *Portraits of Places* (1883), p. 164). The arranged marriage was, moreover, the chief factor in the Gallic double standard in sexual morality. This 'horrible' French way of marrying by family arrangement is declared in *The American* to be 'a chapter for a novel' (ch. 8), as indeed it becomes in that novel. Christopher Newman there argues that the bullying of women and coaxing them into marriage is 'infamous'. He believes there have been only a dozen cases of it in America since independence (ch. 6); yet he finds young Frenchmen able to contemplate it with equanimity, being in fact more concerned with the dowry involved than perturbed by the unfairness of the practice: 'We want to know what we are about when we marry' (ch. 4). At the same time they are not at all cynical with women, but evidently well bred and devoted to romantic honour, masters of the Gallic tradition which combines social virtues with agreeable sensations. Certainly, French women belong to two worlds, the respectable and the *demi-monde*. A member of the former cannot visit or know a divorcee. The French invariably put Mother and the advantage of the family first; hence it is not always the case that French urbanity and French sincerity merge. At the Bellegardes' reception (ch. 16), Newman is treated with 'that soft hardness of good society which puts out its hand but keeps its fingers closed over the coin'. Although Newman is not James, nor Strether, but, rather, an American who had lost money manufacturing washing-tubs (there is no coyness in naming such articles in *The American*) and made it handling railway stock, his voyage of discovery round the French mind amusingly anticipates certain turns in the plot of *The Ambassadors*; the French mind had hardly changed in twenty-five years.

The Reverberator (1888), though its main theme is the abuse of journalism, also focuses on French manners, but from a rather special angle. It studies the postures and defences of a Gallicised American family. The older generation of the Proberts has, through inclination and marriage-ties, adopted the French aristocratic code; the younger generation is given to aestheticism. James has avoided making too direct a satirical attack on the French here, since he felt that it would be 'too cheap, too valueless'; indeed, he insists while planning *The Reverberator* that he will not, after *The American*, do the French collectively again (*Notebooks*, p. 85) – a statement that throws a strong light also on his intentions in *The Ambassadors*. Nevertheless, *The Reverberator* is not like *The Ambassadors*; it is an unsympathetic, caricaturing piece, concerned with specious imitation rather than with the real thing. Old Mr Probert, 'a Gallomaniac of the old American type', is a grotesque, whose family has been so 'completely Gallicised that the affairs of each member of it were the affairs of all the rest' (ch. 3). The Proberts totally lack probity; they fear only exposure of their behaviour, not its moral effects. They use conventional forms for their impulses; devoted evidently to 'the legitimist principle, the ancient faith and even a little the right, the unconscious, grand air', they evince manners which are actually only manner in itself, which may be 'a very misleading symbol' when it corresponds so little to fact (ch. 7). Their conception of the family is particularly rigid. They cannot live with vulgar people. 'Family feeling among them was not a tyranny, but a religion' (ch. 5), so that, in considering the action of a Probert mind, you might have thought 'human beings were susceptible of no attribute but that of a dwindling or thickening consanguinity' (ch. 7). At the same time, they subscribe completely to the French ideas about young girls having to be chaperoned before marriage, but having to be discreet about betrayal after it. It is the kind of world which lies very much in the background and in the shadows in *The Ambassadors*, but which is sufficiently present to cool Strether's francophile ardour. In *The Reverberator*, the young Gaston Probert successfully rejects this world. Gaston belongs to an alternative Parisian set, 'his dawdling coævals' (ch. 3) who give attention to art and revel in the modern, that is the visual, sense. But he is not entirely lost to visual impressionism, turning in the end to the American girl, Francie Dosson, whom he marries.

   The Tragic Muse (1890), written immediately after *The Reverberator*, takes a much more favourable view of French culture. There are long sequences, especially, which are warmly appreciative of the institution of the French National Theatre, of which Peter Sherringham takes such a 'serious view' (ch. 12) and of which the most distinguished representative is the veteran actress Madame Carré, whose habit of ferocious analysis and intellectual joy in having reasons for everything amount to a 'logical passion' (ch. 10). Also, the hero of the novel, Nick Dormer, finds that Paris always has 'the power of quickening sensibly the life of reflection and of observation within him' (ch. 2), a view which James himself continued to hold, though with reservations. Even in *The Tragic Muse*, the increasing influence of the celebrity cult is deplored, particularly in the passage when Mademoiselle Voisin, who is one of the mere 'stars of the drama', is found in the academic 'holy-of-holies' at the National Theatre (chs 20 and 21; see my '*The Tragic Muse*: the objective centre' (1970) for further discussion). Paris is a place where one can live in one's senses and tastes as well as one can imagine, but perhaps not so well in the long run. Forces of trivialisation are at work. Manifestations of luxury and extravagance, especially in architecture, have a depressing effect. In 1899, James wrote from the south

of France to Edward Warren, the architect: 'Wondrous are the re-
sources of this people, but (let us bear up!) hideous – apparently,
mainly – their villas *as* villas. On many questions of taste – !' (see Sir
John Russell, 'Henry James and the Leaning Tower', 1943). Such
broadsides against French taste, delivered in France by James just
before the period of composition of *The Ambassadors*, should caution us
against expecting a romantic view of France in that novel.

James never claimed to know France from the inside. His viewpoint
was that of the intuitive, perceptive visitor. It is sometimes forgotten
that he was the author of a widely used guidebook on France, the
charming *A Little Tour in France* (1884), which, significantly, he had
had reissued, with a new introduction of his own and new illustrations
by Joseph Pennell, in 1900. In this introduction he writes, no doubt
with an eye on his forthcoming novel, that there exists, unfortunately,
no happy mean between the tourist's surface impressionism which his
Little Tour provides and 'the perception of very complex underlying
matters', that is, the perception of 'the inner springs of the subject –
springs and connections social, economic, historic'. James adds that the
time has now passed for him to write a deeper study of France which
would be a 'demonstration' of his interest in that country and its
people. 'There are relations that soon get beyond all merely showy
appearances of value for us,' he says, implying that he has been too
subtly influenced by France all his life to analyse the process explicitly
but must make do with paying an indirect tribute 'behind the altar', by
reissuing his guidebook in an improved version. What James says he
offers is not an analysis of French culture, but a representation of 'the
process – the quieter, mostly, the better – of absorption and assimilation of what the relation has done for us' (pp. v–viii) – a phrase which
would apply to the presentation of Strether's feeling for France in *The
Ambassadors* very aptly. In Strether's case, too, the appreciation of
French influence is not so much analysed as indirectly indicated, built
up as another tribute 'behind the altar'. But the more explicit and
unsystematic Jamesian reactions to the subject in his previous writings
give some idea of the positive and negative components of the
American's relation to France in the novel.

As time went on, James came to see France more and more as
Britain's ally rather than as America's cultural opposite. When the First
World War came, Germany's attack on French soil deeply stirred
James's emotions. In a late essay, 'France', published in *The Book of
France* (1915), he paid glowing tribute to the quality of French civilisa-
tion. He praised France supremely as the modern equivalent of ancient
Greece in that France sums up 'the life of the mind and the life of the
senses alike, taken together in the most irrepressible freedom of either'.
He enthused over Britain's good fortune in being neighboured by a

genius 'so suggestive of wondrous and attaching comparisons, as to keep us chronically aware of the difference and the contrast'. France 'takes charge of those of the interests of man which most dispose him to fraternise with himself, to pervade all his possibilities and to taste all his faculties'. Civilisation, he concluded, has depended on France for 'half its assurances' (*Within the Rim* (1918), pp. 85–92). These comments, though very cordial, are not fulsome. James still holds his corner and keeps his criticisms in reserve.

CHAPTER 3

The Ideas

JAMES AND ARNOLD

T. S. Eliot, praising James two years after his death as 'the most intelligent man of his generation', prefaced the compliment with the remark that James 'had a mind so fine that no idea could violate it' ('In memory of Henry James' (1918); reprinted in *The Question of Henry James*, ed. F. W. Dupee (1947), pp. 125–6). Eliot argued again that James 'did not provide us with "ideas", but with another world of thought and feeling' ('A prediction in regard to three English authors', in *Vanity Fair* (New York), February 1924, p. 29). Although it is true that *The Ambassadors* does not propound ideas in any episodic, Shavian way, the prestige of Eliot's *dicta* should not lead us into doubting the intellectual basis from which James projected his fictional characters and situations. James was well aware of the world of contemporary ideas and he knew which of them he rejected and which he accepted. It is perfectly true that he felt no need to identify himself with the 'cause' of any current '-ism'. But his novels assume the existence of a familiar literature of ideas, and are evidently influenced by it.

James reached adolescence in the mid-Victorian period (he was 16 when Darwin's *Origin of Species* was published). He formed the foundation of his intellectual standpoint at that time and hardly ever modified it again. He rejected Christianity even in its most 'progressive' form, Unitarianism. He believed that the supernatural idea had to be applied only in the moral and critical sphere. Religious faith has no place in *The Ambassadors*. When he enters Notre-Dame Cathedral, Strether has 'no errand in such a place', except to be amused by his cowardice, since it has 'no altar for his worship, no direct voice for his soul' (ch. XVI). It is, however, 'soothing even to sanctity' for his worried nerves and of immense cultural and aesthetic interest to him. Strether's point that justice and injustice, so palpably present outside 'in the hard light' of Paris, were equally absent inside the Cathedral is subtly realist and alert, if not disapproving. For James accepted the competitive version of the animal kingdom and the human world provided by the Darwinists; when 'something in the great world covertly tigerish' comes to Strether across Gloriani's lawn 'as a waft from the jungle' (ch. XI), the tiger is no romantic symbol of creational symmetry, but belongs to the world of the survival of the fittest. James wanted to confront reality as experience, not to see through it to a spiritual sphere. Evolutionary theory offered James a material explanation of his sense of sin and human wrong, which he shared with Hawthorne and the lack of which in Emerson he found so limiting: 'that ripe unconsciousness of evil' (*Partial Portraits* (1888), p. 7) which was so significant in Emerson was also for James the chief weakness in New England transcendentalism, with its calls for a return to nature and to individual independence. Nicola Bradbury, who regards Strether as 'culturally unsophisticated' and 'naïve', finds an echo of H. D. Thoreau's 'living by the sweat of his brow' (*Walden*, 1854) in Strether's wish to buy himself off from 'the sweat of one's brow' (ch. VII) by keeping down the weeds of delusion in Woollett about Chad. The echo, if it is one, seems to me ironical, and the other echoes of Thoreau which she discerns purely fanciful (see her *Henry James: The Later Novels* (1979), pp. 49, 50, 53, 56 and 60). Much of the idealising and spiritualised intellectual atmosphere of his American youth James heartily repudiated.

The expected source of alternative mental stimulation for the much-travelled youth might well have been the Continent of Europe but, though James was taught by the Fourierist Fezandié during 1856 and 1857 in his co-educational 'phalansteric' Institution in Paris and was exposed to revolutionary sentiments from one of the staff, M. Bonnefons (*A Small Boy and Others* (1913), pp. 380–2), Continental socialism never appealed to him. France provided James with 'literature', by means of the *revues*, and with 'life' and society, the 'complex order' in which such contrasts flourished for his discrimination (*Notes of a Son and Brother* (1914), p. 52), but not specifically with the culture of the mind. That item came to him – or, rather, was thrust upon him in its own way – from the old country.

The earlier Victorians James admired affectionately as representing an older England, which was superior in historical colour, social density and types of character to its transatlantic offspring, but he felt no particular respect for his favourite English writers' grasp of ideas. As he read the novels of Dickens, Thackeray, Trollope and George Eliot coming out around 1860 and earlier, he was impressed with their 'genial weight' as enrichments of life and with their authors' 'command of the . . . collective sensibility' (*Notes of a Son and Brother* (1914), p.20), but not with their moral ideas. When James met Dickens briefly in 1867 he felt the force of great passion in a 'single pulse of time', but nothing happened between them except an exchange of platitudes (p. 239). Even the learned George Eliot, whose *The Mill on the Floss* had seemed an all-engulfing and 'incomparably privileged production' to James and his contemporaries (p. 443), was too keen on determinism for James; she underestimated the 'great and novel responsibilities' which consciences may take on ('The Novels of George Eliot' (1866), p. 492). Her concern with the traditional life and shared attitudes of the provincial community made her too conservative a moralist for James. Of the more radical Victorian sages, Carlyle had been condemned as a perverse 'literary desperado' by Henry James senior (see F. O. Matthiessen, *The James Family* (1947), p. 477); and, though James deeply respected and followed Ruskin as an interpreter of actual works of art and also admired Morris for his exquisite designs and legendary poems (*Letters*, Vol. 1, pp. 93–4), he distanced himself from both in their anti-capitalist phase. He regarded Ruskin, when he met him in 1867, as having been 'scared back by the grim face of reality into the world of unreason and illusion' (*Letters*, Vol. 1, p. 103), and he concluded in 1899 that the formula for Morris was 'that he was a boisterous, boyish, British man of action and practical faculty, launched indeed by his imagination, but really floundering and romping and roaring through the arts, both literary and plastic, very much as a bull through a china-shop' (Lubbock, Vol. 1, p. 349). The coolness is clear.

With Matthew Arnold, however, it was altogether different; Arnold had been, when James met him in Rome in 1873, 'in prose and verse, the idol of my previous years' (*William Wetmore Storey and His Friends* (1903), Vol. 2, p. 208). It is, I think, true to say that Henry James was Matthew Arnold's principal disciple. The 'noble influence' is still a strong presence in *The Ambassadors*. It had begun to take effect very early; according to James's autobiography, it was a critical self-consciousness developed while watching performances like that of a dramatised *Uncle Tom's Cabin*, a version of the novel by Mrs Harriet Beecher Stowe, at the National Theatre in New York, which prepared James for receptivity to Arnold's ideas. The James boys went to the theatre not to be beguiled, but to enjoy the experiences 'with ironic detachment' and 'to be amused ourselves at our sensibility should it prove to have been trapped and caught'. This awareness of their 'collective attitude' gave the young James 'his first glimpse of that possibility of a "free play of mind" over a subject which was to throw him with force at a later stage of culture, when subjects had considerably multiplied, into the critical arms of Matthew Arnold' (*A Small Boy and Others* (1913), p. 171). The idea of the importance of ideas to literature is itself the most important of Arnold's legacies to James. Arnold had argued in 'The Function of Criticism at the Present Time' (1864) that the gift of the grand work of literary genius lay in its faculty of being inspired 'by a certain order of ideas' which it presents 'in the most effective and attractive combinations'; for to work freely it must 'find itself amidst the order of ideas' (Super, Vol. 1, p. 261). This theme appears frequently in James's criticism. In his review of Whitman's *Drum-Taps*, James objected to the absence of ideas in his work, since art required above all the 'subordination of one's self to an idea' ('Mr Walt Whitman' (1865), p. 626). Again, he felt it was a defect of Alphonse Daudet 'that he has not a great number of ideas. . . Imaginative writers of the first order always give us an impression that they have a kind of philosophy' (*Partial Portraits* (1888), p. 238). There is every reason to believe, then, that James avoided such a deficiency in his own fiction.

James's hospitality is for ideas in the plural; it is not an identification with any simple cause. Several of James's main characters, including particularly Strether in *The Ambassadors*, themselves embody this hospitality to the life of intelligence. Without being professionally literary, like James himself, Strether endeavours to act like Arnold's ideal critic who finds a pleasure in 'the free play of the mind upon all subjects'. He exercises that criticism or curiosity which Arnold defined as the 'disinterested love' of this very free play of mind ('The Function of Criticism at the Present Time': Super, Vol. 1, p. 268). Strether's errors, which are due largely to temperamental factors and to a certain kind of inexperience, do not invalidate this exercise. It is evident especially in Strether's self-criticism, his attempts to see himself and his immediate preoccupations from more than one point of view, which amount to a conscientious search for disinterestedness. Even the emotional advice about intense living given to Little Bilham in chapter XI contains the admission that Strether may be too much a case of reaction to his own past of missed opportunities; 'the voice of reaction should, no doubt, always be taken with an allowance'. That is a good example of the Arnoldian 'return' upon the self (Super, Vol. 1, p. 267) or 'living by ideas', when one is carried to the opposite side of a question from the one which has one's earnest support. It is significant that in landing on the metaphor of the missed train for the missed opportunities of his past, Strether in the phrase 'I hear its faint receding whistle' comically echoes Arnold's 'I only hear/Its melancholy, long, withdrawing roar' in the passage on loss of faith in 'Dover Beach' (1867). James implies that Strether's loss must not be taken as seriously as Arnold's. Strether's mild and light tone, as he shrugs off the more melancholy mood, is also in line with what Arnold often recommended and desired. James found irresistible the eloquence of Arnold's essay on 'Falkland' (1877), in which he praised a 'martyr of sweetness and light, of lucidity of mind and largeness of temper' (Super, Vol. 8, p. 206). Strether's avoidance of the sardonic and the bitter in his practice of the free play of consciousness also suggests the lesson of Arnold's 'Heine's Grave', a poem singled out by James as one in which, alongside his major prose works,

Arnold 'speaks more directly' to an American, becomes 'nearer and dearer', than 'any other contemporary English writer' ('Matthew Arnold' (1884), p. 241; cf. also p. 246 for allusion to the 'Falkland' essay.) In this poem Arnold deplores Heine's harshness and scornful wit, which mar his enlightened attack on Philistinism, and prefers a milder and more severe life for himself, which will enable him to influence his readers through 'charm'. Strether's tolerant and open-minded approach to people is the main secret, surely, of his charm, and in this respect his tone is representative of his author.

Another poem of Arnold's which James particularly liked was 'Stanzas in Memory of the Author of "Obermann"' (1852). Arnold's 1868 note, in which he characterised Senancour as 'the most perfectly isolated and the least attitudinising' of authors, indicates the appeal of the subject to James. The poem praises the sage who, scanning the 'hopeless tangle of our age', finds the glow and thrill of life not in the world of men's strife, but in the spectator's imagination:

> He who has watched, not shared, the strife,
> Knows how the day hath gone.
> He only lives with the world's life,
> Who hath renounced his own.

In criticising Whitman for merely reiterating facts *ore rotundo*, James added, in this Arnoldian vein: 'He only sings them worthily who views them from a height' ('Mr Walt Whitman' (1865), pp. 625–6). This idea of the elevated, detached observer as the true penetrator of experience undoubtedly influenced James's conduct of his own life as well as his presentation of life through lucid reflectors in his novels. James argued that Arnold's poetry always went 'to the point' and nourished the mind ('Matthew Arnold' (1884), p. 244). After first meeting him in 1873, James referred twice in letters to Arnold specifically as the author of the Obermann verses (*Letters*, Vol. 1, pp. 371 and 381). Strether's image of himself as a spectator who participates in life in his imagination and renounces anything for himself out of the whole affair except his 'wonderful impressions' (ch. XXXVI) is closer, I think, to the Arnoldian ideal than to any Modernist types of anti-hero. So, during his initial fascination with the traces of Chad's way of life in France, Strether checks himself by reminding himself that 'he mustn't dispossess himself of the faculty of seeing things as they are' (ch. VI). The phrase echoes Arnold's definition of the first function of criticism, 'To see the object as in itself it really is', first used in *On Translating Homer* (1861; Super, Vol. 1, p. 140); to achieve a clearer observation of Chad's milieu Strether must sit down less '*with*' Chad's friends, must participate less in their life. When he understands Chad's life in France more fully, he finds a 'point of vantage' alone on his bedroom sofa (ch.

XXXI), regaining detachment for this 'belated vision'. Strether's non-participatory vision is what Madame de Vionnet has to accept when, while she finally breaks down, he is 'conscious of some vague inward irony in the presence of such a fine free range of bliss and bale'. She remarks: 'In spite of your patience, all the same, you'd . . . do everything for us but be mixed up with us' (ch. XXXIII). Strether attains a 'final philosophy' according to which he wishes to do everything 'because he was lucid and quiet' (ch. XXXIV). Such a philosophy undoubtedly has to remove itself 'from practice' and embrace what Arnold called 'the Indian virtue of detachment' ('The Function of Criticism at the Present Time': Super, Vol. 3, p. 274). It has, however, also its positive aspect.

In his autobiography James recalls the circle of friends with whom he spent the summer of 1865 in North Conway, Massachusetts. It was 'a little world of happy and easy interchange', providing the 'right conditions for the play of young intelligence and young friendship, the reading of Matthew Arnold and Browning, the discussion of a hundred human and personal things'. He thinks it uncouth to defend as merely innocent their interplay of relation 'attuned to that fruitful freedom of what we took for speculation . . . as boundless curiosity – as the consideration of life, that is, the personal, the moral inquiry and adventure at large' (*Notes of a Son and Brother* (1914), pp. 426–7). Arnold's thinking was new to James at that time. In his July 1865 review of Arnold's essays James argued that Arnold's definition of the object of criticism, 'to know the best that is known and thought in the world' (Arnold also says, 'a disinterested endeavour to learn and propagate' it, in 'The Function of Criticism at the Present Time': Super, Vol. 3, p. 282), without regard to practical consequences or considerations, was 'doubly applicable in America', where there was no lack 'of experimentalists, of empirics' (*Essays in Criticism* (1865), p. 211). Arnold was 'profoundly conscious of his time' and spoke of all things seriously. Evidently the young James and his friends were attempting to follow Arnold's lead in taking 'high ground'. In *The Ambassadors* Strether is not represented as having enjoyed quite such a cultural opportunity as this one; Strether marries around 1865, makes his first trip to Paris and returns full of hopes of propagating 'the higher culture' which are not fulfilled. But the aspiration is the same, and indeed Strether's journey to Europe in the novel is in part the long-delayed consummation of it.

An essential feature of the critical endeavour as Arnold conceived it was the making of 'fine distinctions', of constructive comparisons between the products of different cultures, which involved for the English critic the dwelling in foreign thought and the possession of at least one foreign literature. Arnold regarded Europe as 'one great federation' ('The Function of Criticism at the Present Time': Super, Vol. 3, p. 284) for intellectual purposes. James's aim in his fiction on his international theme was, in a sense, to bring America into this federation. A federal civilisation is an ideal which implies a balance of mutual respect among the contributory national cultures. This equality seems to be the value glanced at in the ambassadorial metaphor which James assigned to his projected novel of 1900 as its title and which recurs in its text. His cultural ambassadors fall ironically short of the ideal, of course, but indirectly James does define an imagined positive in *The Ambassadors*. Christof Wegelin, in his *The Image of Europe in Henry James* (1958, pp. 86–7), draws attention to an 1877 essay, 'Occasional Paris', reprinted in *Portraits of Places* (1883), in which James says that one set of national customs, 'wherever it may be found, grows to seem to you about as provincial as another' (pp. 75–6), but the process of comparing them may be both instructive and entertaining. The essay contains a defence of the cosmopolite, as an informed observer who thinks 'well of mankind' on the whole, and adds: 'The consequence of the cosmopolite spirit is to initiate you into the merits of all peoples, to convince you that national virtues are numerous, though they may be very different, and to make downright preference really very hard.' Despite its thinness of tone, this early statement clearly indicates James's own moral stance. The cosmopolitan person is a norm against which to set both the local patriot and the exile devoted to a foreign culture. In *The Ambassadors* Strether veers towards francophilia but holds to the cosmopolitan norm in the end, whereas Sarah Pocock represents American provinciality. She sounds too much 'the note of home' (ch. XXIII) and her husband *is* that note, a note comparable with the one that Waymarsh's countenance would have presented to Strether on his first landing in Europe, when he was apprehensive as to what or who would 'prove the note of Europe' (ch I). The use of the word 'note' here is not an allusion to the art of music. Ian Watt, in his subtle explication of 'The first paragraph of *The Ambassadors*' (1960), interprets the passage about the note of Europe as showing us the force of Strether's aesthetic sense, without mentioning the Arnoldian context of ideas in which James worked (p. 266). Arnold, however, discusses his choice of the term 'note' in phrases like his 'the note of provinciality' in a passage in 'The Literary Influence of Academies'. Arnold says it is an expressive theological term used by J. H. Newman in phrases like 'the note of catholicity' (it is based on the Latin *nota*, a mark). The mark of the provincial spirit is that it 'orders its ideas amiss; it is hurried away by fancies; it likes and dislikes too passionately, too exclusively' (Super, Vol. 3, pp. 244, 245, 249 and 468 n). The note of provinciality is shown, according to Arnold, when moderation and proportion are forgotten and 'the fitness, the measure, the centrality, which is the soul of all good criticism, is lost' (pp. 252–3). Strether's criticism of Woollett and apprehensive discovery of the note of Europe are conducted along such authentically Arnoldian lines. When Maria

Gostrey asks him in chapter XVIII, after he has given up Mrs
Newsome's uncomprehending plan, if it is his idea 'to stay out of
curiosity', Maria's 'smile of the most genial criticism' shows that she is
using that word, too, in the positive sense which Arnold wanted it to
be given in English.

Arnold's specific strictures upon American life seem to have been
endorsed by James as salutary, if harsh and satirical. As early as 1861
Arnold had used a neologism, 'to Americanise', to indicate the process
by which a ruling middle class would 'deteriorate' a country 'by their
low ideals and want of culture'. Lacking ecclesiastical and aristocratical
institutions, the Americans, Arnold believed, watched with self-
satisfaction 'a certain mediocre culture diffused with indisputable
breadth' and reacted with incredulity and resentment when in contact
with 'real superiority' (*Popular Education in France*: Super, Vol. 2,
pp. 25 and 161). However, he regarded the American middle class as
also expressing an English middle-class spirit of 'rawness, hardness and
imperfection . . . needing to be liberalised, enlarged and ennobled'
('A French Eton', 1863, p. 319). The portrait of Jim Pocock in *The
Ambassadors* easily lends itself to the illustration of these ideas. Considered by Strether to be 'extravagantly common', Pocock treats his
trip to Paris as 'a regular windfall' and remarks: 'We haven't all the
same at Woollett got anything like this' (ch. XX). Arnold believed that
the basis of American culture was necessarily commercial, but he later
praised America's democratic institutions as complying well with the
form and pressure of modern circumstances ('Civilisation in the United
States', 1888: Super, Vol. 11, p. 351). By the end of his life Arnold was
in turn influenced by his reading of James, whose novels he recommended and praised, especially *Roderick Hudson*. His praise of the
natural charm of manner of American women as 'a real note of civilisation' to be reckoned to the credit 'of American life, and of its quality'
(p. 356), suggests a Jamesian influence. Arnold had been gratified
when James declined to write a reply to his first major essay on the
United States, 'A Word about America' (1882), since James felt 'it was
so true, and carried him along with it' (Super, Vol. 10, p. 450). In that
essay Arnold, while admitting the existence of brilliantly gifted
American individuals, who frequently cross the Atlantic, suggested
that James's Philistine character Striker from *Roderick Hudson* was
more typical of the social order of the smaller cities (p. 7). The two men
were largely in agreement in their evaluation of American civilisation.
It is true that James objected to Arnold's reluctant verdict that
Emerson was not a great writer or 'born man of letters' ('Emerson'
(1884): Super, Vol. 10, p. 172) and countered that 'letters surely were
the very texture of his history' ('The Life of Emerson', *Macmillan's
Magazine*, vol. 57 (October, 1887), in *Partial Portraits* (1888), p. 2),

but James also conceded that Emerson suffered, in fact, from a critical insensibility in several areas. With regard to the Puritan tradition in New England, James's emphasis was less negative than Arnold's. Arnold's reference to American Methodists as people whose minds are 'constantly fixed upon a mind of the third order' ('A Word about America' (1882): Super, Vol. 10, p. 11) would no doubt be too direct and biting for James. James's critical presentation of Puritan principles in *The Europeans* (1878) is not without respect, though the satire on sectarianism in *The Bostonians* (1886) is more in Arnold's sharper vein. Strether's affectionate irony is impregnated with Puritan phraseology, as, for instance, when he refers to Waymarsh as 'the pilgrim from Milrose' (ch. XVII), jokes with Maria about 'the real redemption' of Chad's state (ch. XXII) and tells Sarah Pocock that Madame de Vionnet's amiability was 'a real revelation to him' (ch. XXVII). Yet Ford Madox Ford's observation that James towards the end of his life 'came to think that the society of early, self-conscious New England, with its circumscribed horizon and want of exterior decoration or furnishings, was a spiritually finer thing than the man-nered Europeanism that had so taken him to its bosom' (1937, in *Memories and Impressions* (1979), p. 232) is worth noting as, for once for Ford, probably true. In *The Ambassadors* Strether, when regaining his affection for 'the manner of Woollett' in recognising Mamie Pocock's charming and generous qualities, is given an Arnoldian phrase to mark his readjustment: 'He had never so felt the true inwardness' of the manner of Woollett (ch. XXIV). In the 'Religion new-given' chapter of *Literature and Dogma* (1873), Arnold had defined 'inwardness' as the 'mercy and humbleness' added by Christ to the Old Testament 'judge-ment and justice'. Its practice involved self-sacrifice, attention to 'the *springs* of conduct' and mildness (Super, Vol. 6, pp. 216 and 220–1). Mamie's social delicacy is a product of a New England religious tradition which has been humanised in Strether himself and reveals James's continued appreciation of Arnold's effort to reinterpret Christian ethics for agnostics. It is also Strether's own 'poor old trick of quiet inwardness' which exposes his appreciation of the improvement in Chad to Sarah Pocock (ch. XXIV). James certainly admired Arnold's serious interest in 'the religious life of humanity', especially his remark that the 'paramount virtue of religion is, that it has *lighted up* morality' ('Marcus Aurelius' (1863): Super, Vol. 3, p. 134) and appreciated the fact that Arnold 'was impregnated with the associations of Protestantism' and loved 'biblical phraseology', traits which he felt were 'deeply English' ('Matthew Arnold' (1884), p. 243).

Arnold, of course, also loved France, though with reservations, and here, too, we find James walking in his footsteps. In *Popular Education in France* (1861: Super, Vol. 2, p. 153) Arnold argued that the French masses showed an intelligence 'which the masses of other nations do not possess' and that the cultural origins of this superiority were to be found in the lucid and rational language of modern French law and administration: 'I have myself heard a French peasant quote the Code Napoleon.' He went on in 1864 to liken the French people to the ancient Athenians for their flexibility of intelligence and for having 'a conscience in intellectual matters' ('The Literary Influence of Academies': Super, Vol. 3, p. 236). However, Arnold also came to feel, as Christopher Campos points out (*The View of France from Arnold to Bloomsbury* (1965), pp. 32–45), that the French regard for equality was dependent on tactfully making the most of 'the average sensual man' and confidently propagating the 'pleasurable life of Paris' (*Literature and Dogma* (1873): Super, Vol 6, pp. 390–1), which led to the worship of 'the great goddess Lubricity' ('Numbers' (1884): Super, Vol. 10, p. 155), so that ultimately the French lack of 'a sense for the power of conduct could spoil the French gift for social intercourse and respect for intelligence ('Equality' (1878): Super, Vol. 8, p. 292). In *The Ambassadors* it is Jim Pocock rather than Strether who is tempted by Paris in the profane aspect, 'the great temple, as one hears of it, of pleasure' (ch. XXIII), which forms the background also to Sarah Pocock's flirtation with Waymarsh. On the other hand, Strether's respect for the intelligent conversation of French people obviously reflects Arnold's praise of French civilisation. For instance, he expects the driver of the local *carriole* to converse with a 'genius of response' and 'tell him what the French people were thinking' (ch. XXX). Madame de Vionnet herself is conceived by James as combining predominant French traits such as sociable intelligence and tactful sensuality: 'she was so odd a mixture of lucidity and mystery' to Strether (ch. XXII). Strether's response to France is, therefore, a divided one, finding insincerity and a certain moral hardness alongside excellent taste, wit and attractiveness. The parallels with Arnold are well marked.

Arnold's social analysis of England provided James with what he assumed to be a familiar current terminology. The division of society into three classes, Barbarians, Philistines and Populace, with an enlightened Remnant offering some hope of mitigation of national failings, and, secondly, the perception of English (and American) cultural history as a conflict between Hebraist and Hellenist elements are accepted by James as understood by his readers. The influence of these ideas on James's fiction has been explored by Alwyn Berland in his *Culture and Conduct in the Novels of Henry James* (1981); he sees the opposition between Hebraism and Hellenism as dramatised in the contrast between Mrs Newsome and Madame de Vionnet and notes that it 'is no accident that Waymarsh is described as a "Hebrew prophet"' (pp. 28–37). In fact it is a friend of Miss Barrace's father whom she so calls; she describes Waymarsh as 'the grand old American' of that type (ch. VI). But one takes the point. Equally significant, but not noted by Mr Berland, are the speculations made by Strether on the handsome but 'oddly indulgent' Chad's pagan qualities and their relation to his gentlemanliness (ch. VIII and XII). Arnold had associated paganism with the life revealed by the Pompeii excavations, a life which 'by the very intensity and unremittingness of its appeal to the senses and the understanding . . . ends by fatiguing and revolting us' ('Pagan and Mediaeval Religious Sentiment' (1864): Super, Vol. 3, p. 223). It is natural that Strether's thinking should move in these categories, and indeed perhaps invent memorable phrases of its own in Arnold's style. James believed that it was through Arnold alone that he and his contemporaries had 'grown familiar with certain ideas and terms which now form part of the current stock of allusion': Arnold had given wide circulation to a number of 'expressive phrases' like 'sweetness and light' ('Matthew Arnold' (1884) pp. 244–5). Strether himself likes to repeat expressive phrases both to himself and to his friends, such as 'the sacred rage', 'the visual sense', 'the grand manner', 'the virtuous relation', 'golden nail', 'lovely home', 'supreme respectability', 'bridling brightness' and 'in the picture', all phrases which could serve as titles for pieces of fiction as well as recalling the felicitous formulas of James's favourite writer. In one other detail there may be an Arnoldian influence on James; in *Friendship's Garland* (1866), letter 1, Arnold introduces Arminius to a representative British industrialist '(something in the bottle way)' (Super, Vol. 5, p. 38). The reluctance to be definite about the item of manufacture responsible for the fortune of this 'wiseacre' is the sort of fastidious comic tantalising which James took even farther in the business of not naming at all 'the great product of Woollett' (ch. XXXVI) or Waymarsh's 'extraordinary purchase' in Chester (ch. III).

JAMES AND PATER

After Arnold, the contemporary writer who influenced James's ideas the most was undoubtedly Pater, whose *Studies in the History of the Renaissance* he evidently reviewed in 1873, the year of its publication, though the review was not published and is lost (*Letters*, Vol. 1, pp. 411–12). Significant echoes of Pater's prose occur fairly frequently throughout James's writings. He probably picked up the title for one of his greatest novels, *The Wings of the Dove*, from the Biblical quotation which Pater had set at the beginning of the fourth edition of *The Renaissance* (1893). Also, in the preface to that novel James explains Milly Theale's ordeal of consciousness in terms reminiscent of

Pater's reference to Victor Hugo's *Le dernier jour d'un condamné* in the conclusion to *The Renaissance* (Blackmur, p. 288). The conclusion, containing the propositions that the physical universe is revealed by science to be in a state of flux, that man's mental experience is a series of discrete, momentary impressions, that identity and communication are impossible and that all activity is pointless except that which yields the individual intensely pleasurable sensations, seems the obvious source of many of the ideas to be found in James. Alwyn Berland, for instance, reads Isabel Archer's 'combination of the delicate, desultory, flame-like spirit and the eager and personal young girl' (*The Portrait of a Lady* (1881), ch. 6) as 'James's version of burning with a hard, gem-like flame' in the hunger for experience (*Culture and Conduct in the Novels of Henry James* (1981), p. 99). There would certainly seem to be an allusion to Pater's negative idea: 'This at least of flame-like our life has, that it is but the concurrence renewed from moment to moment of forces parting sooner or later on their ways.' Whether Isabel's 'determination to see, to try, to know' is to be equated with Pater's 'desperate effort to see and touch . . . forever courting new impressions' is more dubious. Alwyn Berland perhaps sees Pater as a more constructive advocate of civilisation than James did; he can argue that Isabel Archer's vocation 'exemplifies the Ruskin–Pater–Arnold sanctification of Culture' (pp. 99–100) and likens Isabel's making over her fortune to the aesthetic Osmond to Marius's saving himself from the heaviness of material vulgarity by following 'the precept of "culture"' (p. 119). But in chapter IX of *Marius the Epicurean* (1885) Pater actually has Marius, confined to the 'closely shut cell' of his own personality, realise 'the true esthetic culture' as 'a new form of the contemplative life' involving a life 'of industrious study', a more extreme, self-absorbed line of conduct than Isabel's. James's allusions to the 'aesthetic' philosophy tend to be reserved or unsympathetic. The long-legged expatriates who 'twanged with a vengeance the aesthetic lyre' in the alley studio across the Seine in *The Ambassadors* (ch. VII) strike Strether as 'queer and dear and droll'. In 1879, Pater himself was said by James to be, on acquaintance, 'far from being as beautiful as his own prose' (*Letters*, Vol. 2, p. 212), and when he died James wrote to Edmund Gosse in 1894 about 'faint, pale, embarrassed, exquisite Pater!' who, like a lucent matchbox, had 'a phosphorescence, not a flame'. He called Pater 'the mask without the face', remarking 'how curiously negative and faintly-grey he, after all telling, remains!' (Lubbock, Vol. 1, pp. 227–8). The extent, then, to which James distances himself from Pater may too often be underestimated.

Jamesian affinities with Pater are naturally most frequently discerned by those who want to stress the subjectivity of James's centres of consciousness and align them with the characters who express themselves in stream-of-consciousness in later Modernist novels. The minds of James's characters are sometimes seen as ever-changing recipients of fleeting impressions. Philip Sicker, for example, argues that the "'self'", for both Pater and James, is merely the sum of its experiences, and, because this experience is a whirlpool of impressions, it follows that there can be no stable source of identity within the conscious mind' (*Love and the Quest for Identity in the Fiction of Henry James* (1980), p. 23). Although certain of James's characters at times do find impressions merging, fluid and blurred, Philip Sicker's use of the word 'whirlpool' seems to me to be unJamesian. After all, James talks in the preface to *The Portrait of a Lady* about the observer's use of a field-glass which ensures him 'an impression distinct from every other' (Blackmur, p. 46). James uses plot and dialogue to correct first impressions. Indeed, he argues that experience consists of the imaginative power of converting 'the very pulses of the air into revelations', of judging 'the whole piece by the pattern' and of being 'one of the people on whom nothing is lost' ('The Art of Fiction' (1884), in *Henry James: Selected Literary Criticism*, ed. M. Shapira (1963), p. 86). This impressionism is constructive and positive, rather than solipsist. Characters in James's fiction whose impressions are swept along by other impressions till 'all melt like water into water' (*Roderick Hudson* (1875), ch. 5) tend to be people on whom something important is lost. Gabriel Nash, in *The Tragic Muse* (1890), who feels we must save as many moments of consciousness as possible 'from the dark gulf' (ch. 2), is a Pater caricature in part. There is, then, a Paterian presence in James, but it tends to be placed, superseded or ironically evaluated.

In *The Ambassadors* this presence of Pater's ideas is at times strong, but it is a mistake to consider it pervasive. Strether frequently interprets his experience aesthetically and impressionistically, though with a readiness for moral criticism which makes him a less hedonistically intense personality than any leading figure in Pater's writings. If he at first suffers an 'assault of images' in Gloriani's garden in the form of signs and tokens 'too thick for prompt discrimination' (ch. X), he eventually makes some sense of them, provisional rather than final and perhaps wrong, but comically ordered. The impressions come to have 'their abundant message' for Strether (ch. XI). If the message only issues in his advice to Little Bilham to live as intensely as he can, Strether later recoils from that urgency as probably morally misleading (ch. XV), in a way that recalls Pater's own failure of nerve when he dropped the conclusion from the 1877 edition of *The Renaissance* in case, as he admitted in a note in the 1888 edition, it 'might possibly mislead some of those young men into whose hands it might fall' (p. 246 n). Strether has his own moments of greatest Paterian intensity when he contemplates Chad's 'pleasant earnest face' (ch. XII), 'the face of one's friend', in Pater's phrase, that sense-stirring impression at which we may well catch while 'all melts under our feet' (*The Renaissance*, conclusion). Chad's 'personal magnificence' (ch. XVII) and his magnificent way of handling the Pococks affect Strether like 'some light, pleasant, perfect work of art' (ch. XX), but of course the development of events in *The Ambassadors* renders such moments of appreciation retrospectively limited by irony. Little Bilham is a more imperturbable aesthete than Strether; when he equivocates about the 'virtuous relationship' between Chad and Madame de Vionnet with the question 'What more than a vain appearance does the wisest of us know?' (ch. X) Little Bilham echoes the Pater of the conclusion, where 'the wisest' were said to spend their interval in 'art and song'. But the novel itself probes beneath the appearance of the relationship. So Little Bilham, though gentle and charming, slips to the margin of the novel's interests. Maria Gostrey's appreciation of him as 'quite beautiful', because he is so consistently and unashamedly inactive (ch. VII), in turn associates her with aestheticism, since she uses the terms of Paterian connoisseurship. As Strether disengages himself from his attachment to Maria, it is significant that he registers the nature of their relationship in rather cool, aesthetic imagery; an hour with her had 'something of the innocent pleasure of handling rounded ivory' (ch. XXXIV) and to sit with her in her dining-room was 'to see life reflected for the time in ideally kept pewter' (ch. XXXVI); comforting thoughts, but not leading anywhere. By this time Strether has grown wary of the impressionistic vision. His belief that elements of the French scene 'composed' themselves pictorially for him had reached its climax during his day in the country, when visual objects seemed to fall into a Lambinet-like composition within the lines of an 'oblong gilt frame' and he had 'the sense of success, of a finer harmony in things' (ch. XXX). However, when the figures 'wanted in the picture' appear, they turn out to be Chad and Madame de Vionnet in a compromising situation. Strether's overconfident sense of a finer harmony is shattered. This sense of a finer harmony is, actually, too complacent and too wilfully, actively fanciful to be truly Paterian, but Strether's general predisposition for 'the task of idleness' and his persistence in 'boring so deeply into his impression' suggest ideas in the conclusion to *The Renaissance*, such as the desire for experience as an end, in which the pulses of life are appreciated by 'the finest senses'. Again, the Paterian mood is a prelude to a comic reversal.

HENRY JAMES AND HIS FATHER AND BROTHER

The James family was its own school of intellectual inquiry. Both James's father and his brother William were authors of outstanding importance in the tradition of American thought. Henry James senior was an unorthodox theologian and social idealist; William James was the leading exponent of the philosophy of pragmatism. James was well acquainted with their ideas both in their published work and in informal communications, and valued them with a combination of affectionate loyalty and amused (or usually amused) criticism.

Henry James senior, reacting against his own father's staunch Presbyterianism, adopted from Swedenborg a view of God as a redeeming agent within the passions of universal man, as the divine natural humanity, and from Fourier an optimistic vision of man's social harmony (Edel 1, pp. 24–36). In works like *Moralism and Christianity: or, Man's Experience and Destiny* (1850), *The Secret of Swedenborg: Being an Elucidation of His Doctrine of the Divine Natural Humanity* (1869) and *Society the Redeemed Form of Man, and the Earnest of God's Omnipotence in Human Nature* (1879), James's father was concerned with mankind in general and its place in the universe. He looked for a regenerated state of human community with the Creator (see F. H. Young, *The Philosophy of Henry James, Sr* (1951), pp. 310–12). He believed neither in individual salvation nor in religious ceremony. He had, furthermore, argued in 1861 in a speech entitled 'The social significance of our institutions' that 'the country of all mankind' was America; hence the inability of an author like Dickens, with his typically European interest in social distinctions and persons, rather than in 'man' himself unqualified by convention, to understand it (cited from F. O. Matthiessen, *The James Family* (1947), p. 61; by Sarah B. Daugherty in her *The Literary Criticism of Henry James* (1981), p. 13). Henry James senior contended that the American state had 'really become the vehicle of an enlarged human spirit'; he was struck by the 'natural or interior refinement' of plain New England people (*Society the Redeemed Form of Man*, ch. 28; in G. Gunn, *Henry James, Senior* (1974), p. 237). This identification of America as the home of a generalised humanity not only influenced the younger Henry James's reviews of Dickens (Sarah Daugherty's point) but surely also informed his presentation of American innocence and cultural thinness in his major works. He writes warmly in *Notes of a Son and Brother* (1914) of his father's 'constitutional optimism . . . fed so little by any sense of things as they were or are, but rich in its vision of the facility with which they might become almost at any moment or from one day to the other totally and splendidly different' (p. 209). The occasion was the sending of James's younger brothers to the experimental co-educational school at Concord, which provided the father with 'a glimpse into that new world wherein dwelleth righteousness and which is full surely fast coming upon our children and our children's children'. James praises his father's philosophic tone here, his ability to catch at any turn 'some flagrant assurance or promise of the state of man transfigured', and his sympathetic insight into the general human condition. James adds that he could not totally disbelieve in the virtue of his father's 'consequent and ultimate synthesis', either, without also betraying himself (p. 214). There seems little doubt that one source of the unstated, implied positive or harmonious relationship and civilisation so strongly felt in James's fiction, but so subtly, indirectly, even obscurely, indicated, lies here.

James's autobiography attributes to his father genial and complex attitudes which one can see reflected in the presentation of Strether's predicament in *The Ambassadors*. The speed with which Strether's moral imagination leads him to assume the best about people suggests Henry James senior's quick and generous insights into what could so easily come about in a state of transfigured human relations. It is significant, too, that Henry James's father always found his sons' mistakes more interesting than their successes. James speculates that the kind of novel or 'personal history' that would have appealed most to his father would have been one 'that should fairly proceed by mistakes, mistakes more human, more associational, less angular, less hard for others, less exemplary for them (since righteousness, as mostly under-stood, was in our parent's view, I think, the cruellest thing in the world) than straight and smug and declared felicities' (*Notes of a Son and Brother* (1914), p. 104). Strether's history certainly fits this case; his confession to Maria Gostrey in chapter III of *The Ambassadors* that he is a 'failure' suggests the very kind of character whom James's father had his own 'manner' of appreciating. The father's idealism was 'the most socialised and ironised, the most assuredly generalised, that possibly could be' (p. 106). The dislike of righteousness is also characteristic. He had a horror of prigs and a love of paradox. He considered moralism or narrow, Puritanical self-righteousness to be the worst failing of America. Legalistic conformism belonged, in his view, to a phase of conflicting impulses within mankind which would be overcome when natural and social needs could be harmonised. So the James boys had the constant amusement:

of hearing morality, or moralism, as it was more invidiously worded, made hay of in the very interest of character and conduct; these things suffering much, it seemed, by their association with the con-science – that is, the *conscious* conscience – the very home of the literal, the haunt of so many pedantries. (*A Small Boy and Others* (1913), pp. 227–8)

In this allusion to his father's criticism of narrow-mindedness James links Matthew Arnold's vocabulary – 'character and conduct' – to his father's satirical term, 'moralism', to which he liked to oppose 'the ideal of the social'. The linkage of ideas underpinning the discussions of Mrs Newsome and the Woollett mentality in *The Ambassadors* is clear enough here surely. Quentin Anderson, who argues for the systematic use of the father's symbolism by the son in his later works, especially in *The Golden Bowl* (1905), refers the treatment of Woollett to Henry James senior's *The Nature of Evil* (1885), where the 'literal or Mosaic' cosmology is condemned as 'a gaunt unhandsome skeleton'. Quentin Anderson's contention that in '*The Ambassadors* the "pinched and wintry Congregationalism" of New England stands for Old Testament righteousness' is overexplicit, but the general similarity of attitude in the father's theological work and the son's novel is certainly remarkable. When Quentin Anderson adds that as an ambassador Strether demonstrates 'that neither persons nor peoples could be saved by righteousness, or any system which affirmed that there were essential differences between individuals' ('Henry James and the New Jerusalem: of morality and style' (1946), p. 554), he is close in meaning to James's text. Strether does not, however, reach the conclusion that there are *no* differences between individuals, as is clear from his final responses to Chad and Maria Gostrey. Quentin Anderson considers that Strether is self-righteous in getting nothing out of the affair for himself at the end; he attributes a new moralism to Strether in his insistence that Chad should stay in France with Madame de Vionnet, which is an interesting point, if rather severe (*The American Henry James* (1957), p. 221). But Quentin Anderson goes too far in attributing to James the perception of a universe without personal problems or distinct entities where only the flow of consciousness is real, 'an insistent and swelling theme' supposed to be derived from his father's works, so that for him James becomes 'the poet of his father's theorising' ('Henry James and the New Jerusalem' (1946), pp. 564–5). Though James enjoyed 'the spirit, the feeling, and the manner' of his father's original and personal system of ideas, he could not, as he told his brother William on the publication of the latter's selection of their father's *Literary Remains* in Boston and New York in 1884, enter into it much himself: 'I can't be so theological nor grant his extraordinary premises . . . nor be sure that the keynote of nature is humanity' (letter of 2 January 1885: Lubbock, Vol. 1, p. 112). James doubted, indeed, whether the spiritual relations which seemed most present in his father's 'schemes of importances' could ever have been successfully incorporated into his own stories (*Notes of a Son and Brother* (1914), p. 160). The human interest to which James was attached as a novelist, though it engaged his father's 'genially alert and expert comment' when actively observed by him, seemed to James to have virtually no place in his father's generalised theory, according to which humanity was 'in its

every fibre the absolute expression of a resident Divinity' (p. 161).
James deeply respected his father, appreciating both his optimistic
temper and his opposition to rigid moralising and self-satisfaction, but
he was not a disciple of his doctrine of redemption through merging
with an undifferentiated spiritual force.

Henry James's relationship with his elder brother William (1842–1910)
was not always easy. For example, at one point, after their father's death, a
disagreement over the will led to the novelist's requesting the philosopher
to limit their correspondence: 'I write this with a clear understanding that
you will write to me after this as little and as briefly as possible' (letter of 11
February 1883: *Letters*, Vol. 2, pp. 404–5). Leon Edel even suggests
(Edel 5, p. 305) that they had been 'like Jacob and Esau', both relapsing
'into petty illnesses when they had to be together for too long a time'.
When after the publication of *The Golden Bowl* (1905) William James
criticised Henry James's mustiness, fencing and evasiveness in his novels,
Henry James replied on 23 November 1905 that he always hoped his
brother would not read anything of his – 'you seem to me so constitutionally unable to "enjoy" it (and so condemned to look at it from a point of
view remotely alien to mine)' (Edel 5, pp. 310–11; Lubbock, Vol. 2,
p. 44). Despite, however, fairly constant criticism from his brother on the
lack of solidity and explicitness in his fiction, James did, in later life, come
warmly to appreciate the works in which William James expounded and
rounded off his philosophy of pragmatism. In 1907 he read his brother's
Pragmatism: A New Name for Some Old Ways of Thinking, which cast a
'spell' on him; he 'was lost in the wonder of the extent to which all my
life I have (like M. Jourdain) unconsciously pragmatised. You are
immensely and universally *right*' (Lubbock, Vol. 2, p. 85). Since M.
Jourdain is the character in Molière's *Le Bourgeois Gentilhomme* who
learns from a philosopher that he has all his life been speaking prose
without knowing it to be such, James may be meaning here that he has
throughout his career been thinking and writing like a pragmatist without being aware of the word for it. If so, there was not so much an
influence of William James's ideas upon Henry James's fiction as a
coincidental affinity of James's practice as a novelist with his brother's
philosophical thought. It was certainly a barbed compliment on Henry
James's part to call himself an unconscious pragmatist in view of
William James's dislike of his style. And he repeated it. On reading
William James's *A Pluralistic Universe* (1909), James thanked his
brother 'with pride', adding that as an artist he could catch on to
pragmatism and 'work in the light of it and apply it' (F. O.
Matthiessen, *The James Family* (1947), p. 344). In the same year he
found his brother's *The Meaning of Truth* (1909) 'of thrilling interest',
feeling that it played into his artistic vision with 'inspiration' (Lubbock,
Vol. 2, pp. 145–6). By the time of these letters, James's major novels

had been written several years back, however. The application of pragmatism to them has to be examined with the benefit of hindsight. William James contended that an idea is true so long as to believe it is profitable to our lives. Truth is 'whatever proves itself to be good in the way of belief' for assignable reasons (*Pragmatism* (1907), p. 76). The argument that Maggie Verver in *The Golden Bowl* (1905) is a rigid absolutist who is devoted to a preconceived idea which exemplifies what William James calls the 'essential foreignness and monstrosity' of the static, timeless absolute was advanced by Joseph Firebaugh in his essay 'The Ververs' (1954, p. 415). But Maggie may also be seen as a pragmatist who gradually makes the idea of her marriage come true. If so, she groups with a number of James's flexible, open-minded, extemporising characters, such as Strether, whose consciousness that truth is a process better called truth-making contrasts favourably with the fixed ideas of his various moral absolutists. William McMurray suggested that William James's distinction between the easy-going and the strenuous mood in the moral life of man was paralleled in James's fiction by the distinction between characters who take things easy and characters who take things hard, such as Basil Ransom and Olive Chancellor, respectively, in *The Bostonians*; monistic absolutism is destructive in Henry James's pluralistic world; James urges a pragmatism that would free us from limiting reality 'by keeping life "open"' ('Pragmatic realism in *The Bostonians*' (1962), p. 344). Richard A. Hocks in his *Henry James and Pragmatistic Thought* (1974) develops this critical theme by interpreting several of James's stories in terms of his brother's thought. William James's view of experience as an immediate flux which furnishes material for later reflection certainly seems relevant to Henry James's narrative centres of consciousness. Richard Hocks argues that Henry James's '"cordial" or open-ended' fiction corresponds to William James's thesis that knowing is made by 'the ambulation through intervening experiences' (p. 41): Henry James's ambulating mind is genuinely devoted to the pluralist ideal (p. 45). Furthermore Richard Hocks regards *The Ambassadors* as 'the textbook illustration' of this relation between the brothers' work. Strether is a pragmatist in abandoning the preconceived moral absolutism of Woollett in favour of 'his new and ongoing experience of Europe' (pp. 152 and 156). In France, Strether relocates his moral seriousness contextually, instead of *a priori*, and the fact that he can be deceived bespeaks his openness. He preserves a 'pragmatic cordiality to multiple meaning and awareness' (p. 171) and refuses to distinguish 'the confluently related elements of experience', which he cannot empirically divide (p. 173). It is this cordiality which makes him such an attractive character to the other characters in Europe as well as to the reader. Jamesian pragmatism is, of course, as Richard Hocks points out, somewhat more positive than Paterian impressionism; whereas Pater embraces flux as an end in itself, 'William James embraces it as a means of making it yield something workable while, in his prospective view, never denying the *possibility* of some final goal' (p. 67). This view of the potential of William James's perceptual flux is, significantly, rather tentative, however. Strether, while abandoning a predetermined norm, still has constantly to adjust his ethical sensibility and remains too uncomfortable to be only a neutral pluralist; he does not refuse to distinguish the confluently related elements of the pluralistic world for ever, in my view, nor would I go as far as Richard Hocks does when he identifies Strether's way of thinking with Henry James's. Clearly the novelist is not deceived in the way that Strether is. However, the similarity between Strether's interpretation of experience and William James's accounts of the ideal pragmatist is evidently considerable. Yet it may be, as Dorothea Krook suggested, that James's view of a reality in which everything is internally related with everything else was taken, not from his brother's pragmatism nor from his father's Sweden-borgism, but just 'from the ambient air of nineteenth-century specula-tion, whose main current was the preoccupation with the phenomenon of self-consciousness' (*The Ordeal of Consciousness in Henry James* (1962), p. 411). One could say that it may, probably, equally have been contributed to that air by him as taken from it. The amalgam of ideas that is James's own, a core of moral self-criticism, civilised harmony and cultural breadth enhanced by an ironical consciousness of experi-ence as delicate, variable, subtle, many-sided and subject to revision, is more than a reflection of impressionism, aestheticism or pragmatism. It stands clearly in relation to the thought of Arnold, Pater, Henry James senior, William James and others, and recognisably it stands by itself.

CHAPTER 4

The Form

THE PSYCHOLOGICAL NOVEL AND *ERLEBTE REDE*

The Ambassadors is generally agreed to be a difficult work to read, particularly at the first attempt. The difficulty is felt to appertain partly to the language of the novel (not so much to the vocabulary as to the syntax) and partly to a certain obliqueness in the form.

Perhaps the difficulty arises because the form is in one sense so pure. *The Ambassadors* is prose fiction and nothing else (one character, Gloriani, with his wife, strays in from another James novel, *Roderick Hudson*); elements of verse, historical reporting, journalism, authorial commentary, song, pictorial illustration, dramatic inset, parody, fantasy, story-within-the-story, epistolary communication, diary-keeping, mock-pedantry and verbal display are totally excluded. A telegram is quoted in chapter XVIII; a preface and two frontispieces were added to the New York Edition. But otherwise *The Ambassadors* is pure fictional narrative with no time-shifts; it conveys what was thought in the story, what was said, what was felt and what was done. There is some very economical recollection of the past, but the narrative sticks closely with Strether during his four or five months' visit to Europe. Wherein, then, is the lack of straightforwardness?

One characteristic of *The Ambassadors* which strikes everyone is that there is hardly any action. The physical content of the novel seems confined to strolling, talking, eating and sitting. Even compared with other James novels, in which people do fall ill, have miscarriages, see ghosts, have accidents, break things, witness fires, cheat one another, shoot themselves, paint pictures, face the public, fall in love, propose, marry and die, *The Ambassadors* is very short on incidents. Various Americans come to Europe; a young American eventually leaves his French mistress; her daughter's engagement to a Frenchman is announced. That is about all. Undoubtedly, Chad and Madame de Vionnet make love during the course of the story, but that is quite out of view. Indeed, their mere appearance together in the same rowing-boat has the effect of a major sensation. Meetings of people are the most important events in the novel, both first meetings and meetings after a lapse of time. Two of these meetings are such coincidences that in another novel they might suggest a metaphysical dimension, but not here. That the woman whom Strether meets by chance in a Chester hotel should turn out to be an old schoolfriend of Chad's mistress and that Strether should come upon the very spot in the French countryside where Chad and his mistress are out together are chances which are felt to be not significant in themselves, but only aids to the clarification of the situation. In fact the clarification of the situation is the plot of the novel, or such plot as it has, for the clarification is not absolutely complete. The obscurity of motivation on the part of some of the characters undoubtedly contributes to the difficulty of *The Ambassadors*.

As a novel of situation *The Ambassadors* is by no means unique. Obviously it has influenced many subsequent novels, where the plots may be even thinner, but it also has affinities with Jane Austen's comic novels, where the plots decidedly thicken, such as *Pride and Prejudice* (1813). That, too, is about changing judgement of a situation and characters. In its early version, probably in epistolary form, it was entitled 'First Impressions' (see the 1970 Oxford English Novels edition of *Pride and Prejudice* edited by F. W. Bradbrook, introduction). Though its plot turns on much firmer incidents, like proposals, an elopement and marriages, than those that we find in the James novel, *Pride and Prejudice* also has little action and much strolling, talking, eating and sitting. But, in first obscuring and then clarifying the Darcy–Wickham relationship from the point of view of the intelligent and sympathetic Elizabeth Bennet, whose personal interests are vitally involved in the outcome, Jane Austen preserves a pattern of guidelines for the reader which James in his novel largely requires him to do without. Jane Austen gives and withholds precise information in the role of a reliable but calculatingly ironic narrator, she uses letters to clear up misunderstanding and convey correct information, she traces the stages in Elizabeth's change of opinions through soliloquy and dialogue, she flanks Elizabeth with one character who cautions her against haste *before* she knows the truth and one who persists in Elizabeth's error *after* she knows the truth, she works towards a happy ending which indicates which characters have learned their lessons and which not, and she reports Elizabeth's reflections on the situation (for example, in Volume III, chapter 2, when she tries to 'make out' her feelings towards Darcy) in prose which is analytic, formally patterned, undistracted by sensual perception or chance thoughts and free from intonations suggesting authorial reservations. James, though prejudiced himself in considering Jane Austen's heroines to have 'undoubtedly small and second-rate minds', still found them interesting for their expression of 'simple undistracted concentrated feeling' (letter to George Pellew of 23 June 1883: *Letters*, Vol. 2, p. 422). Jane Austen goes behind her main characters' appearance, gestures, actions and speech to explore their feelings and composed thoughts, and so contributes to the transformation of the epistolary form of the eighteenth-century novel into the psychological form of the nineteenth-century novel. But James did not find her work an immediate model.

James always felt that his task as a novelist was to represent the inner life of imaginative people, the personal history of lively and cultivated imaginations. His aim, as explained in his autobiography, was to catch 'the man of imagination' in his novels and represent the light in which an imagination 'might so cause the whole scene of life to unroll'. In the end, in order to achieve this effect in a novel like *The Ambassadors*, James had to draw this character 'forth from within' and to turn himself 'inside out' to make it objective, for objectivity was 'the prize to be won'. He leaves it to the reader to judge if he has failed (*Notes of a Son and Brother* (1914), pp. 344–6). With such an end in view, James predictably admired George Eliot's and Hawthorne's practice in drawing their characters from within. The desired effect of intelligent realism in fiction was, in James's view, dependent on the inner psychological representation of intelligent, cultivated characters (see Sarah B. Daugherty, *The Literary Criticism of Henry James* (1981), p. 47). Therefore, he especially admired George Eliot's 'full portrait' of Dr Lydgate in *Middlemarch* (review in *Galaxy*, 15 March 1873, p. 427) and the deep psychological penetration shown in Hawthorne's novels. Indeed, James considered Hawthorne's preoccupation with internal possibilities, the landscape of the soul, to be characteristically American; Hawthorne presented the drama of consciousness, which depends on the extent to which characters are aware of themselves and of each other and their sins. It was in this sense that Hawthorne collected 'mosses' and could 'see in the dark' (*Hawthorne* (1879), p. 88) like a cat. James believed that a self-conscious, cultivated character should be at the centre of novels and constitute their main subject. This element was essential to produce the illusion in readers that they were enlarging their experience, that while reading the novel they had 'lived another life' (*Partial Portraits* (1888), p. 227). Novelists who presented stock characters lacking psychological depth, like Daudet and Zola, were consistently criticised by James for doing so. He believed that a novel should look inwards.

Flaubert, however, was a difficult case for James, for here was a novelist who, especially in *Madame Bovary* (1856), combined exploration of the inner consciousness of a central character with ironic authorial detachment. Despite his distaste for the petty and sordid experience of Emma Bovary in Flaubert's novel, James acknowledged that she is a 'powerfully conceived' and extremely realistic figure ('The Minor French Novelists' in *Galaxy*, 21 February 1876, p. 227; cited in

Sarah B. Daugherty, *Literary Criticism*, p. 52). Emma Bovary's romantic attitudes are not merely satirised by Flaubert, but also acquire an added dimension of irony from Flaubert's 'irritated sensibility to the life around him', which underlies both his detailed naturalism and his stylistic artistry, Flaubert's imagination thus works indirectly upon the reader, even if it is a fact that, in James's view, the nature of his heroine's consciousness is still 'really too small an affair' (*Notes on Novelists* (1914), pp. 76 and 81; from James's introduction to W. G. Blaydes's translation of *Madame Bovary* (New York, 1902), pp. v–xliii). George Eliot, no doubt influenced by Flaubert's example, followed a similar practice of irony with regard to certain characters like Hetty Sorrel in *Adam Bede* (1859) and Rosamond Vincy in *Middlemarch* (1871–2), both of which impressed James, although these unsympathetic figures are not central ones in the design of the novels, in her case.

The style which allows these novelists to present the thinking, feeling and inner attitudes of such limited characters while also controlling the narrator's distance from them is called *le style indirect libre* (first identified by Charles Bally in the *Germanisch-Romanische Monatschrift*, vol. 4 (1912), pp. 549–56 and 597–606) or *erlebte Rede*. This style differs from indirect speech ('he thought that') by omitting introductory verbs and conjunctions and transposing direct speech-form into the past tense colloquially, at the same time varying the vocabulary and syntax from those appropriate to the character to those appropriate to the narrator. It is this varying which is free and subtle – indeed, not always definite. The indirect free style is, as Bally says, 'une forme intermédiaire' (p. 597); he cites several instances from *Madame Bovary*. Flaubert uses the style to interpose himself between his personages and us (see M. Lips, *Le Style indirect libre* (1926), p. 193). It avoids the rhetoric of inner soliloquy and allows the narrator to convey placing and generalising meanings not available to the character. Flaubert uses it not only to convey impulsive emotion, but also to reveal insincerity and to caricature weaker traits in characters (see S. Ullmann, *Style in the French Novel* (1957), pp. 106–10). In English there are traces of *erlebte Rede* in Scott, Thackeray and others, but the first novelist to fulfil all the conditions for developing this style is George Eliot; she first combines representation of the inner life with authorial analysis, allowing characters' self-consciousness to reach us through a critical, comparative and objective filter (see Lisa Glauser, *Die erlebte Rede im Englischen Roman des 19. Jahrhunderts* (1948), pp. 117–19; and Roy Pascal, *The Dual Voice* (1977), ch. 6, p. 1). Henry James was, predictably, very fond of this technique. It is used with particular success in *Washington Square*, where the inexperience and toughness of the dull Catherine Sloper are both sensitively caught and ironically assessed as the narrator slips his own phrases unobtrusively in among hers. However, *Washington Square*, influenced by the French tradition in the novel, is not typical of James's fiction; it lacks an intelligent, cultivated centre of consciousness close to the author and was excluded from the New York Edition.

The difficulty with *The Ambassadors* is that here James uses the indirect free style virtually exclusively, but applies it to the case of a character, Strether, who is not distinctly limited like the characters discussed above, but who is highly intelligent, intuitive, capable of learning and tender in conscience. Strether's very flexibility and self-critical openmindedness make the reader's task of responding to the nuances of the free indirect style highly problematic. Extreme attentiveness is necessary, and also careful balancing of the ambiguities. In order to achieve his aim of intelligent realism in the novel, James has to foreshorten the distance between narrator and central consciousness, so that the psychological exploration is less judged than many readers expect and want, and may sometimes seem to be, or to amount to, unintentional self-revelation on the part of the narrator.

The psychological novel is not, of course, exclusive of description of the external world. The impersonal historical and scenic background description used by Scott, for example, tends in later, more psychological novels to be subsumed in the characters' responses to natural scenery and to aspects of culture and society. These responses are made either in the course of characters' pursuit of personal relationships and, indeed, of employment or else simply in their capacity as tourists. Indeed, some of the most impressive instances of the presentation of the relationship between the individual and the environment in Victorian fiction come during accounts of characters' reactions to places, works of art and public spectacles. In her classic though brief article, 'A note on literary indebtedness: Dickens, George Eliot, Henry James' (1955), Q. D. Leavis selected such passages from Dickens's *Little Dorrit*, George Eliot's *Middlemarch* and Henry James's *The Portrait of a Lady*, in which the heroine responds to the sights of Rome, and argued that James was indebted to the other two. Rhetoric, indicating the author's view of a young girl, comes between the reader and the character in the case of the Dickens, but in the George Eliot example we share the girl's 'experience of disorder', which is 'both precipitated by and dramatically enacted by the concept "Rome"' (p. 426). The James example Q. D. Leavis finds comparatively diluted and generalised, diffusing merely a melancholy charm and leaving the heroine's postulated suffering unrealised. Though extremely perceptive, these strictures on James lose something from the fact that his heroine reaches a crisis of perception similar to George Eliot's heroine at a later point in the novel and not during the passage cited by Q. D. Leavis. In *The Ambassadors* there is a whole series of scenes in which James improves on his early handling of this technique. It is certainly true both of George Eliot and James that the central figures in the major novels convert items of sense impression into images which recur at moments of crisis and act as correlatives of acute feelings. James's richly metaphorical style requires such sensuous responsiveness in his characters. Sometimes the process is reversed, as when the tired metaphor in the phrase 'in the same boat' becomes an ironic symbol when Strether finds himself not in the actual boat being used by Madame de Vionnet and Chad (ch. XXXI). This point is not articulated by Strether, however, only silently indicated by the narrator. The consciousness of a character like Strether is a linguistic world in which phrases and images drawn from literary and colloquial usage (some carrying overtones not present to the character) merge, exchange and clash with expressions used or just being found to describe landscape, buildings and people. It is surely the interaction between interior reminiscence and self-questioning on the one hand and the stimuli provided by the surrounding human world on the other which gives the dramatic consciousness of Strether its immediacy and life, making the novel such fascinating reading, despite the evident density and complexity of its prose. So James exploits the potentials of *erlebte Rede*.

POINT OF VIEW AND INDIRECTION IN *THE AMBASSADORS*

Although the narrator does not withdraw completely as a commenting presence in *The Ambassadors*, we are given his point of view very sparingly indeed. To the virtual exclusion of any other character's point of view the point of view in the novel is Strether's. Strether is an observer of and participant in the action as it happens. Information about previous action or occurrences elsewhere is either given through his memory and intuition or reaches him during dialogue. Indications as to the time and place of incidents may have an authorial stamp, especially when intervals of time are passed rather rapidly over, but there is no consistent attempt to balance Strether's point of view against that of any other figure. James does not go behind any other figure to dramatise an alternative centre of consciousness. Franz Stanzel defines this narrative situation in *The Ambassadors* as 'figural', lacking narrator's summaries, prefigurations and transitions; this is the reason, he says, why most of its chapters 'end in the middle of a dialogue' (*Die Typischen Erzählsituationen im Roman*, trans. James P. Pusack as *Narrative Situations in the Novel* (1971), p. 106). James prefers the reader to draw his own conclusions from the point reached in the exchange of speeches rather than to expound them for him in the manner of the omniscient author.

James's fiction previous to *The Ambassadors* exhibits a variety of narrative situations from the use of the omniscient narrator to the use of letter-writers and first-person or autobiographical narrators. His methods all tend, however, to let his fictional situations speak for them-

selves without authorial commentary and to reduce as much as possible
the number of characters from whose point of view the situation is seen.
These two principles of composition are termed by him 'impersonality'
and 'economy', respectively. He objects to the self-conscious novel, in
which the narrator freely discusses the conduct of the fiction, as
violating his ideas of intelligent realism; for James, as for George Eliot,
the novel conveys a series of probable and possible truths about human
relationships which is just as conscientiously serious as the findings of
the historian. In an essay of 1883 he characterised Trollope's intrusive
confessions of make-believe as 'little slaps at credulity', which were as
damaging and shocking as admissions would be on the part of a
historian that he, too, had made something up (*Partial Portraits* (1888),
pp. 116-17). James disliked the role of the self-conscious author-
narrator. But, if the broad sweep, slice-of-life effect achieved by
omniscient narration seemed to James to lack concentration, form and
artistic propriety, its opposite, first-person narrative, also had in his
view its disadvantages. In the preface to *The Ambassadors* he deplores
'the terrible *fluidity* of self-revelation' involved in the autobiographical
technique – a looseness of form associated here with an undue interest
in the self on the part of the hero, as he has to convey information and
confesses weakness in embarrassing detail, presuming on the
sympathetic indulgence rather than on the critical awareness of the
reader (Blackmur, p. 321). In the first-person novel the central figure
both experiences the action and narrates it, being equipped, in James's
phrase, with 'the double privilege of subject and object'; he has,
implicitly at least, to justify his own selection of material from his
fictional past, both trivial and significant, for narration. In point-of-
view narration, however, this responsibility is removed from the central
figure and assumed entirely by the all-but-absent narrator; a convenient
and clever tactic.

James's method has the advantage of presenting experiences, which
he defines as 'our apprehension and our measure of what happens to us
as social creatures' (Blackmur, pp. 64–5), from the point of view of an
intelligent, finely aware individual, without this reporting consciousness being felt to be preternaturally knowing or identical with the
author's. In certain instances these Jamesian reflectors are on the
periphery of the action as observers, in other instances they cluster
round the central figures but are not to be confused with them, and in
some cases they are themselves centres. Sometimes there are only two
or three of them to a novel; their points of view alternate. In *The
Ambassadors* there is only one, Strether's and it is central; this novel
employs 'one centre . . . keeping it all within my hero's compass', and
the narrator's role is to simplify that part of the value of Strether's
adventure which the projection of his own consciousness upon it still

leaves 'unexpressed' (Blackmur, p. 317). This 'rich rigour' in narrative technique gives the novel both unity and intensity. The formal consistency of *The Ambassadors* enabled James to estimate it as 'frankly, quite the best, "all round"', of his novels (p. 309).

To say that Strether's is the central point of view does not mean that he is the sole central subject-matter of the novel, however. Centrality in James's theoretical parlance is envisaged as a point from which to see the world, not as a spot on which to narrow the focus. The subject-matter of a James novel is some aspect of interconnected human relations; his subject, he says, is 'the related state, to each other, of certain figures and things', and the form of the novel draws a circle within which those relations appear to stop, although they really 'stop nowhere' (p. 5). Not all of those relations, however, 'directly minister to interest', and the felicity of the form depends on the writer's appreciation of 'the degree of that directness'. In general, James felt that most of the obvious facts, incidents and processes of human life – proposals, weddings, childbirth, deaths and funerals, lovemaking, dreaming and rejoicing, doing work, playing sport and fighting enemies, elements which fill up classic nineteenth-century novels – did not 'directly minister to interest' in the way he knew *he* could make things interesting. Such physical and ritualistic elements of human relations are interesting, he believed, only if presented indirectly, through memory, allusion, discussion, anticipation or an alternative point of view. A prime instance of such Jamesian indirection is the presentation of Milly Theale's illness in *The Wings of the Dove* (see my '*The Wings of the Dove*: the main image', 1979), where the novel dispenses with Milly's consciousness just before the sick-room would inevitably begin to dominate it. James's subtlety in this instance has misled certain critics into doubting whether Milly is ill at all, though there is no doubt that her illness is acutely present to the imagination of Merton Densher, to whose point of view James hands us over. Even when there is no shift in the point of view, James's predilection for indirection can give rise to ambiguities; in several James stories certain vital facts are never established with certainty. Neither the occasional use of the narrator's own comments nor the (frequently negative) outcome of the plot gives enough clues to what actually happened or what people really thought and felt. In these cases the figures from whose point of view the story is told are employed not so much to be 'the most polished of possible mirrors of the subject' as to be conveyors of the uncertainty and anxiety which a relationship with a weak, indecisive or secretive personality produces. James identifies Strether as an 'unmistakeable' example of such mirrors '(*he* a mirror verily of miraculous silver and quite pre-eminent, I think, for the connexion)' (Blackmur, p. 70). Though there is some obscurity in the motivation of the characters in *The*

Ambassadors, especially in the case of Chad, the main subject-matter of
the novel – the morals and manners of various Americans brought into
relation with French tradition – is too broad to be seriously obfuscated
or brought into doubt. The main problem is that Strether is himself a
component of the subject-matter; he underestimates himself and cannot by himself express the full value of the critique of America which
the novel conducts. His consciousness leaves a part of the value of his
adventure 'unexpressed' (Blackmur, p. 317).

In order to clarify these problems of indirection, James developed in
his three late major novels the use of what he called *ficelles*, characters
like strings or wires which the novelist manipulates to firm the structure of meaning in the work. These *ficelles*, of whom the main examples
in *The Ambassadors* are Maria Gostrey and Waymarsh, are said by
James to belong, from the point of view of the novel as a whole, less to
his 'subject' than to his 'treatment of it'; they are the reader's friends
'much rather' than they are Strether's friends (Blackmur, p. 322).
James's exposition of his idea of the *ficelle* in his preface to the novel is
full of traps for the unwary, since he uses the word 'subject' to mean
'central recording consciousness' rather than 'subject-matter', for
which he uses words like 'theme', 'image' or 'object'. The *ficelles*, then,
or confidants appertain to the treatment of Strether. They are aids to
lucidity in the sense of enabling James to relieve the figure from whose
point of view the story is told from tedious inner confession and to
bring to his notice elements in the situation which have escaped it,
especially with regard to himself. In the preface James gives as an
example the way the referential narrative is waved away 'with energy'
when Maria questions Strether on his past. However, the free development of the 'artistic process' of writing the novel may give such subordinate, functional characters more life and interest than was at first
expected of them. James admits that Maria Gostrey 'achieves, after a
fashion, something of the dignity of a prime idea', and the same can be
said of Waymarsh. As characteristic American types, they help to
define Strether's own type by what they are not and by their relationships with other characters which are different from his. *Ficelles* may,
therefore, enrich the pattern of significance in a novel, even though
their primary function is formal.

A *ficelle* like Maria Gostrey functions mainly in dialogue. The
abundance of dialogue in *The Ambassadors* is one of its most attractive
features. There is, generally, an equal balance struck between episodes
of reflection and response to visual experience in Strether's consciousness, on the one hand, and episodes of often bantering dialogue on the
other. Rather confusingly, James termed the latter episodes 'scenes'
and the former 'pictures' (an analogy, probably, with the stage and the
film); one tends, of course, to think of episodes like the description of

the gathering in Gloriani's garden (ch. X) as a 'scene', whereas in James's terms it is not, or only partly so towards the end. Consideration of this feature of the novel is further confounded by James's insistence that the consciousnesses of his central characters are dramatised by his narrative technique; so, he can say he takes his 'subject for the stuff of drama', meaning that his 'pictures', too, are dramatic (but not scenic). 'Pictures' which he especially approved in *The Ambassadors* were those in which Strether meets Chad in the theatre (ch. VII) and in which Strether comes across Mamie in the hotel salon (ch. XXIV). Such 'pictures' are all 'discriminated preparation', he felt, for the scenes which follow them and also have 'representational virtue' in their own right, though the 'direct presentability' of Chad is thereby 'diminished and compromised' (Blackmur, pp. 322, 323 and 325–6). James believed that the variation or opposition between picture and scene con- tributes, by its intensity, to the dramatic effect of the novel. The analogy here is probably with dramatic contrasts in musical form.

The typical chapter in *The Ambassadors* begins with a few paragraphs of picture and then modulates into scene. Over half the chapters mix the two methods one way or another, and over half of these have a pre- ponderance of scene. Thirteen of the thirty-six chapters use scene vir- tually exclusively, to be set against a mere four (chs. V and XXX– XXXII) where there is no dialogue. James had come to feel after seeing a performance of Ibsen's *John Gabriel Borkman* in 1896 that the 'scenic scheme' was the only one he could trust to get his novels completed within a reasonable word-limit (*Notebooks*, p. 263). *The Awkward Age* uses this scenic method all the time. *The Ambassadors* certainly relies on it to a great extent and looks as though it does so, as one turns the pages, in a way that *The Wings of the Dove* does not. It is, in fact, more of a dialogue-novel in form than anything else. The distinguishing factor is that Strether not only takes part in every single dialogue in the novel, but also interprets to himself what his interlocutors say and how they say it. *The Ambassadors* is thus a remarkable example of technical virtuosity and plausibility.

A NOTE ON JAMES'S STYLE IN *THE AMBASSADORS*

The difficulty in James's later style has two aspects: density and ob- scurity. The prose is both full of imagery, allusion, complicated syntax and personal vocabulary and also lacking in repetition, identification, elucidation and summary. A technical account of this language is pro- vided by Seymour Chatman in his *The Later Style of Henry James* (1972); it deals with James's psychological nominalisations, obliquity, deixis, expletives, ellipsis and colloquialism. The dialogue tends to be easier to comprehend than the long paragraphs of reported reflections, since it uses short sentences and phrases and is dominated by question-and-answer exchanges. Yet even in the dialogue there is a great deal of abstraction and indirection, as people and ideas are represented by pronouns and circumlocutions and sometimes mistaken by the other speaker. The dialogue is marked by mutual admiration among the parties as they catch on to the apt phrase, the fashionable colloquialism, the refined allusion, the novel metaphor or the heightened cliché. Much of the comic tone of the novel depends on the linguistic aware-ness of Strether and his interlocutors as they search for definitions, postpone conclusions, dispose of objections, elaborate similes, and complete and revise each other's meanings. Conversation in *The Ambassadors* is an ironic art with much fencing, probing, ambiguity and surprise. The participants take pleasure in understanding each other's speculations without having to confirm facts and spell out names. At one point James attributes to Strether the image of the toy-puzzle to indicate this process: 'Considering how many pieces had to fit them-selves, it all fell, in Strether's brain, into a close, rapid order. He saw on the spot what had happened and what probably would yet; and it was all funny enough' (ch. XXVI). Conversations begin abruptly, with the subject known intuitively to both parties. For example, while Little Bilham is watching Sarah Pocock at Chad's party, Strether suddenly asks him what she makes of it all:

'By which I mean on what terms does she take it?'
'Oh, she takes it, I judge, as proving that the claim of his family is more than ever justified.'
'She isn't then pleased with what he has to show?'
'On the contrary; she's pleased with it as with his capacity to do this kind of thing – more than she has been pleased with anything for a long time. But she wants him to show it *there*. He has no right to waste it on the likes of us.'
Strether wondered. 'She wants him to move the whole thing over?'
'The whole thing – with an important exception. Everything he has "picked up" – and the way he knows how. She sees no difficulty in that. She'd run the show herself, and she'll make the handsome concession that Woollett would be, on the whole, in some ways the better for it.' (ch. XXV)

This snatch of dialogue is typical of *The Ambassadors*, sparing in attri-buting the speeches to the speakers and witty in establishing the motives of a third party with satirical guesses. The language is dis-tinguished by its abstract moral vocabulary ('terms', 'claim', 'right', 'better') and deictic nouns and pronouns, that is, ones which have an indicative function but no independent content ('it all', 'this kind of thing', 'Everything'). The reader has to substitute his own explicatory references for phrases like 'to show it *there*', which means 'to show his new cultivation in America', or 'an important exception', which means 'Madame de Vionnet herself'. The speakers take up each other's phrases and refine the meaning without necessarily revealing all that they imply and infer. They agree on the words, words whose content is vague or minimal, but retain different private interpretations. As Ruth Bernard Yeazell has pointed out, (in *Language and Knowledge in the Late Novels of Henry James* (1976)), the Jamesian common code of words like 'wonderful', 'extraordinary', 'splendid', 'prodigious', and so on, distinguishes a social world 'in which each member has potentially his own secret' (p. 73). Strether being so inclined temperamentally to postpone conclusions and delay the impact of known facts, the reader's pleasure consists substantially in detecting and anticipating possible truths behind the deixis and periphrases, while responding to the interruptions and inversions in the sentence-structure as expressive of a reluctant, hesitant, exploratory and evasive state of mind.

The style of the dense 'picture' episodes in *The Ambassadors* has been the subject of several excellent analyses, to which all students of James must be indebted. The first notable one is Ian Watt's 'The first paragraph of *The Ambassadors*: an explication' (1960), in which five distinctive features of James's prose are distinguished: a fondness for nontransitive verbs, frequent abstract nouns, much use of 'that', elegant variation to avoid an excess of personal and possessive pronouns, and the presence of many negatives and near-negatives. He finds the average length of sentences in the first paragraph of the novel to be forty-one words, and notes the delayed specification of referents and the predominance of mental ideas and states of being over concrete subjects performing finite actions affecting objects. David Lodge made a related study of the two opening paragraphs of chapter XXXI in his *The Language of Fiction* (1966, pt 2, ch. 5), choosing a passage where, in the second of the two paragraphs, facts do break in on Strether's consciousness. He finds that, in the first six sentences of the first paragraph of chapter XXXI, Ian Watt's categories do generally prevail, as expected, but in the next six sentences there are fewer non-transitive verbs, more concrete subjects and a succession of regular subject–verb–object constructions. David Lodge concludes that the violation of Strether's consciousness by facts 'is conveyed by the partial violation, at the moment of recognition, of the linguistic norms of the novel' (p. 204), so that the latter part of his first sample paragraph has an unusual effect of clarity and alertness, concerned as it is with events in a physical continuum, grasped in the mental continuum of Strether's consciousness. Strether's style is characterised as grandly vague, grand because of the nobility of his 'vision of social beauty' and vague 'because it failed to take into account some brutal facts of human nature' (p. 213). Critical understanding of James's style has also been advanced by Ruth Bernard Yeazell in the work referred to above. She chooses the *last* paragraph of chapter XXXI, calling the whole episode 'a recognition scene with a vengeance'. Close analysts of the language of the novel have understandably tended to focus on the Cheval Blanc chapters, because of their crucial relevance to the assessment of the theme. David Lodge's essay, which seems to me the most decisive defence of *The Ambassadors* that we have, is designed to answer F. R. Leavis's sceptical question as to the value of the experience of life which Strether has missed ('Is it anything adequately realized?': *The Great Tradition* (1948), p. 161). David Lodge's analysis of the style establishes that 'what is being realized in the greater part of *The Ambassadors* is the experience of a man who has himself not fully "realized" the total implications of that experience' (p. 194). Stylistic analysis is also relevant to the argument that Strether does, after the Cheval Blanc scene, recognise the implications. The impatience we feel with Strether is a necessary and proper effect of the elaborate style and narrative tone of affectionate humour, as both Ian Watt and David Lodge convincingly demonstrate, and it is James's use of our impatience which gives the Cheval Blanc scene its power.

CHAPTER 5

The Evolution of *The Ambassadors*

THE NOTEBOOK SKETCH OF 1895

On 31 October 1895, James wrote in his fifth notebook a long entry (*Notebooks*, pp. 225–8) concerning a possible story to be called 'Les Vieux'. Jonathan Sturges, who was staying with James in a Torquay hotel at the time, had set the novelist's imagination working with some information about William Dean Howells. Eighteen months previously Sturges had met Howells in Paris, where he was on a short visit to his son. Brooding on his sense of the newness of life in Paris, Howells had told Sturges:

> Oh, you are young, you are young – be glad of it: be glad of it and *live*. Live all you can: it's a mistake not to. It doesn't so much matter what you do – but live. This place makes it all come over me. I see it now. I haven't done so – and now I'm old. It's too late. It has gone past me – I've lost it. You have time. You are young. Live!

This private speech of Howells of 1894, reported by Sturges on 30 October 1895, and avowedly amplified and improved by James the next day in his notebook, is the initial idea of *The Ambassadors*. Some of its phrasing is preserved intact in Strether's speech to Little Bilham in chapter XI. The emotional situation of an older man's enjoining a young fellow-American to live intensely as he himself had failed to do becomes the first climax of the novel (though not its 'center', as the editors of the *Notebooks* assert, p. 229). Two other features of the Howells speech are especially significant: its temerity (it implicitly condones moral indifference – 'It doesn't so much matter what you do'), which gives rise to guilt and modification, if not retraction, in Strether; and its evocation of Paris ('This place makes it all come over me') as the city where certain people's way of life exemplifies intensity of living *par excellence*. In the novel this impression of Paris is the leading, but not the only, one. After writing *The Ambassadors* in 1901, James confirmed in a letter to William Dean Howells (Lubbock, Vol. 1, p. 384) that the incident of his having spoken those words to

Sturges 'during a call at Whistler's' was 'the faint vague germ' of the novel's subject, though as an idea it had immediately 'got away from' Howells and 'become impersonal and independent'.

To get it away from Howells, James had first to tie the incident to an invented American character. The 1895 notebook entry proceeds to explore the possibilities of an imaginary 'figure of an elderly man who hasn't "lived"'. In view of Howells's profession, the new character could not be a novelist. In turn James rejects the claims of a fictitious clergyman to the role (too obvious), a journalist, a lawyer (too experienced), a doctor, an artist, a businessman (not intellectual enough), a professor (too knowledgeable about the young), and settles for the 'Editor of a Magazine' as most suitable (though not perhaps as far away from Howells as he had hoped). This intellectual, '*fine*, clever, literary almost', is Strether in embryo; and the idea of the tale is to be 'the revolution that takes place in the poor man'. At first, then, James conceives of the Strether figure as a kind of routine Puritan who 'has never really enjoyed – he has lived only for Duty and conscience – his conception of them; for pure appearances and daily tasks – lived for effort, for surrender, for abstention, sacrifice'. He is one who has not been particularly self-conscious, since James does not see him as 'having battled with his passions' or suspected what he was missing. 'The alternative wasn't present to him.' But when the central figure of the projected tale comes into the presence of this 'alternative', having come out to 'decide some question with regard to some one, in the sense of his old feelings and habits', then the new influences 'make him act just in the opposite spirit – make him accept on the spot, with a *volte-face*, a wholly different inspiration'. This reversal in the direction of pleasure amounts to no more in the end, however, than 'the sense that he may have a little supersensual hour in the vicarious freedom of another'.

This preliminary sketch of Strether, though it prefigures one of the main turns of the plot of *The Ambassadors*, contains some emphases that are subtly modified in the novel. There Strether has been to Paris before and has developed a more critical, liberal awareness of Woollett before, or else instantly after, he comes out again (he knows that the failure of Woollett is general); similarly, his surrender to new influences is never intellectually complete. There is more continuity in Strether than the original idea of a revolution in him or a volte-face suggests; he is complex both before he comes out and after.

In his notebook James toys with the idea that his projected hero may have oppressed in the past a younger relative or ward, whose desire to live intensely he has failed to understand. The young man would now be dead, and the hero, from his new point of view, guilty and bitter about it. This part of the scheme is dropped in the novel, no doubt because it would have made Strether too repressively active in the past and hence less capable of detachment.

James is not yet entirely sure that the new influences which open his hero's eyes need be French. It is somewhat obvious and banal, he feels, to use Paris to provide the revelation. London or Italy might do, or just 'the general impression of a summer in Europe'. However, on second thoughts, James decides that if the hero is an American ('he might be an Englishman') 'I'm afraid it must be Paris'. This indecision provides evidence that the theme of French life does not have priority over the theme of Anglo-Saxon anti-hedonism in the conception of *The Ambassadors*, but derives from it.

For the occasion of his hero's visit to Paris, James now devises the 'little illustrative action', 'the little drama', of what is to become the Newsome family. 'Say he "goes out" (partly) to look after, to bring home, some young man whom his family are anxious about, who won't *come* home, etc. – ', but then under the new influence tells the young man after all to stay on in Paris:

> Say our friend is a widower, and that the *jeune homme* is the son of a widow to whom he is engaged to be married. *She* is of the strenuous pattern – she is the reflection of his old self. She has money – she admires and approves him: 5 years have elapsed since his 1st wife's death, 10 since his own son's. He is 55. He married at 20! Displeasing the strenuous widow is a sacrifice – an injury to him. To marry her means rest and security *pour ses vieux jours*. The 'revolution' endangers immensely his situation with her. But of course my denouement is that it takes place –

In the novel Strether's son's death (of diphtheria, at school) occurs after, not before, his wife's, and Strether blames himself for neglecting the boy in the excess of missing his mother, but both these deceased characters are very pale presences. A more marked change is in James's handling of the strenuous widow, Mrs Newsome, who was originally planned to be 'the reflection' of Strether's 'old self'. In *The Ambassadors* she is felt to have dominated Strether in America, but not exactly reflected him; indeed, she had exhausted him, leaving him 'one of the weariest of men' and 'distinctly fagged out' (ch. V). The Strether of the novel realises he had felt 'done for' at the point of departure for Europe rather than being about to enter into a state of rest and security. Particularly in its cultural aspirations Strether's old self is presented as having been distinct from Mrs Newsome's, though its negativity and ineffectuality as envisaged in the 1895 notebook entry are preserved in the novel. Again, the fact that in the novel the old self is perceived only in Europe and therefore only when it is changing to the new is not precisely anticipated in the original note. Of course, this retrospective approach to the old self inevitably makes the development of Strether more elusive and complex than the preliminary sketch suggests.

THE SCENARIO OF 1900

On 1 September 1900, Henry James signed a completed typescript, 'Project of a Novel by Henry James', which was subsequently seen by his literary agent, J. B. Pinker, and sent to Harper & Brothers, the New York publishers, as a 'statement drawn up on the basis of the serialization of the work' (James's letter to H. G. Wells of 15 November 1902, in *Henry James and H. G. Wells: A Record*, ed. Leon Edel and Gordon N. Ray (1958), p. 84). This preliminary statement or scenario (a shorter scenario, written in 1899, is lost: Edel 4, p. 320) runs to over 20,000 words on ninety typed pages. James himself refers to its exceptionally extreme detail and length. Having been retained at Harper's, it was published in part in *Hound and Horn*, vol. 7, no. 3 (April–June 1934), pp. 541–62, edited by Edna Kenton, and in full in *The Notebooks of Henry James* (pp. 370–415). The scenario is in three sections with a preface; altogether it contains a sketch of the genesis of *The Ambassadors*, full notes on characters, summaries of scenes, examples of dialogue, and an overall outline of the plot. It is not, however, as claimed by Edna Kenton, 'almost the preface itself to *The Ambassadors*', proving that before the act of creation James's 'intention was crystal clear'. Rather, the scenario is virtually a short story in its own right, a version of the subject by no means identical with the novel itself. In places, especially when James is inventing characters who are treated indirectly in the novel, the prose of the scenario is actually superior to that of *The Ambassadors*, and its dialogues, mostly dropped when it came to writing the novel, are arguably crisper and more dramatic than what later emerged. The scenario is more than a statement, as James told Wells it was, 'full and vivid, I think, as a statement could be, of a subject as worked out'. It is an earlier, abbreviated, somewhat different version of the novel which was to be completed in 1901.

In the introductory four paragraphs which form the unnumbered preface of the scenario, James repeats the story of the Howells speech as providing him with 'a vivid and workable theme'. It describes the enclosed old garden in the Faubourg St-Germain where Sturges had heard the speech, during a 'charming June afternoon in Paris' (in the novel the scene in Gloriani's garden takes place in April). It refers to Howells merely as a distinguished American acquaintance of his own, a 'rather fatigued and alien compatriot', whose 'slow rush' of an outburst may have been occasioned in particular by the 'presence of a charming woman or two, of peculiarly "European" tradition'. The women as well as the 'slow rush' reappear in the novel.

This second, amplified and improved version of the speech (*Notebooks*, pp. 373–4) repeats the points made in the first in the same order, expands one of them and adds two more. The reference to Paris is expanded to: 'This place and these impressions, as well as many of those, for so many days, of So-and-So's and So-and-So's life, that I've been receiving and that have had their abundant message, make it all come over me.' In the novel this new allusion to other people's lives in Paris as affecting Strether's mood is tied specifically to Chad and people whom he has seen 'at *his* place' (ch. XI) and the impressionist phrasing, the 'abundant message' of impressions, is retained. The first entirely new point in the scenario version of the speech is that the mature American admits that his own life 'couldn't, no doubt, have been different for me – for one's life takes a form and holds one' – a concession to determinism retained in the novel in the inelegant metaphor of the 'tin mould' into which the 'helpless jelly' of consciousness is poured. The new emphasis on not being able to help things in the past serves to diminish Strether's feeling of guilt. James's position on the Free Will and Determinism controversy was possibly close to G. H. Lewes's doctrine of Limited Will, as exemplified by sailors who are 'free to move to and fro' on the deck of a ship but not free to prevent the ship from being 'swept onwards by the waves' (G. H. Lewes, 'The study of psychology, (1879), p. 103) – a useful compromise allowing for variation of emphasis. The speech in the novel has a lot to say about the freedom of the people whom Strether has been meeting and observing in Paris, a freedom not to miss the train of life, which may only be an 'illusion of freedom', but which is an illusion whose memory is worth having and whose memory Strether does not have. This admiration of a limited exercise of freedom is implicit in the scenario version. The second new point in the scenario version of the speech is Strether's assurance to the young man (here provisionally called Glenn Burbage) that he knows he is not stupid, 'or I shouldn't be saying these awful things to you'. This insertion, which is retained in a slightly altered form in the novel, reduces the element of temerity in the speech, suggesting that the young man will not misinterpret Strether's advice too self-indulgently or immorally.

The speech in the scenario runs as follows:

Oh, *you're* young, you're blessedly young – be glad of it; be glad of it and *live*. Live all you can: it's a mistake not to. It doesn't so much matter what you do – but live. This place and these impressions, as well as many of those, for so many days, of So-and-So's and So-and-So's life, that I've been receiving and that have had their abundant message, make it all come over me. I see it now. I haven't done so enough before – and now I'm old; I'm, at any rate, too old for what I see. Oh, I *do* see, at least – I see a lot. It's too late. It has gone past me. I've lost it. It couldn't, no doubt, have been different for me – for one's life takes a form and holds one: one lives as one can. But the point is that *you* have time. That's the great thing. You're, as I say, damn you, so luckily, so happily, so hatefully young. Don't be stupid. Of course I don't dream you *are*, or I shouldn't be saying these awful things to you. Don't, at any rate, make *my* mistake. Live!

The main difference between this version and the next is that nothing is said here explicitly about freedom. Again, in *The Ambassadors* Strether asks Little Bilham to allow for the possibility that he is over-reacting to his past restraint. Also, in the novel the style is more figurative, with references to a clock, a station, a whistle, a train, a line, an embossed tin mould, a jelly and a 'great cook'. The speech gains a great deal of irony from its context in the novel, following upon the account of the trick of 'social art' played by one of Madame de Vionnet's companions and preceding the rejoinder of Little Bilham, who tactfully reassures Strether that he would not like to be 'too different' from Strether at his age. In the scenario the theme of Strether's missed opportunities is still being worked without any substantial qualification.

Section I of the scenario corresponds to the first four chapters of the novel, called by James 'My Preliminary'. It deals with Strether himself, his relation with Mrs Newsome, his reunion with Waymark (Waymarsh) and his new friendship with Maria Gostrey. The account of the central figure, named now for the first time as Lewis Lambert Strether, is much more closely aligned with the role of Strether in *The Ambassadors* than with that proposed for the Puritan figure of the notebook entry. The subject of the novel is to be the picture of 'some six months or so, in the history of a man no longer in the prime of life'. James intends to risk representing everyone in the novel, 'rather monotonously', as liking him. He is to be a contemporary New Englander, 'sufficiently typical', with 'many earnest and anxious experiments' to look back on, but little success. 'Educated, with excellent gifts, intelligent', he is highly esteemed in the 'rather provincial' world of Worcester, Massachusetts, or some similar town (not the seat of a large college). Unlike the figure in the notebook entry, this Strether is 'vaguely haunted by the feeling of what he has missed' even before he comes to Europe. He has already been to Europe 'once or twice' before:

His traditions, associations, sympathies, have all been the liberal and instructed sort, on a due basis of culture and curiosity; he has not been too much mixed up with vulgar things; he has always been occupied, and preoccupied, in one way and another, but has always, in all relations and connections, been ridden by his 'New England conscience'. (*Notebooks*, p. 375)

The allusion here is to a refined Arnoldian tradition, adapted to the United States and overbalanced perhaps by Protestant-style strictness, but also with links back to the Enlightenment, a tradition certainly embodying a critical historical understanding, but lacking in academic precision, and, even more, lacking in experience. As James wittily puts it, Strether is disenchanted in America 'without having known any great enchantments, enchanters, or, above all, enchantresses'. He is, however, widely read in literature, has tutored at college for a while (there is no reference in the scenario to the tutoring of Mamie Pocock) and has had hankerings 'for "study", for serious literature, for serious journalism', before taking up the editorship of the review. The review itself is taken by all the American colleges and goes to Europe; in another of the superbly comic passages in which the scenario abounds, but which can hardly be accommodated in Strether's own thoughts in the novel, James describes the review as being 'devoted to serious questions and enquiries, economic, social, sanitary, humanitary' and remarks that 'they believe it to have attracted attention in high quarters' in Europe (*Notebooks*, p. 383). For all that kind of innocent optimism, the Strether of the scenario is a man of genuine insight; he has, 'with imagination, perception, humour, melancholy', the sense of what he has lost or only just 'caught the last whisk of the tip of the tail of', that is, pleasure; he is very critical of the late Mr Newsome, who in his business dealings had been 'the reverse of over-scrupulous' and left a name of a savour not 'ideally sweet' (*Notebooks*, p. 379). Mrs Newsome's father was a similar type. Compared with Mrs Newsome, Strether even regards himself as 'a man of the world', and he has a theory, different from her own, that her son Chad 'is not a little, really, alas, of an egoist and even a brute'; all this before Strether leaves on his mission. The one area in which this much more familiarly recognisable Strether reverts to the figure of the notebook entry is the connection with his dead son. This time the boy survives his mother and dies at the age of 16 in a swimming accident. But Strether does penance for having brutally blundered about certain 'tender and sensitive things in the lad', for not having truthfully allowed for the boy's 'nature, temperament, tendencies'. In the novel, on the contrary, the boy is said to have been *dull*, because he had been banished by Strether, so that the compunction is less bitter, though still painful. In the scenario the pointing up of Strether's deep, probably morbid, feeling about his son tends to contradict the new Arnoldian view of him as disinterested; it 'had been his idea of himself, above all, that he has been fundamentally indifferent and detached, fatally unable really to care for anything'

(*Notebooks*, p. 382). Here we have the self-conscious and self-critical observer who is to be developed in the novel ('a period of conscious detachment' had occupied 'the gray middle desert of the two deaths; ch. IV) and is essentially formed thus in America before he sets out on his mission.

In the scenario, Mrs Newsome is presented with brilliant clarity and analytical sharpness, though without the metaphoric suggestiveness of the novel. She is no longer the reflection of Strether's old self, but a figure over against which that self begins to define itself. She fully evokes, as James says, Strether's 'background and setting', the 'cluster of circumstances' in which he is involved. James characterises her convincingly with his inventive rhetoric; she is the widow of Worcester, 'domiciled and dominant', aged 51:

> a really remarkable woman: high, strenuous, nervous, 'intense' (oh, a type!) – full of ideals and activities, many of them really, in respect to her husband's career, of a decidedly fine expiatory or compensatory nature. She is many other things besides; invalidical, exalted, depressed, at once shrill and muffled, at once extremely abounding and extremely narrow, and of an especial austerity (in spite of herself almost, as it were, and of some of her imaginations), an especial refined hardness and dryness of grain and strain.

She is haunted by her rather dreadful image of Chad's French mistress, whom she fancies low and mercenary, a 'ravening adventuress'. She has fallen in love herself with Strether, who has become necessary to her and whose mission to Europe on her behalf relieves her of a task which proved to be too much for her nerves. Lest this sketch should promise too vivid an element in the novel, however, James warns his publisher that we are to see Mrs Newsome only in Strether's consciousness, 'altogether in this reflected manner' (*Notebooks*, p. 381). He claims that she will be put just as distinctly before us by the indirect method as by the method now being used in the scenario: 'lively element as she is in the action, we deal with her presence and personality only as an affirmed influence, only in their depicted, represented form . . . always out of it, yet always of it, always absent, yet always felt'. It is not made clear yet to what extent Mrs Newsome will be represented in dialogue by her daughter, who in the novel is regarded at times as being almost indistinguishable from her. In one other point, also, the detail of Strether's relationship with Mrs Newsome differs in the scenario from what emerges in the novel itself. In the scenario both she and Strether accept in good faith that the mission may well fail, in which case honour will have been saved by the practical effort to save Chad. In the novel Mrs Newsome appears as more peremptory since it is admitted soon after the outset that Strether's failure would put his future with her in jeopardy; he stands to lose 'everything' (ch. IV).

James undertakes in the scenario to specify in the novel the 'vulgar article of domestic use' which is manufactured by the Newsome firm, but in the novel he actually exploits his decision not to specify it. On the other hand, the details of Chad's free use of money from the firm, while he is in Paris, and his independence of his mother owing to a legacy left him by his maternal grandfather are retained exactly in the novel. In the scenario the commercialism of Worcester is spelled out satirically by James in a manner which is too direct to be Strether's own: 'The bustling business at home, the mercantile mandate, the counter, the ledger, the bank, the "advertising interest", embody mainly the special phase of civilisation to which he must recall his charge' (*Notebooks*, p. 396). Such a catologue is too narrow to do justice to the Woollett of the novel, which, despite its faults, is in the end felt to be capable of change and which, despite its censorious moral traditions, which have to be rejected, is also felt to be capable of a 'lovable' manner and a 'true inwardness' (ch. XXIV).

In the scenario, the first person whom Strether meets in Europe is Waymark (*sic*), not Maria Gostrey. We are given the words of a tele-gram he sends to Waymark from Queenstown in Ireland: 'No – not Liverpool; wait for me at Chester – like awfully to be with you there a day or two' (*Notebooks*, p. 376), the prissy tone of which hardly makes its absence from the novel a loss. Waymark and Strether spend a Sunday (the day of arrival is not named in the novel) walking on the walls and in the Rows of Chester and 'talk, talk, talk', before meeting Maria Gostrey 'on the rampart'. It is Waymark's first trip away from America, and he has been 'overworked' in Europe, whereas in the novel Waymarsh seems, less satisfactorily, to be in Europe merely on a 'wild hunt for rest', vaguely dogging his separated wife (ch. II). In the scenario considerable space is devoted to explaining how Miss Gostrey had known Waymark in New England: in the novel Waymarsh has no recollection of any previous acquaintance with her, an early detail which tends to diminish our sense of her reliability as a reporter of the exact truth. Indeed, the priority of presentation which James accords to Maria Gostrey in *The Ambassadors* over Waymarsh works paradoxically to check any impressions we might gain to the effect that he is less important or considerable than she is in the balance of forces playing upon Strether. In the scenario Waymark is treated with delightful, verbally fecund satire with Arnoldian overtones, as one who,

unamenable, unadjustable, to a new and disarranging adventure . . . fails to react, fails of elasticity, of 'amusement', throws himself back on suspicion, depreciation, resentment really; the sense of exteriority, the cultivation of dissent, the surrender to unbridgeable difference. Waymark's office in the subject is, in other words, that of a contrast and foil to Strether – (*Notebooks*, p. 377)

But in the novel Waymarsh's function is more ironically complex than this passage suggests, since Strether eventually ends up feeling out of tune with Europe in a way that partly recalls Waymarsh's.

In the scenario James, while anticipating fairly closely the attributes of Maria Gostrey's personality (her 'slightly battered' quality and 'semi-cynical helpfulness') and her function as an extractor and conveyer of information for the reader, gives a much more explicit and comic account of her business as an 'amateur-courier' than we can find in the novel. This attempted verisimilitude is not all gain, however, since there is something inherently improbable in the economic background of Maria's services. 'She comes over with girls. She goes back with girls. She meets girls at Liverpool, at Genoa, at Bremen – she has even been known to meet boys. She sees people through. She shops with them in Paris. She shops with them in London, where she has a tailor of her "very own". She knows all the trains. She meets a want' (*Notebooks*, p. 378). It is unlikely that she could be so organised and yet so free, so much in demand and yet so disdainful of commercial strategies like advertising. In *The Ambassadors* Maria Gostrey is only a 'superior "courier maid"' who does nothing for money (ch. I), and her occupations are suspended during Strether's visit. This vagueness at least deters one's sceptical investigation. Her developing fondness for Strether is mentioned in the scenario, of course, as well as their jointly ironic observation of Waymark and her eliciting from Strether the fact that there is an understanding between Mrs Newsome and himself amounting to an engagement. In the scenario, however, but not in the novel, Maria Gostrey urges Strether not to disappoint Mrs Newsome, who can guarantee his future: 'Therefore he mustn't let her back out' (*Notebooks*, p. 386), and consequently he *must* capture Chad for her, she urges. James offers a specimen of the dialogue between Maria and Strether which will conclude the part of the novel set in England:

'Oh, I see what you're thinking – that Paris is an awful place, and that it may be awfully difficult. But it will be all the more fun.'

'Fun?' poor Strether rather ruefully echoes.

'It's just the sort of job,' she replies, 'that's really, I assure you, in my line and that I should be quite ready to hand in an estimate for. Upon my word, I'd take the order.'

'I wish to goodness then you would!' her companion laughs. 'It would save me a lot of trouble!'

'Well, I'll save you', she responds, 'all the trouble I can.'

In *The Ambassadors* Maria Gostrey doesn't hand in estimates or save trouble quite as serviceably. In the lengthy dialogue throughout chapter IV there is much discussion about Mamie's role in the rescue of Chad and about the increasing mildness of the spirit of the age in Woollett; at the end Maria promises to be Strether's till death, but only to prevent his losing everything – a much more negative commitment. We have there much more of a sense of Maria's 'general human awareness and competence' (*Notebooks*, p. 385) at the receiving end of checks and surprises.

Section II of the scenario covers events in Paris up to the arrival of the Pococks, though there is little evocation of the glamour of the city. Instead Strether is taken about by Burbage (Bilham) to places like cafés, restaurants, even to the 'Folies-Bergère' (*Notebooks*, p. 388), where one can hardly imagine him in the novel, unless forced to go there with Jim Pocock. He also enjoys himself with one or two of Maria Gostrey's friends, none of whom appears in the novel. There is no scene at the Théâtre Français, no party at Chad's apartment, no encounter in Notre-Dame. The romantic background is largely left out. Chad simply 'comes on the scene', prodigiously transformed, of course. Far from having been brutalised by some horrible woman, he appears as charming and good-natured, but not the fascinating pagan of the novel. As in the novel, however, Strether discovers that Chad's 'manners at least have extraordinarily improved', as he postpones discussion of the main issue. But there are 'inscrutabilities' about Chad: he is not as simple as Strether had expected, but 'the note of the *changed* creature . . . overlies everything else'. The 'difference in Chad' is what James gives: James admits to his publisher that Chad is 'a special figure – difficult to do, but to be unmistakeably done; and I don't pretend here to construct him for you. For that you must wait for the book.' In fact, Chad still remains somewhat unconstructed and mistakable in the book, so that James's own postponement of elucidation in this case, contrasting with the treatment of several other characters in the scenario, is significant.

James introduces Madame de Vionnet in a snatch dialogue between Maria Gostrey and Strether not unlike that at the beginning of chapter IX of the novel, where they discuss the good woman who has 'held her own' with Chad and accounts for him. In the scenario, the phrasing is cruder; she is some woman 'more or less feeding on him' who has 'saved' Chad. There is no play with the idea of a virtuous attachment or *ces dames*. It is Maria Gostrey and Strether who suggest that Madame de Vionnet may be planning a match between Chad and her daughter, though it is explained that she does not know the lady's name because Strether got it wrong or did not pronounce it in speaking of her – a circumstance accounted for more plausibly in the novel by the fact that

Chad had kept the name from Strether also. As in the novel, Strether meets Madame de Vionnet and her daughter during a scene in the garden of a 'prime celebrity' (Gloriani) just before the representation of Strether's 'moral "dishing"' (*Notebooks*, p. 393) in the speech about living intensely. Madame de Vionnet is charming, sympathetic, 'young (that is, she is thirty-eight)', and the cleverest thing about her is that she does not alarm Strether by being 'dazzlingly clever'. On the other hand, she is not the kind of person with whom Strether is likely to fall in love – a complication which, in *The Ambassadors* itself, is surely felt to be a possibility. 'Her charm is independent of that for him, and gratifies some more distinctively disinterested aesthetic, intellectual, social, even, so to speak, historic sense in him, which has never yet been *à pareille fête*' – at the same time Strether is confused as to the nature of Madame de Vionnet's relationship with Chad. Maria Gostrey brings out the details of Madame de Vionnet's past during a walk home (not in the garden); the details correspond to what we learn in chapter XII, except that in the scenario Maria's cleverness at school is not qualified as being bookless. Chad, when pressed by Strether, duly denies that he is in love with Jeanne de Vionnet or intends to marry her. Madame de Vionnet then becomes the cause of a process of change in Strether 'which is of the core of the subject' (*Notebooks*, p. 395); his estimate of the value of her relationship with Chad rises. Madame de Vionnet comes 'to stand, with Strether, for most of the things that make the *charm* of civilization as he now revises and imaginatively reconstructs, morally reconsiders, so to speak, civilization'. Madame de Vionnet's positive qualities are stressed without any dark hints at all: James calls her 'a magnificent little subject, and the artist must be left alone with her. There is much in her – alas, for the artist's ease, *too* much' (*Notebooks*, p. 396). As with Chad, James's uneasiness suggests that there may be less in the character than he expects. The element of *promise* in this passage in the scenario indicates that charm by itself was going to prove hard to handle on such a scale, without more ambiguity.

The second section of the scenario ends with an account of the events which precipitate the Pococks' arrival – something Strether is said not to have 'thought of', though in the novel he expects at least Mamie to come (ch. IX). Waymark is not involved in communications with Mrs Newsome about Strether. Strether himself lets Mrs Newsome know that Chad will not return to America without him, and Strether stays on, obscurely coerced by Madame de Vionnet. On receipt of the ultimatum from Worcester, Strether urges Chad to stay on and promises to see him through, instead of asking Chad to stand by him, as in the novel (ch. XVII). He then cables to Mrs Newsome, recommending her to come to Paris, yet privately expecting to go back to America on her summons instead. In the novel he gets Chad to cable to his mother that he declines to return (ch. XVIII). These changes in the action all tend to make Strether more passive, more of a drifter, in the novel, knowingly but indirectly precipitating the second embassage, more by omission than by commission.

In section III of the scenario James takes the story of his projected novel through to its conclusion. The Pococks are presented vividly and fairly fully. They are called 'fresh emissaries' whose office is 'that of rather tacitly, coldly and austerely superseding and suspending Strether in *his* function' (*Notebooks*, p. 400), Sarah being 'empowered to speak and act, conscientiously, lucidly, indignantly, if necessary, for' her mother and arriving, therefore, 'with a great deal of accumulated resentment, disapproval, virtue, surprise'. This irony is essentially reproduced in the novel with longer metaphoric flourishes and a less cryptic quality. Also, Sarah develops the same relationship with Waymark as in the novel. Jim Pocock, however, is given more to do in the scenario than in the novel itself; he talks continually to Strether in their walks about 'matters at home', especially about Chad's father, and brings to his notice 'two or three facts, illustrative of the deceased's character and practices', which disgust Strether and convince him that Mrs Newsome is a woman rich in connections that 'grow ugly and smell badly, for him' (*Notebooks*, p. 407). Thus, the corrupt element in American commerce is given a stronger emphasis at this stage in the plot than at the corresponding stage in the novel, where Jim mentions no such facts. Sarah's nastiness is enhanced in the scenario by the incident there in which she suggests to Strether that Chad may be deliberately engineering a split between Strether and Mrs Newsome by which Chad himself might 'pecuniarily profit'. Mamie Pocock is much less prominent than in the novel. There is no scene with her and Strether in the hotel in which he revises his opinion of her upwards. She is represented merely ridiculously as 'the little Pocock', the cause of a row between Chad and Sarah on the latter's folly or 'humiliating futility' in supposing him amenable to 'any such bait'. This idea is said to have been surrounded by 'ignorant complacencies' and 'fathomless fallacies' (*Notebooks*, p. 401). There is no sign of any respect for Mamie in the scenario at all. Consonant with this anti-American bias in the scenario is the playing down of the arranged marriage for Jeanne de Vionnet. The engagement is said to be 'markedly congruous and suitable'; it is to a 'candidate presented' by Jeanne's father, whereas in chapter XXII of the novel her father takes no trouble over the matter and merely has to accept what Chad has arranged. Nor is Strether's disapproval of the match mentioned in the scenario; he reacts only by rebuking Maria Gostrey for making a gross mistake about Chad's supposed love for Jeanne, whereupon Maria admits that she deliberately deceived Strether about it. In *The Ambassadors* Strether and Maria agree amiably that the news simplifies the situation (ch. XXIII) and that Chad did once think it would be nicer if he '*could* care' for Jeanne, implying self-questioning in Chad over his attachment to Madame de Vionnet.

In the scenario Strether goes on hoping that some turn of events may make Chad's marriage to Madame de Vionnet possible. He supports her without qualification, saying to himself: 'As between Madame de Vionnet and the advertising-department, then, I decide for Madame de Vionnet, and if my expression, my action *is* to tip down the scale, why, let it tip' (*Notebooks*, p. 408). After seeing her with Chad 'in a suburban village' in a position 'indubitably intimate with the last intimacy', Strether is staggered and ashamed, but not depressed, as in the novel, for the upshot is 'to confirm Strether's vision of the influence and the benefit the situation has represented for Chad'. In the scenario Madame de Vionnet visits Strether at this juncture (not vice versa) and 'proves to him, how good she is for Chad', so that Strether defends Chad to Sarah Pocock. The Pococks then depart for America, with Waymark, all scandalised, and Chad stays with Madame de Vionnet: Strether himself prepares to return to a hostile Woollett, 'to all the big Difference, over there' (*Notebooks*, p. 412), but not before a farewell interview with Madame de Vionnet in which he receives her gratitude, 'probably the most beautiful and interesting morsel in the book', though one which, no doubt fortunately, never materialised, since this climax to which the 'action marches straight from the first' was dropped from the scheme of the novel. With Chad's deciding to go home, the valedictory scene between Strether and Madame de Vionnet is, in the novel, combined with the previous scene with her (ch. XXXIII), in which she affirms that she and Chad now 'bore' Strether, the only certainty in her own future being that she will 'be the loser'. The last chapter, however, is much as projected in the scenario; Strether rejects marriage with Maria Gostrey because it 'would be almost of the old order' (*Notebooks*, p. 415), but James gives us his 'moment of hesitation' and 'their lingering, ripe separation'. James admits, too, with some embarrassment, that almost all the women in the story have been 'agreeably and favourably affected' by Strether, even to the point of proposing to him. He had not fully reconciled the value and attractiveness of Strether with the defeat of things American which the conclusion reached in the scenario entailed.

H. M. Alden, the reader for Harper's, wrote an unfavourable memorandum on James's project, reacting no doubt to the anti-American emphases which recur throughout the presentation of characters and plot:

The Scenario is interesting, but it does not promise a popular novel. The tissues of it are too subtly fine for general appreciation. It is subjective, fold within fold of a complex mental web, in which the reader is lost if his much-wearied attention falters. A good proportion of the characters are American, but the scene is chiefly in Paris. The story (in its mere plot) centres about an American youth in Paris who has been captivated by a charming French woman (separated from her husband) and the critical situations are developed in connection with the efforts of his friends and relatives to rescue him. The moral in the end is that he is better off in this captivity than in the conditions to which his friends would restore him. I do not advise acceptance. We ought to do better. (*Notebooks*, p. 372)

Though condemned as 'a masterpiece of miscomprehension' by the editors of the *Notebooks*, Alden's memorandum at least lays bare the lack of ambiguity in the scenario's core. The inability to respond to the point-of-view technique reveals Alden as insensitive to James's originality as a writer, but the implication that the moral content of the story was objectionable as well as likely to prove unpopular may have had a lot to do, not only with the two years' delay before publication, but also with James's decision to alter many details in the direction of ambivalence and reroute the whole ending. James, no doubt, wished to forestall criticisms like Alden's.

THE FOUR MAIN EDITIONS OF *THE AMBASSADORS*

The Ambassadors appeared in three versions in 1903. It was serialised in twelve monthly parts in the *North American Review* between January and December 1903. Two sets of uncorrected proof-sheets of the first nine parts of this version were deposited in 1903 in England for copyright purposes, one in the library of Cambridge University and one in the Bodleian Library, Oxford. (These proofs were discovered by Brian Birch; see his 'Henry James: some bibliographical and textual matters' (1965). I adhere closely to his argument.) The novel appeared in book form in September 1903, published by Methuen in England, and again in November 1903, published by Harper in America. James had written to his literary agent, J. B. Pinker, on 13 August 1903, referring to copy for the Methuen edition; he was going to send his English publisher the eight parts of the *North American Review* version so far published, together with an interpolation, and 'a duplicate Type-Copy of my M.S., which I fortunately have clung to, and have not sent him hitherto because the printed text of the Serial contains inevitable little amendments and alterations. (Besides this I am afraid I lack duplicates of some passages omitted in the serial form and subsequently supplied to Harpers for insertion in the Book.)' (*Selected Letters of Henry James*, ed. Leon Edel (1956), p. 131) The passages referred to as omitted from the *North American Review* serial are four pages of chapter V, giving Strether's account, largely hypothetical, of Chad's experiences in

Paris hitherto, the whole of chapter XIX, the whole of chapter XXVIII and the whole of chapter XXXV. The serial version is, however, based on thirty-two and half chapters of James's original typescript (now lost), with a few minor cuts near the ends of instalments undertaken so that the text could finish at the foot of a page. In its abbreviated form the novel makes a more obscure impression than otherwise since virtually all the omitted sections are about Chad; but not too much can be made of this fact, for the restored versions were available in book form on both sides of the Atlantic before the serialisation in the *North American Review* was complete. By the autumn of 1903 the cut and full versions were becoming available, in effect, simultaneously. The evidence does suggest, however, that James considered that the novel could still stand up without the additional material presenting Chad. Chapters VIII, IX, XII and XVIII do also present Chad directly, but more delicately than the sections omitted from the serial. James may have experienced a certain nervousness about the manner in which the fuller exposure of his immoral young American expatriate would be received in the United States.

The first English edition, since its Parts One to Eight are based exactly on the corresponding parts in the *North American Review* which James sent to Methuen for copy, reproducing even the minor cuts made to suit pagination in the finished periodical, may seem intermediate. It can, nevertheless, with respect to its Parts Nine to Twelve and to the passages dropped from the periodical version but restored to it, be considered the earliest text of *The Ambassadors*. The last third of the Methuen version and the restored passages throughout it are almost certainly based on James's carbon copy of his typescript. This carbon copy, though it may have carried a few corrections by James, was unaffected by the alterations which he had made to the typescript sent to Harper in New York, many at the proof stage. Consequently Parts Nine to Twelve of the Methuen edition do not reproduce the minor cuts made to suit pagination in the periodical. The most significant of these minor cuts is one near the end of chapter XXIV, in which Mamie Pocock has the momentary effect on Strether of making everyone else in the whole affair seem 'stupid'. The most distinctive features of the Methuen text are its extended treatment of Chad's putative love-life in Paris prior to Strether's arrival in chapter V and its abbreviated account of Strether's last minutes with Chad in chapter XXV. In the English text Chad's irregular sex-life in Paris is referred to as a 'fever in his blood, early recognised, yet so difficult to account for', breaking out into a 'chronic affection', and the number of his girlfriends is said probably to have exceeded 'those of mere modest clock-faces', that is, twelve; both these rather prurient ideas are dropped from the Harper text. Also dropped is a longer passage in which Mrs Newsome is credited with the knowledge that Chad had moved back into the expensive district of Paris in 'scandalous notorious company', making 'bolder pushes and taking larger freedoms,' having reached there 'almost like a Pasha – save that his palanquins had been by no means curtained and their occupants far from veiled' (ch. V); such fanciful details throw a lurid light on the Woollett imagination as well as attributing to Chad a taint of indecency. James can be assumed to have felt that they would not particularly amuse his American readers; they tend to discredit the American side too much, and they had to go.

In chapter XXXV, however, the Methuen text lacks an important piece of dialogue between Strether and Chad and an account of Chad's reassuring gestures as Strether leaves his flat with him for the last time. Their conversation breaks off in the Methuen text with Strether's declaring himself to have been made in the first place 'portentously solemn', but in the Harper text Chad goes on to say that no one could have been good enough to make Strether better, for he never needed improving, and 'what *is* beastly, at all events', was losing Strether, who then admits, laughingly: 'I am, certainly, prodigious.' This exchange underlines the influence Strether has had on Chad and aligns the two characters more positively, as does a statement added to a Chad speech a little later: 'Haven't I been drinking you in – showing you all I feel you're worth to me?' In the Methuen text Chad merely shows Strether an 'intention of kindness' as 'a protest and a promise', but in the Harper text it becomes 'a protest against doubt and a promise, positively, of performance'. The revision undoubtedly gives Chad a better image; indeed, it almost gives him the benefit of the doubt. Yet another addition in the Harper text goes some way to explain his break from Madame de Vionnet: in the Harper text he says he cleaves to her 'to the death', adding good-humouredly, 'the only thing is . . . that one can't but have it before one, in the cleaving – the point where the death comes in', a remark which, allowing for irony, expresses plausibly Chad's growing awareness of the impermanence of his relationship with Madame de Vionnet. The changes make the Harper text of *The Ambassadors* a version that is subtly more favourable to Chad than the Methuen one and make it even more remote than that is from the scenario in presenting a balanced opposition between America and France.

The Harper text is derived, bibliographically, from James's typescript, but it embodies corrections, made either to the typescript or to the proofs, which are not to be found in the Methuen text. For example, in chapter XVIII, Maria's compliment to Strether, 'You look exquisite!', becomes in the Harper text 'You look divine!' In chapter XIV, Gloriani's reference to Chad as 'our young friend' becomes in the Harper text *notre jeune homme*. At the beginning of chapter XXXVI in the Methuen text Strether has 'another report to make', but in the

Harper text it is, more poignantly, 'another separation to face'. The opening sentence of chapter XXX is, however, spoiled in the Harper text, owing to the omission of an 'only'. The Harper text also sees the restoration of the minor cuts in Parts One to Eight which had been made in the *North American Review* for convenience in pagination. However, in restoring the major cuts which had been made to the typescript for the periodical version, the Harper editor made an egregious blunder. He inserted chapters XXVIII and XXIX in the reverse order. The error no doubt arose because chapter XXIX opens with a reference to an incident in the afternoon of the day on which Sarah Pocock had visited Strether in the morning, whereas chapter XXVIII opens with a reference to an incident in the evening of the same day. Afternoon would seem to precede evening; had the Harper editor read on more carefully in chapter XXIX, however, he would have seen that the afternoon incident is dismissed, for the chapter to focus on a similar incident on the next day.

The trouble is that the error remained unnoticed until 1950, when Robert E. Young drew attention to it in his article, 'An error in *The Ambassadors*'. The chapters continued to be printed in the wrong order in all reprints up to and for some time beyond 1950, although now all current reprints have them in the correct order. Unfortunately, James himself used the Harper edition when making his revisions for the New York Edition of 1909. He made many minor corrections to the punctuation in the exchanged chapters, even to passages which alert one to the error, such as at the beginning of the second of the two chapters, but did not notice that the whole chapters were in the wrong order. Robert E. Young argued that it was James's radically wrong writing style which had 'managed to obscure the error' from the author, his editors and the critics (p. 253); he felt the mishap was ironic in view of the fact that James regarded *The Ambassadors* as his most perfectly constructed novel. James has, however, had his excusers, notably S. P. Rosenbaum in his Norton Critical Edition of *The Ambassadors* (1964), which records the variants in the textual notes. The controversy had gained currency because it was featured in Richard J. Altick's *The Art of Literary Research* (1963, p. 49), a work widely read by postgraduates in English and American literary studies.

The New York Edition of *The Ambassadors* (1909), then, contains the exchanged chapters in the wrong order, but it is in other respects the definitive edition since it contains James's final revisions and the renaming of the twelve Parts as Books. In those passages discussed above where the Harper text differs significantly from the Methuen text James not only follows the Harper text for the New York Edition but further alters them in minor ways. Most of the changes in the New York text concern punctuation; James tended to remove commas when revising, sometimes complicating the meaning as well as lightening the effect. Another tendency of the corrections is to use metaphors or expansive phrases in place of simple words; Gloriani's testing look is referred to by Strether as an 'inquiry' in the 1903 versions, but in 1909 it becomes a 'plummet' (ch. X). In chapter XXIII, Strether's 'manners' in the Harper edition become his 'forms and usages' in the New York Edition. At the end of chapter XXXI he finds himself 'supposing every-thing' in the Harper edition, which becomes in the New York Edition 'supposing innumerable wonderful things'. The changes made for the 1909 edition are, therefore, largely refinements. The loss of the con-secutive numbering of the thirty-six chapters for the sake of subdivision of the new Books is, in my view, a defect. But, in general, the New York Edition is closely aligned with the first American edition, and most modern versions reproduce its text, except the Signet edition, New American Library (1960), which uses the 1903 Methuen text with bracketed passages and footnotes providing variants. It is clear that each of the four early editions of *The Ambassadors* has its individual textual interest and value and that none is without disadvantages.

THE PREFACE OF 1908

Scribner brought out the New York Edition of the Novels and Tales of Henry James in twenty-four volumes during 1907–9. Volume XXI, the first of the two devoted to *The Ambassadors*, was published in 1909 with a preface of nineteen pages (pp. v–xxiii), which James had composed the previous year (Edel 5, p. 339). Like all the prefaces, it is a unique combination of anecdote, self-judgement and critical theory. Handling as it does the ramifications of point-of-view technique in the novel in which James practised it most consistently, the preface to *The Ambassadors* is arguably the most impressive of the whole unsystematic set. But it is not that aspect of it which concerns me here but, rather, the view of *The Ambassadors* which it presents. Each preface is, among other things, a telling of 'the story of one's story itself' (Blackmur, p. 313), a reminiscent account of the origin and development of the plot and characters in James's mind. James's recollections are not necessarily accurate, of course. The main drift of the preface takes no account of the process of redressing an anti-American bias, as traced in this chapter. It regards the novel, rather, from a late position, towards which the phases of revision had tended.

The preface contains yet another version of the Howells speech, which is identified as the salient 'situation' and as a major contributing factor to the subject of the novel, without being precisely that subject. This speech, which is also said to contain 'the essence' of the novel, runs in the preface as follows:

Live all you can; it's a mistake not to. It doesn't so much matter what
you do in particular so long as you have your life. If you haven't had
that what *have* you had? I'm too old – too old at any rate for what I
see. What one loses one loses; make no mistake about that. Still, we
have the illusion of freedom; therefore don't, like me to-day, be without the memory of that illusion. I was either, at the right time, too
stupid or too intelligent to have it, and now I'm a case of reaction
against the mistake. Do what you like so long as you don't make it.
For it *was* a mistake. Live, live!

This version is, no doubt, a late recollection of Sturgis's report of
Howells's speech as well as a condensation of Strether's, and it lacks,
therefore, the corrective note provided in Little Bilham's reply in
chapter XI. It preserves the element of moral permissiveness, which is
in the notebook version, but drops the reference to 'This place', the
Paris scene, as the chief stimulus to the conversion. It lacks also the
bracketing of Chad and his friends with the place as an example of life
lived intensely which is found in both the scenario and the novel
versions. It includes the reference to the 'illusion of freedom' (without
raising the question of determinism) and the admission that the speaker
is a case of reaction against his own past and, by implication, may
therefore be exaggerating the attractiveness of intense living, none of
which is to be found in the notebook version, either, but which features
in the scenario and in the novel. It is, then, something of a hybrid, putting more emphasis on the complex American forces behind Strether
than on the French ones before him, as one would expect at this late
stage in the evolution of James's view of his subject. The prospectus of
the New York Edition had, after all, advertised him as *'par excellence*
the American novelist. In the words of no other writer have American
types of character and ideas appeared in such high relief and been
characterised with such definite reference to *nationality'*, his foreign
backgrounds setting off with such marked effect 'his American
characters and American point of view' (Edel 5, p. 331).

Strether's praise of the intense life is not presented in the preface as
the whole message of *The Ambassadors*. James is careful to distinguish
the speech as a situation suggesting the wealth of a 'whole case'. The
idea of the novel resides in the fact that 'an hour of such unprecedented
ease should have been felt by him *as* a crisis' (Blackmur, p. 307): James
adds that Strether now *sees* an affront has been stupidly put upon his
character by forces back home, 'so that the business of my tale and the
march of my action, not to say the precious moral of everything, is just
my demonstration of this process of vision'. This fictional process of
vision is the 'shadow projected' by the seminal material drawn from real
experiences; it coincides with the process of expression, 'the literal

squeezing-out, of value' (Blackmur, p. 312). In this sense the subject seems to be identical with the whole of the novel, which could be summarised as what Strether is and what he learns, or the reassessment of his American moral inheritance. The preface, however, does not, in general terms, stress the complexity of that process.

The account of Strether in the preface, however, does justice to the complexity of James's fictional product. Strether is described as 'perhaps after all constitutionally qualified for a better part' than the one envisaged for him by Mrs Newsome. The reference is not to his physical constitution but to the constitution of his intellect and feelings as conditioned by his own American experience. Strether has intellectual power, tempered by human values, and weakened by a tendency to be readily shocked and then hastily sanguine. James now defends his choice of a 'hero so mature' whose 'thickened motive and accumulated character' gave him so much to work on. Strether is 'a man of imagination', at least comparatively so; he is not one in whom imagination *predominates* (Blackmur, p. 310), for he has been put in a false position. James characterises him wittily as a 'belated man of the world – belated because he had endeavoured so long to escape being one, and now at last had really to face his doom' (Blackmur, p. 315). Strether's enlightenment is in this sense predetermined. Since his note is already the special 'note of discrimination', his 'drama of discrimination' belatedly follows, set off by what he makes of Europe. The difference between Chad's actual situation and what Strether had been expected to find strikes Strether's imagination, and exercises his 'analytical faculty', as he is thrown forward 'upon his lifelong trick of intense reflexion' (Blackmur, p. 316). Nevertheless, Strether's appreciation of the facts is not immediate and comprehensive; he acquires only a 'more or less groping knowledge of them'. The concentration on point-of-view technique, therefore, leaves a part of the value of his 'intimate adventure' still unexpressed both for himself and for us (Blackmur, p. 317). The remaining significance, which is not available to the reader through the projection of Strether's consciousness upon the situation, has to be expressed ('every grain of it') by other characters in dialogue. It is certainly possible that this remainder is, or largely comprises, a sense of Strether's own worthiness as an intelligent American. That is a more substantial point, which by the nature of things he cannot make himself, than any details of his Woollett life extracted from him by Maria Gostrey.

The preface includes no satirical account of Woollett; it does not emphasise only its failings; Strether is said to have been propelled to Europe by 'complex forces' which are associated with the 'whole situation at Woollett' (Blackmur, p. 323). Mrs Newsome is said to have 'her finger on the pulse of Massachusetts', but in the preface James is much more concerned to defend his indirect presentation of her, 'away off', but 'felt as to be reckoned with' (Blackmur, p. 319), than to simplify her significance. He does say that Strether, 'our rueful worthy', having issued 'from the very heart of New England', is primed by her 'with a moral scheme of the most approved pattern which was yet framed to break down on any approach to vivid facts; that is to any at all liberal appreciation of them' (Blackmur, p. 315). The charge of illiberalism is levelled against Mrs Newsome then, but 'the very heart of New England' is a phrase which suggests, if not an alternative view of her, then a warmer response to her American context. In line with this more positive account of America is the prominence given by James to Mamie Pocock near the end of the preface, where, although the main point is to illustrate a technique of presentation, the argument also refers, clearly approvingly, to Mamie's concentrated study of the sense of matters bearing on her own case, affirming that she 'gives her appointed and, I can't but think, duly felt lift to the whole action' (Blackmur, p. 326). The 'lift' must refer here to the more favourable view of home which Mamie's perceptiveness opens up for Strether.

The tradition that James was concerned in *The Ambassadors* to present the essence of France draws some warrant perhaps from a hint or two in the preface. He refers to the setting of the seminal incident, the old Paris garden, as a token in which were sealed up 'values infinitely precious' contributing to the 'note' he wanted. But there is another view of Paris in the preface: as representing the world, it is a 'boundless menagerie'. It is also the city to which cynical hypocrites resort in 'hundreds of thousands' for immoral pleasure. Strether's enthusiasm for the intense life is to be distinguished from any inclination towards such vulgar, trivial temptations, 'any *bêtise* of the imputably "tempted" state' (Blackmur, p. 316). Paris suits James's purpose perhaps because it exposes Strether's sensibility to so many vivid assaults that he responds with 'the play of wildness and the development of extremes'. When he applies his moral scheme there, Strether is alarmed by 'a variability so violent' as he sways from one judgement to another. It is Strether's American perception of France that is dramatically interesting in the novel rather than France itself. James emphasises this point when he explains in the preface that 'Another surrounding scene would have done as well for our show could it have represented a place in which Strether's errand was likely to lie' (Blackmur, p. 316). The surrounding Parisian scene in the novel is 'itself a minor matter, a mere symbol for more things than had been dreamt of in the philosophy of Woollett'. This pronouncement throws the critical emphasis back on American tensions as the main subject. It amounts to a final Jamesian disclaimer of any intention to dramatise French life in depth in *The Ambassadors*.

In its discussion of the *ficelle* characters, Waymarsh and Maria Gostrey, the preface deals rather evasively with their thematic significance. While defining their function as characters who draw out information from Strether in dialogue, thus enabling the author to avoid 'referential narrative' and self-revelation on Strether's part (Blackmur, p. 321), James also makes certain ambiguous comments on their roles. They are the reader's friends, aids to lucidity, he says, belonging, 'in the whole business, less to my subject than to my treatment of it', more to the package, as it were, than to the contents, but technique is so integral to subject in James that this distinction is rather apparent than real. The *ficelles'* feelings may not be explored independently, but the fact that they represent American types different from Strether helps to clarify our response to him. James seems to admit this possibility when he says that Maria Gostrey, the 'lively extractor' of Strether's 'value and distiller of his essence', doubtless achieves, 'after a fashion, something of the dignity of a prime idea'. She is still a subordinate character, but she represents an idea, the Europeanised American, in its own right. Hence, evidently, the meaning of James's enigmatic comment on chapter XXXVI, whose function, he says, 'is to give or to add nothing whatever, but only to express as vividly as possible certain things quite other than itself and that are of the already fixed and appointed measure' (Blackmur, p. 324). The last scene's true importance, that is to say, resides, not in the outcome of Maria's romantic plan for Strether and herself, but in Strether's dissociation of himself from what she is, prior to his return to Woollett and the 'difference' at Woollett. Both Waymarsh and Maria Gostrey are, in other words, seen to stimulate as well as merely to register Strether's power of discrimination, and in the process are themselves critically placed.

The preface records James's pleasure with the consistency with which he had sustained Strether as the central consciousness of *The Ambassadors*. This method is said to have had the advantage of economy of expression, grace of intensity and 'a large unity' (Blackmur, p. 318), as well as exemplifying the aesthetic value that there is in composition itself. For this reason, James recorded his estimate of this novel 'as, frankly, quite the best, "all round", of my productions' (Blackmur, p. 309), a judgement which may be felt to rest too much on aesthetic considerations and which has, therefore, probably hindered appreciation of the work in its totality. James's late preoccupation with artistic form diverts his attention from any systematic defence of his novel's substance.

One further interesting point in the preface is the reference to the 'small compositional law' deriving from the serialisation of *The Ambassadors* in the *North American Review*; James states that he had been open 'to any pleasant provocation for ingenuity that might reside

in one's actively adopting . . . recurrent breaks and resumptions'
(Blackmur, p. 317). Examples of such ingenuity include the picking up
of the idea of 'the sacred rage' at the beginning of Part II from the end
of the third Chester chapter, which had appeared a month before; the
use of recollection at the beginning of Part III to cover the experience
expected at the end of Part II; a month's suspense between Chad's
appearance and Strether's first spoken communication with him (Parts
III and IV); and a similar gap between the scene at the Cheval Blanc
and Strether's coming to terms with it (Parts XI and XII). Such
exploitation of a publishing method to enhance narrative tension is
perfectly legitimate but perhaps unexpected and also a somewhat
unsubtle feature of the plot of *The Ambassadors*. For once in the
preface, James's candour fixes our attention, briefly and simply, on an
enjoyable element in the novel which, otherwise, one suspects, might
have tempted him to a rarefied and oblique vindication.

OTHER POSSIBLE SOURCES

In addition to James's earlier works on the international theme and the
various works discussed above, James is thought to have had several other
works in mind during his composition of *The Ambassadors*. Thackeray's
Henry Esmond (1852), where the hero abandons Beatrix and marries her
mother, Lady Castlewood, has been proposed as providing a possible
source of the involvement of Chad with Madame de Vionnet's daughter as
well as with herself (Cargill, p. 332,n. 30); and George du Maurier's *Trilby*
(1894), with its brilliant but doomed art student, Little Billee, may provide
a source for the rather gallant figure of Little Bilham (Cargill, p. 331,
n. 27). Oscar Cargill argues the case for Ibsen's *Rosmersholm* (1886) as an
influence on *The Ambassadors*, particularly stressing the hero's rejection of
Puritan morality and his inability to escape the haunting presence of his
dead wife, Beata, whom his present companion, Rebecca, had induced to
commit suicide. The analogy is too loose for *Rosmersholm* to be considered
'one of the major sources of *The Ambassadors*' (Cargill, p. 306), but it is true
that the Ibsen theme of a tradition of self-discipline subject to questioning is
also present in the novel. Michael Egan, in his *Henry James: The Ibsen Years*
(1972), is left largely unconvinced by Cargill's argument (p. 115), con-
tending that in *Rosmersholm* traditional values, 'grimly vigorous as they are',
triumph (p. 73). Certainly James handles the conflict of values with much
more subtlety and spontaneity than Ibsen.

   Among James's own works the one which is closest in date to *The
Ambassadors* is *The Sacred Fount* (1901). The two novels can be considered together since both are dominated by central observer-
characters who make questionable assumptions about other people's
personal relationships. The narrator in *The Sacred Fount* is used with

exclusive first-person technique, however, and lacks personal interest, identity, nationality and self-analysis, apart from moments of alarm over his extreme reactions to the situation which he seems to observe. That situation involves the vampiric draining of one of a pair of lovers by the other; in the scenario James has Strether referring speculatively to Chad's mistress as 'some woman, playing a great part in his life, and more or less feeding on him' (*Notebooks*, p. 389), but it is doubtful if the vampiric theme materialises clearly in *The Ambassadors* itself, apart from the superficial effect of Chad's appearing older and Madame de Vionnet younger than Strether had expected. Madame de Vionnet does more for Chad than she takes from him, and vice versa too. Bernard Richards, however, argues interestingly that in chapter XXXIII Madame de Vionnet 'does in a sense confess to the emotional vampirism' ('*The Ambassadors* and *The Sacred Fount*: the artist *manqué*' (1972), p. 230), when she asserts that it is never a happiness to take, as the 'only safe thing is to give'. Richards considers that Strether also 'is living off others', particularly off Maria Gostrey. He has a very unfavourable view of Strether as 'a man who is timid, self-centred, ungenerous, over-diplomatic, untrustworthy and on many occasions untrusting' (p. 224). Though underestimating Strether's self-correctiveness and commitment to critical values, Richards's argument establishes that there are considerable psychological connections between the narrator of *The Sacred Fount* and Strether.

CHAPTER 6

What Happens in
The Ambassadors

THE INCIDENTS

In this summary I follow the enumeration of the chapters in the first English edition, September 1903, with alternatives noted. I also adhere to the contents of this edition. Suggested chapter headings are my own.

PART FIRST.I. *Strether arrives in England and meets Maria Gostrey.* (In *North American Review*, Part I.I; in first American edition, Part First.I; in New York Edition, Book First.I.)

Strether, having sailed from the United States to Liverpool, England, by steamer, arrives at a hotel in Chester. He learns at the reception-desk that his friend and fellow-American Waymarsh, whom he is to meet, will not reach the hotel before evening. Strether is not put out by this news, as he had not wanted the sight of Waymarsh to be the first thing to greet him in Europe. An American lady overhears Strether's inquiry and accosts him, claiming Waymarsh, a lawyer from Connecticut, as a mutual acquaintance. She quickly makes friends with Strether. In the sunshine of the spring afternoon, they walk along the city wall of Chester, having exchanged personal cards. She has a French, presumably Parisian, address, and is called Maria Gostrey. He tells her he comes from Woollett in Massachusetts, where people fail to enjoy things, but in her he has someone to show him how to enjoy things. Maria explains that she acts as a general guide for Americans in Europe. She asks him to trust her, and he passes his hand into her arm, but draws it out before they regain the hotel, where Waymarsh greets them joylessly.

PART FIRST.II. *Strether renews his acquaintance with Waymarsh.* (In *North American Review*, Part I.II; in first American edition, Part First.II; in New York Edition, Book First.II.)

Waymarsh, it emerges, having been absorbed in prospering in his profession, has not seen Strether for five years. He fails to remember having met Maria Gostrey before. He detains Strether late in his hotel bedroom, irritated by the fact that standards of comfort are lower in Europe than in America. He elicits from Strether the vague communication that there is more to his visit to Europe than his desire to be with Waymarsh. Strether explains that he is not trying to escape from Mrs Newsome; he is coming on her business and plans to take Waymarsh with him, in the first place to London, so as to benefit from his opinions of things. He tucks Waymarsh in, lowers his lamp, and leaves.

PART FIRST.III.   *Shopping in the Rows in Chester.* (In *North American Review*, Part I.III; in first American edition, Part First.III; in New York Edition, Book First.III.)

Maria Gostrey delays her departure by train for London at Strether's request. She agrees to spend a day with them in London. Waiting in the Chester hotel's garden for breakfast, Maria and Strether chat about her system of returning unappreciative American visitors home to America as quickly as possible. She tactfully gets Waymarsh to eat an English-style breakfast. Later in the morning she accompanies the two friends on a ramble in the Rows of Chester. Strether buys himself a pair of gloves. Miss Gostrey and he monopolise the conversation. Waymarsh, distrustful of the influence of 'society' and refined taste, dashes suddenly into a jeweller's, presumably to make an expensive purchase, the nature of which he does not disclose. Maria and Strether analyse the incident as an expression of Waymarsh's sacred rage, his desire for freedom; they ironically compare their own lack of worldly success with his.

PART SECOND.IV.   *At a London theatre with Maria.* (In *North American Review*, Part II.IV; in first American edition, Part Second.IV; in New York Edition, Book Second.I.)

On the third day of his short stay in London, Strether accompanies Maria Gostrey to the theatre. They dine at his hotel, he inwardly comparing her low-cut dress with Mrs Newsome's customary black dress and catching himself in the act of liking Maria's red velvet throat-band. He thinks of the death of his wife and son, and his subsequent solitude. In the theatre Strether notices the English types, represented as much in the audience as on the stage. The play shows a weak young gentleman in evening dress under the influence of a bad woman in a yellow frock. Strether speculates on the possible analogy with Chadwick Newsome's situation. During the intervals, Maria guesses rightly that Strether's mission in Europe is to separate Chad from a wicked woman.

Strether gives her details about the Newsome family: that Mr Newsome has been dead for ten years, that there is a married daughter, Sarah Pocock, aged 30, of whom Strether is perhaps a little afraid, and that Chad is 28. He tells her that Chad has had access to a great deal of money and now is the time for him to go into the family business. The Newsome business is a great industry on the way to becoming a monopoly, but its product, a familiar domestic article, Strether keeps postponing identifying. He does affirm, however, that Chad's grandfather was an old swindler. He explains also that Mrs Newsome pays for the review which he edits. After the play, waiting with Strether in the theatre vestibule for a four-wheeler, Miss Gostrey guesses that Chad likes Strether and that his Parisian milieu may have refined rather than brutalised him. He admits that he want to get Chad home not only for the chance of a share in large profits but also to be married to Mamie Pocock, Sarah's husband's sister. Strether hints at his need of Maria's aid in this mission. In the vehicle ordered for her, before he walks away in the rain, she promises Strether her support, in case he should lose everything by failing in his mission.

PART SECOND.V. *Strether's first impressions of Paris.* (In *North American Review*, Part II.V, with three paragraphs missing; in first American edition, Part Second.V; in New York Edition, Book Second.II.)

On his second morning in Paris, Strether, accompanied by Waymarsh, picks up his mail at an American bank, including four letters from Mrs Newsome, and, leaving Waymarsh at the bank reading the American newspapers, he walks across Paris to the Luxembourg gardens, where he reads the letters. He reflects in a dissatisfied mood upon his life in America. He recalls his previous visit to Paris in the 1860s. He recalls a letter from Chad of five or six years ago in which the latter announced his decision to stay on in Paris, possibly to study painting. He speculates on the succession of Chad's French mistresses. Strether, passing the bookstalls of the Odéon arcade, decides not to buy a book. He reaches the Boulevard Malesherbes, in an expensive district, where Chad has a third-floor flat with a balcony. From the opposite side of the street Strether contemplates the flat's windows, recalling that, six months before, he had written to Chad telling him he might turn up and that Chad had replied assuring him of a welcome. Chad was not expecting him at any particular time. Strether enjoys looking at the house in the March sunshine and realises that Chad might not find it easy to give this flat up. He notices a young man, not Chad, stepping out of the flat on to the balcony to smoke a cigarette. Strether and the young man observe each other curiously, before Strether enters the house to go up.

PART THIRD.VI.   *Chad's friends in his flat, Little Bilham and Miss Barrace.* (In *North American Review*, Part III.VI; in first American edition, Part Third.VI; in New York Edition, Book Third.I.)

The same evening, over dinner in their hotel, Strether tells Waymarsh what he had found out in the morning, that Chad was away in Cannes, probably with a woman, and that the young man whom he had seen on the balcony was John Little Bilham, an American art student and friend of Chad's, at present occupying his apartment. Strether had liked Little Bilham and had agreed to breakfast with him on the next day; Waymarsh was invited also. Waymarsh urges Strether to stop interfering in Chad's affairs, but Strether is forced to admit that, unless he persuades Chad to return to the family business, his understanding with Mrs Newsome will be jeopardised and he will lose everything. The next day Waymarsh accompanies him to breakfast in Chad's flat at noon with Little Bilham and a friend of his, Miss Barrace, a sharp, mature lady, another American expatriate. Strether and Miss Barrace privately discuss Waymarsh as an American type and smoke Chad's cigarettes. Strether feels that, by associating pleasantly with these admiring friends of Chad, he is condoning the impropriety of Chad's way of life.

PART THIRD.VII.   *Strether visits the American artists' colony and the Théâtre Français, where Chad appears unexpectedly.* (In *North American Review*, Part III.VII; in first American edition, Part Third.VII; in New York Edition, Book Third.II.)

Miss Gostrey having arrived in Paris, Strether visits her chambers, expresses his delight in seeing her again and says that he finds himself to be in need of her. He explains that he has made a friend of Little Bilham, whom Maria asks to meet. She is reluctant to mix with Chad's female associates, though she points out that Cannes is not the sort of place to which a young man would take a common mistress. When Strether introduces her to Little Bilham during a morning hour spent at the Louvre, she expresses her approval of this new friend. It emerges that Little Bilham has abandoned his vocation of painting. The next day Little Bilham shows Strether and Maria his studio across the river, where, over tea, they meet several more young expatriate American artists. Two or three nights later, Strether and Waymarsh, with Maria, attend a performance at the Théâtre Français in a box lent to her. She has also offered, by message, a seat to Little Bilham, but without response so far. She speculates that Chad may have been deliberately using Little Bilham to soften Strether's critical judgement. Then Chad enters their box and identifies himself. During the first act of the play,

Strether has silently to take in the change in Chad, the grey streaks in his hair, his refined ways of doing things. He makes Strether feel awkward and young. After the play, Strether and Chad repair to a café, where Strether determines to come straight to the point.

PART FOURTH.VIII.   *Strether opens negotiations with Chad.* (In *North American Review*, Part IV.VIII; in first American edition, Part Fourth.VIII; in New York Edition, Book Fourth.I.)

In the café Strether tells Chad that he has come to fetch him home immediately for very good reasons. Chad asks him if he thinks him improved and then whether Strether is now engaged to his mother. Chad seems different, mature and newly retouched, to Strether. With his wide-brimmed hat pushed back, he strikes Strether as a man marked out by women. Strether now says he is prepared to take as many days in Paris as Chad likes, to answer the latter's questions. Chad pats his arm. Under a street-lamp near Strether's hotel, Chad next strikes Strether as a young pagan, but also as a gentleman. Chad equivocates when Strether asks if he is in the hands of some woman. At the door of the hotel, Chad imputes to Woollett a low mind. Strether has to go to bed with Chad's vague assurance that he is all right.

PART FOURTH.IX.   *Strether discusses Chad's virtuous attachment.* (In *North American Review*, Part IV.IX; in first American edition, Part Fourth.IX; in New York Edition, Book Fourth.II.)

For ten days, Strether keeps seeing Chad, as well as reporting about him by letter to Mrs Newsome and in person to Maria Gostrey. He explains his funny relationship with Maria to Chad, who has never become acquainted with her. He conveys to Woollett Chad's assertion that he is free from binding ties with a woman, and he imagines Sarah Pocock's reaction to this news as confirmation of her doubt in Strether's competence to find Chad's mistress. Strether informs Maria that he has assured Mrs Newsome that Chad will still return to America. But Maria gives it as her opinion that Chad is not free, but wants time to shake off the mistress, whom Strether, if he met her, would probably like, provided he didn't judge her. As the days pass, Strether feels that Waymarsh is watching him to see if he will succumb to the immoral spell of Chad and his circle. One day, after tea with Chad in his apartment, Miss Barrace takes Waymarsh off on her own, and Strether walks to a café with Little Bilham. There, Strether asks him about the woman behind the change in Chad, but Little Bilham equivocates, suggesting that Chad is not happy in his metamorphosed state and really wants to go back to the United States and take up a career in business. Strether gives the waiter in the café too large a tip. Little Bilham then tells Strether that Chad is not free because he is held by a virtuous attachment. Strether does not press Little Bilham further. Maria Gostrey confirms in turn that Little Bilham's account of Chad's relationship with the unknown woman as a virtuous attachment will do. A few days later, Strether learns from Chad that two particular friends of his, a mother and a daughter, are due in Paris, hoping to meet Strether. He asks Strether not to bring the matter of his return to a crisis until he has met them. Maria Gostrey, learning of this development from Strether, agrees with him that the attachment must be innocent if it is to the two of them. They speculate, in her apartment, that Chad may want to marry the daughter. Strether thinks, however, that Mamie Pocock would be a more acceptable match for Chad in his mother's eyes because of her ability to deal with Woollett, a quantity which a young French girl might not want to handle. He argues that Chad has been helping him along so that these friends can meet him. Maria Gostrey then speculates on the French lady's marital status, and throws doubt on the innocence of Chad's attachment to her and on Little Bilham's veracity.

PART FIFTH.X. *In Gloriani's garden.* (In *North American Review*, Part V.X; in first American edition, Part Fifth.X; in New York Edition, Book Fifth.I.)

On a fine Sunday afternoon of the following week, Strether is taken by Chad to an at-home in the private garden of Gloriani, a successful Italian sculptor now settled in Paris. Chad promises Strether the pleasure of meeting there his two friends, now named as Madame de Vionnet and her daughter, who, he confirms, are French, and English-speaking. Strether is deeply impressed by the character of the place, and by the physiognomy of Gloriani, whose penetrating look seems to test Strether. Gloriani moves off politely to speak to Chad, while Little Bilham approaches Strether, identifies their fellow-guests for him and describes them as people who collect acquaintances. With regard to Madame de Vionnet and her daughter, Little Bilham now tells Strether that their relationship with Chad passes as virtuous, and he does not deny Strether's asseveration that Chad is in love with the daughter. He does, however, inform Strether that Monsieur de Vionnet is alive. Miss Barrace turns up and alludes wittily to Little Bilham's conversion to French ways. She prophesies that Strether, too, will eventually be converted, but Waymarsh, whom she has taken off Strether's hands and shown to her friends as an American aboriginal, never. Strether accuses her and Little Bilham of relying too much on the visual rather than the moral sense: he is concerned with what people really are, especially Madame de Vionnet, whom he is about to meet.

PART FIFTH.XI.   *Strether meets Madame de Vionnet and her daughter Jeanne, and tells Little Bilham to live all he can.* (In *North American Review*, Part V.XI; in first American edition, Part Fifth.XI; in New York Edition, Book Fifth.II.)

Chad leads Strether towards the steps of Gloriani's house, where he sees a fair young lady, dressed in black, descending. It is Madame de Vionnet. Chad introduces them and goes to fetch her daughter, Jeanne, whom she has left inside with Maria Gostrey. They sit on a bench together and exchange a few words. Three rather bold acquaintances of hers accost her and take her off, excluding Strether. Little Bilham joins him on the bench, offering to make new introductions, but Strether declines, saying it is too late for that. In a long outburst he enjoins Little Bilham to live all he can, since it is a mistake to have missed one's opportunities, as Strether himself has. Little Bilham protests his appreciation of Strether, who rises self-deprecatingly. Chad approaches, escorting a pretty girl in white, Jeanne de Vionnet. Strether is convinced that Chad's virtuous attachment must be to her. Jeanne invites Strether, on her mother's behalf, to visit them. Strether assumes that Madame de Vionnet wishes to discuss with him her daughter's future with Chad. Chad quickly takes Jeanne off to be with her mother, who is about to leave. Little Bilham also quietly slips away.

PART FIFTH.XII.   *Strether discusses Madame de Vionnet with Maria and with Chad.* (In *North American Review*, Part V.XII; in first American edition, Part Fifth.XII; in New York Edition, Book Fifth.III.)

Miss Gostrey joins Strether on the garden bench, informing him that Chad has left with his two friends. She explains that the elder of these friends has turned out to be an old schoolfriend of hers, whom she has scarcely met for years. Maria, however, will not be at home to Madame de Vionnet when she calls on her. The reason, she tells Strether, is that she wants no part in recommending her to Strether. She then tells him what she knows of Marie de Vionnet's history, her unsettled background, her marriage to and judicial separation from a blameworthy count, and her subsequent, apparently faultless and well-connected life in Paris with her daughter. She suggests that Madame de Vionnet has formed the new Chad as a match for her daughter. Maria advises Strether to call on Madame de Vionnet, but as they leave Gloriani's garden he admits that it would have been simpler if that lady had been a worse type. The next morning Chad calls on Strether at his hotel and proposes that they have coffee together in an adjacent café, evidently in order to avoid Waymarsh. There, with a new seriousness, Chad urges Strether to visit Madame de Vionnet. He denies that he is secretly

engaged to her daughter. He says he wants Strether to stay on in Paris
to get to know and like Madame de Vionnet. To leave her, to whom he
owes so much, Chad now earnestly confesses, will be the greatest of
sacrifices for him. Strether, sensing Chad's impudence and hardness,
gets him to agree that he will surrender himself to Strether, if Strether
surrenders himself to Madame de Vionnet. They leave the café and
Strether lights a cigarette. Chad states that the lady is not directly
against his interests in America. On Chad's assurance that his relations
in France are good ones and that Madame de Vionnet's life is without
reproach, Strether agrees to be picked up by Chad at a quarter to five
that afternoon to go with him to see her.

PART SIXTH.XIII.　*Strether calls on Madame de Vionnet and promises to
save her.* (In *North American Review*, Part VI.XIII; in first American
edition, Part Sixth.XIII; in New York Edition, Book Sixth.I.)

Somewhat after five o'clock that evening, Chad and Strether call on
Madame de Vionnet at her home in the rue de Bellechasse. Chad soon
leaves them alone. She asks for Strether's trust, and he feels moved by
the evidence in her expression that she is troubled. She says it was
Chad's idea that she should take it upon herself to influence Strether
against his mission, but she judges that Strether is not open to that kind
of influence. Nevertheless, she implies that she thinks it possible that in
the end Mrs Newsome may give Strether up. He discovers that she
wants him to keep Mrs Newsome patient, but she will not say what are
the facts about her own relationship with Chad. She does tell him that
she does not wish Chad to marry Jeanne. She asks Strether to find out
for her if her daughter is in love with Chad. Strether, impressed with
Madame de Vionnet's rare beauty and the wonderfully good effect she
has had upon Chad, promises to save her if he can.

PART SIXTH.XIV.　*After dinner in Chad's apartment, Strether talks to
Jeanne de Vionnet and to Miss Barrace.* (In *North American Review*, Part
VI.XIV; in first American edition, Part Sixth.XIV; in New York
Edition, Book Sixth.II.)

Ten days later, Strether dines with other guests in Chad's apartment.
This social occasion has been arranged by Chad so that Strether can
meet Madame de Vionnet and her daughter, without calling on her
again. Strether has written to Mrs Newsome to inform her that, though
he has called on Madame de Vionnet and found her attractive, he will
not repeat the visit. After the dinner, Chad asks Strether to go through
to the *petit salon* to meet Jeanne. Strether spends ten minutes with her,
winning her trust and deducing that she is too well bred to insist on her

own strong feeling about any young man, if indeed she has any. Gloriani enters the *petit salon*, praising Chad's artistic taste, inspecting a small French landscape-painting and speaking with a hollow civility which puts Strether at his ease but does not deceive him. Gloriani takes Strether's place beside Jeanne. Miss Barrace engages Strether in conversation, remarking that she has just left Madame de Vionnet and Waymarsh together, neither of whom makes anything of the other. Miss Barrace says that Madame de Vionnet will never get a divorce in order to marry Chad. She warns Strether not to believe everything he hears about Monsieur de Vionnet. In reply to Strether's question about the innocence of Madame de Vionnet's relationship with Chad, Miss Barrace briefly remarks that Madame de Vionnet is all right with Chad. She tells him that Waymarsh has been buying her flowers when they have been out together; Strether feels a pang at the thought that he has done nothing like that. He says that he has no life of his own; for instance, he does nothing for Miss Gostrey.

PART SIXTH.XV. *Strether decides that Chad ought not to give Madame de Vionnet up.* (In *North American Review*, Part VI.XV; in first American edition, Part Sixth.XV; in New York Edition, Book Sixth.III.)

Madame de Vionnet comes up to Strether, looking showy though fine, and betrays herself by talking to Miss Barrace like the hostess. Miss Barrace obligingly leaves them together. Madame de Vionnet mentions Maria Gostrey's sudden departure from Paris. Strether informs her that Maria is visiting a sick friend in the south of France. Madame de Vionnet suggests that Maria's principal reason for going was to avoid meeting her again. She alludes to Maria's feelings for Strether. Strether does not respond to this hint. Madame de Vionnet then gets Strether to admit that Chad owes her something. He begs her not to interfere with Jeanne's feelings; she promises, as a favour to him, not to want to know what they are. As she turns away, Strether feels morally tied to her. Little Bilham comes up, and Strether, sitting with him, urges him to pay court to Jeanne de Vionnet. But Bilham rejoins that neither the Vionnets nor Chad would approve of him in that role. Strether wonders what Chad has to do with Jeanne's future, seeing that he is not in love with her. He tells Little Bilham that he now understands in what way Chad's attachment to Madame de Vionnet is virtuous – it is a refined friendship. Little Bilham says that now, after three years of it, Madame de Vionnet cares more than Chad does. He adds that Chad has recently told him that he is now ready to return to America and a new life. Strether now exclaims that Chad ought not to give Madame de Vionnet up, Little Bilham having let slip that Chad has been in love with her.

PART SEVENTH.XVI.   *Strether comes across Madame de Vionnet by chance in Notre-Dame and takes her on to lunch.* In *North American Review*, Part VII.XVI; in first American edition, Part Seventh.XVI; in New York Edition, Book Seventh.I.)

Twelve days later, Strether visits Notre-Dame, not for the first time, alone. Maria Gostrey has been at Mentone for three weeks. They have corresponded with each other, rather evasively. Strether has had tea with the American artists over the river once; he has bought himself a seventy-volume run of Hugo's works very cheaply. He goes to the cathedral, not for religious consolation, but to escape his problem. He contemplates a lurking female figure sitting in a chapel, who turns out to be Madame de Vionnet. She recognises him on her way out, speaks to him and sits beside him. They talk about Notre-Dame and Hugo. Later as they view the building from the outside, he asks her to lunch in a riverside restaurant which he knows but where she has never been. There, while enjoying her company and the meal, Strether feels he is losing his grip on the situation. He explains that what he has done in the way of saving her has been to write to Mrs Newsome favourably about her, and about what she has done for Chad. He says he is contemplating returning to America without Chad to give an account of Madame de Vionnet. She asks him not to go in case Chad should then break up. He then suggests Chad should go home to plead for her himself. Madame de Vionnet is anxious lest Chad, back in America, should get married. She argues that Strether is in honour bound to support Chad in his resistance to the idea of his marrying anyone other than herself. Strether agrees to see Chad through in this sense, feeling once again morally tied to Madame de Vionnet, though not against his judgement, in view of what Chad owes her.

PART SEVENTH.XVII.   *Strether gets a telegram, but persuades Chad to stay on.* (In *North American Review*, Part VII.XVII; in first American edition, Part Seventh.XVII; in New York Edition, Book Seventh.II.)

Three days later, Strether receives, at his hotel, a telegram from Mrs Newsome in Woollett, recalling him. Waymarsh approaches him without a greeting and then watches him with his telegram from the reading-room. They dine together, without mentioning the telegram. Strether tries to answer it in a letter that night, but tears up the pages. Chad arrives at his bedroom early the next morning, sees the telegram and announces that he is ready to return to America with Strether. When Strether tells him that Mrs Newsome has become impatient, he urges speed. Chad learns that Miss Gostrey has been back in Paris for two days. Strether is getting dressed to go out. He dismisses the subject of Miss Gostrey, but hesitates about Chad's return. He asks Chad if he is tired of Madame de Vionnet. Chad infers that Strether does not want Mrs Newsome to come herself. Strether asks Chad to stay on in Paris with him, because he himself is not ready to return to Mrs Newsome, he so feels the charm of life in Paris. Chad offers to go home leaving Strether in Madame de Vionnet's care, but Strether threatens to follow him at once in that case. Chad agrees to stay on, noting that Strether's expected marriage to his mother is now very much at risk. Strether leaves the hotel, without seeing Waymarsh.

PART EIGHTH.XVIII.   *The Pococks are coming.* (In *North American Review*, Part VII.XVIII, and Part VIII.XIX; in first American edition, Part Seventh.XVIII; in New York Edition, Book Seventh.III.)

That afternoon, Strether visits Maria Gostrey. He tells her he guesses that Waymarsh has written secretly to Mrs Newsome about him; hence the telegram. Strether says that Chad has cabled home, declining to leave France yet. Now, he is sure, the Pococks will come, producing new reasons for Chad's return. Strether, having left Miss Gostrey, cables to Mrs Newsome, telling her he judges it best to take another month. Two days later, Chad tells him of a communication from Woollett announcing that the Pococks are coming in a fortnight's time. Strether continues to write to Mrs Newsome, but without reply now. He talks critically of Mrs Newsome to Maria, who says he no longer needs her own help. She hints that there will be something he can do for her one day. He awaits Sarah Pocock's arrival apprehensively.

PART EIGHTH.XIX.   *Strether and Chad drive to the station.* (Not in *North American Review*; in first American edition, Part Eighth.XIX; in New York Edition, Book Eighth.I.)

Waymarsh does not admit to Strether that he has intervened between him and Mrs Newsome, but significantly avoids him. Strether does a little touring in France on his own. Both Chad and Madame de Vionnet are out of town. But Chad is back when the Pococks are due at the station. He calls for Strether, who has just asked Waymarsh to help him with the Pococks. As Chad and Strether drive to the station, Strether stresses how well Waymarsh will get on with Sarah Pocock. Chad says that it is to meet Madame de Vionnet that Sarah has come out. Strether wonders if Madame de Vionnet will charm Sarah. He tells Chad that he does not intend Sarah to meet Maria Gostrey.

PART EIGHTH.XX.   *The Pococks see no change in Chad.* (In *North*

American Review, Part VIII.XX; in first American edition, Part Eighth.XX; in New York Edition, Book Eighth.II.)

At the station Strether is relieved that Sarah Pocock greets him affably. He is impressed with Mamie Pocock's festal vitality. Chad take them in his cab, and leaves Strether to accompany Jim Pocock, who is grateful to him for giving him the chance of some fun in Paris. Strether decides that the Pococks do not notice or understand the improvement in Chad and that Jim leaves the moral question to the ladies. He tells Jim that Chad is the man to take over the advertising side of the Newsome business in America. Jim warns Strether not to go back, since Mrs Newsome is furious with him.

PART EIGHTH.XXI. *In Sarah Pocock's salon.* (In *North American Review*, Part VIII.XXI; in first American edition, Part Eighth.XXI; in New York Edition, Book Eighth.III.)

Strether, having spent that evening with Chad, Waymarsh and the Pococks in their hotel, calls on Sarah in her salon the following morning, to find both Waymarsh and Madame de Vionnet already there. Madame de Vionnet offers her services to Sarah in Paris. Her manner tends to compromise Strether. Sarah, though unbending, avoids sarcasm and undertakes to call on Madame de Vionnet. Madame de Vionnet tells her that Strether and her daughter have become friends. She asks that Jeanne may meet Mamie and complains that Strether never calls on her. She says he spends too much time with Maria Gostrey. Waymarsh assures her that there is no harm in Maria, but that she does love Strether. Strether blushes. Waymarsh jokingly refers to Miss Barrace as someone interested in himself. Strether is now certain that Sarah and Waymarsh are in collusion. Strether accepts an invitation to call on Madame de Vionnet on Tuesday. Before escorting her down to her carriage, he undertakes to say what he can to assist in arranging Sarah's and Mamie's visit to her and Jeanne.

PART NINTH.XXII. *Jeanne's marriage is arranged.* (In *North American Review*, Part IX.XXII; in first American edition, Part Ninth.XXII; in New York Edition, Book Ninth.I.)

Keeping his engagement to call on Madame de Vionnet, Strether tells her that Sarah Pocock is watching him wriggle. But, he adds, Chad is spending a lot of time with Jim, who may counteract Sarah's spell: in turn, Chad will look after Mamie, while Waymarsh escorts Sarah. Strether advises Madame de Vionnet to let Jeanne and Mamie get to know each other well. He also suggests she should show the Pococks her possessions in her home. Madame de Vionnet then brings it out that Chad and she have arranged a marriage between Jeanne and a certain young man. Strether, somewhat shocked, says he hopes that they can bring it off, but morally feels it to be quite the wrong way to deal with Jeanne. Madame de Vionnet says that Jeanne is pleased and that Chad wouldn't hurt either her daughter or herself for the world. Strether, bemused, says he will not speak of the matter yet to Chad, and leaves.

PART NINTH.XXIII.   *Maria names Jeanne's fiancé.* (In *North American Review*, Part IX.XXIII; in first American edition, Part Ninth.XXIII; in New York Edition, Book Ninth.II.)

Early in the evening of the following Friday, Strether, having spent all day with the Pococks, calls for half an hour on Maria Gostrey, who again makes clear her fondness for him. He reports that Waymarsh is treating Sarah expensively in Paris. That evening they are going to the circus. But Waymarsh is not falling in love with her. They simply feel an affinity with each other. Strether also reports that Chad is taking Mamie about and Mamie does care for him, but he has no particular hopes. When Maria in turn reports that Jeanne de Vionnet is to marry Monsieur de Montbron, Strether blushes, admitting that he already knows that. He argues that Chad's part in establishing Jeanne in life is a sign to Madame de Vionnet of his attachment to herself. He believes that Jim Pocock's awful personality is influencing Chad against wanting to return home. Neither Sarah nor Mrs Newsome realises it, but Mamie does. Strether leaves to accompany Jim to the Variétés.

PART NINTH.XXIV.   *Strether and Mamie Pocock.* (In *North American Review*, Part IX.XXIV; in first American edition, Part Ninth.XXIV; in New York Edition, Book Ninth.III.)

Two days later Strether, on entering Sarah Pocock's salon, at first thinks no one is there and is reminded by the sight of one of Mrs Newsome's letters that he no longer receives any of them. He then notices Mamie looking out from the balcony; he recalls having taught her English literature in Woollett. Mamie reveals that she is waiting for Little Bilham. Strether, judging her charming if rather too consciously dressed, senses that she is on his side, not on Sarah's. He divines that Mamie, unlike Sarah and Jim, understands the change in Chad. It emerges from their dialogue that she has met Monsieur de Montbron with Jeanne and has perceived that he is in love with Jeanne, but that Jeanne does not know if she reciprocates it, only that her point of duty is to please her mother. He leaves, admiring Mamie's penetration and tact.

PART TENTH.XXV. *A party at Chad's.* (In *North American Review*, Part X.XXV; in first American edition, Part Tenth.XXV; in New York Edition, Book Tenth.I.)

Three evenings later there is a large party at Chad's, with hired singers. Strether has the impression that Sarah may be about to cease participating in the round of amusements laid on by her brother. Little Bilham suggests to Strether that she wishes Chad to move the scene of his social success to America. Strether says that Chad ought to marry Madame de Vionnet, when it is possible, and not Mamie. He then urges Little Bilham to propose marriage to Mamie. Little Bilham says that Mamie no longer wants Chad in so far as that would mean taking on another woman's work, but he gives no positive sign of an interest in Mamie, on his own part. Miss Barrace now takes Little Bilham's seat beside Strether. She says that Sarah Pocock has had her triumph in taking Waymarsh away from her. Miss Barrace then urges Strether to keep Chad on in Paris. She says that Madame de Vionnet is now being charming to Jim Pocock, which shows how much she must care for Chad.

PART TENTH.XXVI. *Waymarsh smooths the way for Sarah's visit to Strether.* (In *North American Review*, Part X.XXVI; in first American edition; Part Tenth.XXVI; in New York Edition, Book Tenth.II.)

One morning within a week of the party (it is now late June), Waymarsh, by way of a change, comes to Strether at breakfast in their hotel. Waymarsh has already been out with Sarah, and wears a rose which has, no doubt, been bought by her. Strether notes ironically how much Waymarsh is now enjoying his stay in Paris, which had been Strether's original intention for him. Waymarsh informs Strether that Mrs Pocock wishes at last to see him alone at his hotel in an hour's time. Waymarsh says that he is joining the Pococks immediately on a trip to Switzerland: they plan to return to America at the end of July. He denies (Strether believes falsely) knowing what Mrs Newsome has been cabling to Sarah. He advises Strether not to say anything to Sarah he may regret and again urges him to quit it all. Waymarsh is less firm than usual, however, since he feels awkward about accompanying the Pococks to Switzerland.

PART TENTH.XXVII. *Sarah repudiates Strether.* (In *North American Review*, Part X.XXVII; in first American edition, Part Tenth.XXVII; in New York Edition, Book Tenth.III.)

Sarah and Strether sit together in the hotel reading-room to have it out.

She gives him one day to signal to Chad that he may leave, since he is only waiting for Strether's signal. She calls Strether's throwing doubt on Chad's duty to his mother and sister an outrage. He in turn irritates her by praising Madame de Vionnet, which she calls an insult to her mother. Sarah says she will be happy to leave Madame de Vionnet with Strether. She thinks Chad's development under her influence hideous. Strether says that in that case all is at an end for himself. Sarah agrees, and departs without looking at him.

PART TENTH.XXVIII. *Chad is still undecided.* (Not in *North American Review*; in first American edition, Part Eleventh.XXIX; in New York Edition, Book Eleventh.II.)

Later that evening Strether goes to Chad's apartment and waits for him, thinking of what he himself missed as a young man. On coming in, Chad admits that he told his sister that he and Strether were judging the situation together. Strether says that Mrs Newsome and Sarah Pocock still want Chad back; the Pococks came out primarily to check on Strether. Chad says he will go back to America if Strether thinks he should. They agree that they both stand to lose money. Chad says that Sarah and his mother hate him to be in Paris with Madame de Vionnet and he has genuinely tried to stop liking Madame de Vionnet, but they go far in wanting him to repudiate her. Chad asks if Strether can't tip the scale in favour of his returning home, since he can't imagine what Strether gains by doing the opposite.

PART ELEVENTH.XXIX. *Strether parries Maria's questions about his feelings for Madame de Vionnet.* (In *North American Review*, Part XI.XXVIII; in first American edition, Part Eleventh.XXVIII; in New York Edition, Book Eleventh.I.)

In the afternoon of the next day, Strether repeats a visit which·he had paid to Maria Gostrey the previous afternoon. Strether has seen Sarah Pocock again in her hotel that morning. Jim has been to tea with Madame de Vionnet. Madame de Vionnet and Chad are to see off the Pococks, Waymarsh and Little Bilham (who goes to accompany Mamie) at the station that evening for their fortnight in Switzerland. Maria agrees to stay on in Paris a bit longer so that Strether can continue to meet her. She says she admires Madame de Vionnet for not telling him anything to her detriment. Strether says that he has asked Sarah for another month before deciding whether to release Chad. He believes that Chad doesn't want to go back. Strether admits to being shocked by Mrs Newsome's lack of imagination. Maria harps on her own interest in Strether and asks if he is in love with Madame de

Vionnet himself. He eventually answers that Madame de Vionnet hasn't yet had that effect on him.

PART ELEVENTH.XXX.   *Strether in the country.* (In *North American Review*, Part XI.XXIX; in first American edition, Part Eleventh.XXX; in New York Edition, Book Eleventh.III.)

A few days later, Strether, on his own, goes by rail into the country, for an hour and twenty minutes' journey from Paris, to a station picked by chance. He is looking for a landscape to remind him of a Lambinet painting he once coveted at a Boston dealer's. He finds such a place, walks about and falls asleep on a hillside during the sunny summer afternoon. He reflects approvingly on the freer tone at which he has arrived in his recent conversation with Madame de Vionnet. At six o'clock Strether orders a meal in the village *auberge*, the Cheval Blanc, enthusing to himself over the quintessential Frenchness of the experience. While waiting for the meal in a garden pavilion, he sees something absorbing on the river.

PART ELEVENTH.XXXI.   *Strether comes upon Madame de Vionnet and Chad in a compromising situation.* (In *North American Review*, Part XI.XXX; in first American edition, Part Eleventh.XXXI; in New York Edition, Book Eleventh.IV.)

What Strether sees is a pair of lovers in a rowing-boat, who by sheer coincidence turn out to be Madame de Vionnet and Chad. On realising it is he, they hesitate long, and he has to call to them. They are also booked for a meal at the Cheval Blanc, and, although they return by train with Strether to Paris after it, it is evident from the lightness of Madame de Vionnet's dress that they had arranged to spend the night together somewhere else in the country. Strether broods on the incident at night in his hotel: he is shocked to have to face the truth that Madame de Vionnet is Chad's mistress and both relieved and distressed by the amount of make-believe required of him by their falseness.

PART TWELFTH.XXXII.   *Strether accepts Madame de Vionnet's invitation to call.* (In *North American Review*, Part XII.XXXI; in first American edition, Part Twelfth.XXXII; in New York Edition, Book Twelfth.I.)

The next morning Strether receives a note from Madame de Vionnet asking him to call on her that evening. After hesitating, he sends his acceptance. At the telegraph office he feels himself amusingly involved with the sinister side of life in Paris. After nine on a thundery evening he arrives at her house. He thinks of historical scenes of violence. Madame de Vionnet treats the previous day's deception as a matter of good taste and intimates that she wants to know where he stands with her.

PART TWELFTH.XXXIII. *Madame de Vionnet reluctantly accepts Strether's leavetaking.* (In *North American Review*, Part XII.XXXII; in first American edition, Part Twelfth.XXXIII; in New York Edition, Book Twelfth.II.)

Madame de Vionnet asks Strether if he may not possibly live near her and Chad in Paris. She admits she feels wretchedly selfish. Strether, telling her she ought to feel easy, senses her passion for Chad and her fear. She breaks down into tears. She tells him she cares about his opinion of her and had wanted him as a friend. Strether says that she has had him as one, and leaves.

PART TWELFTH.XXXIV. *Strether and Maria discuss the end.* (In *North American Review*, Part XII.XXXIII; in first American edition, Part Twelfth.XXXIV; in New York Edition, Book Twelfth.III.)

After two days, in which Strether waits in vain for Chad to come and see him, Strether begins taking Maria about Paris. He waits on, feeling himself abandoned by Chad. Four or five days later, on a wet evening, Strether calls on Maria. She announces that Madame de Vionnet has called and, this time, has been received by her. Maria evidently knows now that Strether is aware of the nature of Madame de Vionnet's relationship with Chad. She feels uncertain of her own prospects with Strether. She tells him that Madame de Vionnet has not seen Chad for some days. Maria explains how she avoided lying about the virtuous attachment; Strether adds that Little Bilham did not. Strether says he feels it is none of his business. He says he is leaving because he and Madame de Vionnet could have been friends.

PART TWELFTH.XXXV. *Chad implies to Strether what his future plans are.* (Not in *North American Review*; in first American edition, Part Twelfth.XXXV; in New York Edition, with seven short paragraphs and several sentences added, Book Twelfth.IV.)

Leaving Maria's place, Strether waits in a café and then goes round by Chad's flat. He sees Chad on the balcony, and walks upstairs. Feeling that Chad would be willing to put him up in the flat indefinitely, Strether warns him not to leave Madame de Vionnet cruelly. Chad equivocates, admitting that he has been to England. Strether states that he is about to write to the Pococks about his departure. Chad indicates that, though he is not tired of Madame de Vionnet, he may not wish to continue with her until he is. He praises Strether's efforts on his behalf. Having escorted him to the street, Chad reports that in London he has been getting information about advertising. Chad mentions being tempted by the money in it, but does not admit to being ready to give Madame de Vionnet up for it. Strether, scarcely paying attention to Chad's plan to see him the following day, parts from him.

PART TWELFTH.XXXVI. *Strether turns down Maria's offer of service.* (In *North American Review*, Part XII.XXXIV; in first American edition, Part Twelfth.XXXVI; in New York Edition, Book Twelfth.V.)

Two days later, Strether breakfasts with Maria Gostrey in her dining-room. She declines to hear named the article produced by the Newsome firm. She suggests that Chad will possibly return to Woollett now. Strether, not disagreeing, says nothing can heal the breach between himself and Mrs Newsome. He has written to Sarah Pocock and told Chad it would be infamous of him to desert Madame de Vionnet. Maria offers to serve Strether, to do anything for him. But he declines, stating that it would be wrong to get anything for himself out of the whole business.

THE TIME-SCHEME OF *THE AMBASSADORS*

The novel appears to cover about five months in 1899 or 1900 (since Strether, aged 55, had, just after the American Civil War, i.e. almost certainly in 1865, previously visited Paris as a young bridegroom with a bride 'who was much younger still' (ch. V), which would put Strether at 19 or 20 then; surely no younger). The events are envisaged by James as generally contemporary with his writing the text.

Strether arrives in England in mid-March and reaches Paris in the last week of March. He first sees Chad at the beginning of April. The scene in Gloriani's garden occurs on a Sunday fairly well on in April (about the third week) and the dinner at Chad's is held at the beginning of May. Strether gets his telegram in mid-May. The Pococks come at the beginning of June, probably on a Saturday. Sarah's visit to Strether's hotel takes place 'at the end of June'. Strether's visit to the country takes place in the first week of July. Chad visits London in the second week in July. Strether takes his leave of Maria in mid-July, and the Pococks sail back to America, presumably with Chad, at the end of July.

James makes frequent references to the time elapsing between incidents in the novel, but his sums do not add up exactly to a calendar.

THE LOCATIONS

The Chester chapters (I–III) are placed mainly in a hotel; probably the Queen Hotel, close to the railway station, where James had stayed in 1872. The 'smooth lawn' and 'tight, fine gravel' of the garden, where Maria observes Strether's appearance, and the hall, in which she shows him her card, can still be seen, though the 'glass cage' of the receptionist has been removed. The Chester city walls and the Rows, also featured in these chapters, are still important tourist attractions.

The London chapter (IV) has no distinctive topography.

The French chapters (V–XXXVI) were mostly written with very precise locations in mind. Strether's operations in Paris are centred on the Place and Avenue de l'Opéra. His modest hotel, with its glass-roofed court, is near there in a by-street from the rue de la Paix, probably the Hôtel Chatham in the rue Daunou or the Hôtel de Calais in the rue des Capucines, both of which are in business today. The American bank in the rue Scribe so beloved by Waymarsh is still prominent, though under new management. The 'congested Boulevard' referred to in chapter V is probably the Boulevard des Italiens, with the Café Riche on its north side on a site now occupied by the Banque Nationale de Paris. The Théâtre Français is at the south end of the Avenue de l'Opéra; the café where Strether and Chad talk in chapter VIII after the performance at the theatre was probably the Café St-Roch, number 31, now occupied by a travel agency. The Café de Paris, also no more, at number 41 seems too famous for Chad to select as 'discriminated from others', but it *may* have been meant, as it certainly had 'brilliant halls' (ch. VII). The other café in the Boulevard a few steps from Strether's hotel where he and Chad feel the plash of hot milk 'in the air' (ch. XII) is no doubt the Café de la Paix, by the Opéra, still a central tourist resort, number 12 Boulevard des Capucines.

Chad's third-floor flat, where Little Bilham is first glimpsed, is no doubt on the east side of the Boulevard Malesherbes, some way up, since its windows catch the midday sun. The Postes et Télégraphes office where Strether goes in chapter XXXII to write his reply to Madame de Vionnet's *petit bleu* is the nearest one to his hotel, 'the big one on the Boulevard'; it was possibly the one at number 6 Boulevard Malesherbes. There was also one at number 2 Avenue de l'Opéra; both are converted to commercial uses now. The Quartier Marbœuf, where Miss Gostrey's *entresol* is situated, lies immediately to the south of the Champs Elysées, at the back part of which Strether thinks of sitting with Madame de Vionnet on 'a penny chair' in chapter XXXII. Miss Barrace's residence can be taken to be in that area, too, on the north side of the Champs Elysées, at number 42 Avenue Gabriel, near the Elysée Palace (that certainly is where her original, Henrietta Reubell, lived). The rue Montaigne, where Miss Barrace remembers meeting the American minister to the Tuileries Court at her father's (ch. VI), is a little to the north of there, now renamed the rue Jean-Mermoz.

The station where the Pococks arrive from Le Havre is the Gare St-Lazare (they would use the Lignes de Normandie). Sarah's large hotel, in which her suite overlooks the Tuileries gardens, is the Hôtel Meurice in the rue de Rivoli, numbers 228–30. The Tuileries Palace, which Strether remembers (ch. V), had been burned down in 1871. Adjacent to its site is the Louvre with its galleries. The Variétés, where Strether takes Jim Pocock (ch. XXIII), still functions today on the Boulevard Montmartre, as does the Théâtre de Gymnase, visited by Strether and Waymarsh in chapter V, a little further to the east. Close by, at number 32 Boulevard Poissonière, is the Taverne Brébant, a restaurant where, it is speculated in chapter XXIII, Chad and Mamie may dine out. The more expensive Bignon's Restaurant, where Waymarsh and Sarah may 'scarcely touch' a hundred francs' worth of food and drink is the Café Riche again, on the Boulevard des Italiens, which was managed by Louis Bignon. The circus to which they go on is likely to have been the New Circus at number 251 rue St-Honoré, now the Ministry of Justice.

Strether's walk to the Left Bank in chapter V must have taken him across the Seine by the Pont Royal or the Passerelle de Solferino, past bookstalls on the Quai Voltaire, and up the rue de Seine to the Luxembourg gardens, as is clearly indicated in the novel. There he reads Mrs Newsome's letters and thinks about Chad's brief stay in the Latin Quarter nearby, on the Montagne Sainte-Geneviève, in the vicinity of the Panthéon. He proceeds north to the Odéon Théâtre, whose 'old arches' were then occupied by bookstalls and cafés. Nearer the river on the Left Bank is the Faubourg St-Germain, where Gloriani's house and garden pavilion are placed right at the centre. They were suggested to James by Whistler's garden-house in the rue du Bac, near a school for missionary priests. Madame de Vionnet's period residence opposite a coach-house on the rue de Bellechasse is situated a little to the west of Gloriani's. The restaurant where Strether takes Madame de Vionnet after their meeting in Notre-Dame, the 'place of pilgrimage for the knowing' (ch. XVI) on the Left Bank, is the Hostellerie de la Tour d'Argent, number 15 Quai de la Tournelle, just east of the Pont de la Tournelle. The Marché aux Fleurs, visited by Waymarsh and Sarah in chapter XXVI, is close by Notre-Dame on the Ile de la Cité, from where also it was possible to board a penny steamboat, or *bateau-mouche*, to which Strether devotes an hour with Maria Gostrey in chapter XXXIV, when he does not drive her in the Bois de Boulogne.

I owe these details to Karl Baedeker's *Paris*, 15th edition (Leipzig, 1900). James's characters seem to use horse-drawn transport in *The Ambassadors*. In fact, however, the Métro, begun in 1898, was already in operation in 1900 from the Cours de Vincennes to Porte Maillot, with stations at the Tuileries gardens and the rue Marbeuf and trains running every four minutes. One cannot imagine Strether's getting about that way. There was also an Exposition that year in the Champ de Mars in the shade of the Eiffel Tower, which, again, Strether would have to ignore.

The scenes in the French countryside (chs. XXX–XXXI) are difficult to locate, and possibly owe more to examples of landscape painting than to spots actually known to James. Several paintings have been suggested as analogous to the Cheval Blanc scene; the sort of Lambinet which Strether had in mind was often an untitled landscape.

CHAPTER 7

Interpretation of
The Ambassadors

PRESENTATION OF AMERICA IN *THE AMBASSADORS*: THE HEROIC PAST, WOOLLETT, THE EXILES

James's reliance on Strether's point of view in narrating the events outlined in the previous chapter lends to the overall subject-matter of the novel a certain elusiveness. It may seem helpful to say that the subject of *The Ambassadors* is Strether himself and Strether's mind, but a little reflection convinces us that that idea does not take us far, since Strether is not presented as merely self-conscious. If anything, on the contrary, he is self-effacing. A more attractive and apparently more objective interpretative idea is that the theme has to do with juxtaposing two cultures; *The Ambassadors* compares the quality of life in France with the quality of life in the United States of America. But this idea, too, is unsatisfactory, since virtually only one of the characters in the story is French and yet at the same time not one of its scenes takes place in America. In a subtle way, however, it is the true idea; in particular, the idea of an embassage is in line with the title. An ambassadorial mission, as Strether's is (humorously) described as being, involves a meeting of the two cultures; not an equal descriptive comparison, but the working of mutual influences, the development of a meaningful relationship between them. Here, then, is a viable working idea.

A simple way of proceeding is to explain Strether's mission in moral terms, to apply to it the allegory of Innocence and Experience. Certain of James's own comments appear to endorse this view. And it does, up to a point, work to fit *The Ambassadors* into the Innocence–Experience framework, with its idealistic and mild American protagonist coming, painfully and comically, to appreciate the richness, contrasts and colour of French life, especially with regard to the relation between the sexes. Strether does find the experienced Madame de Vionnet fascinating and he does consequently reject the narrower, more dogmatic Puritanical traditions associated with New England. This pro-French view of the novel, as it may not unfairly be called, is certainly easy to accept at first. It depends especially on emphasising two scenes in *The Ambassadors*: the scene in Gloriani's garden (ch. X–XII), containing, notably,

Strether's speech in which he advises Little Bilham to live all he can and not to make Strether's mistake, which was not to have lived; and the scene (ch. XXXV) near the end where Chad lets Strether know that he is leaving Madame de Vionnet to return to America. These scenes seem to bring out, through positive rhetoric in the one case and negative irony in the other, the failure of America to produce a life of value, even when given every aid, and, of course, by way of contrast, the success of French civilisation, the brilliance of Paris and the appeal of cultivated French women. But to make these scenes carry so much weight is really misleading, because the presentation of France in the novel as a whole does not substantially support them.

What James is doing principally with Strether's visit to Europe is to make a study of America *in absentia*, as it were. Though much of *The Ambassadors* purports to be about France, the primary role of France in the novel is to provide the setting and context for an indirect presentation of America. The French react to Americans abroad, and the French scene sets off remembered America. France is sufficiently there to be an agreeable and an alien object, but the subtlest political and moral criticisms and praise appertain to America. This is the positive imbalance in the novel to which its title alerts us. The work functions by representing one country in another. It conveys home thoughts from abroad, not in the sense of nostalgia but in the sense of a fearlessly constructive, loving analysis.

This analysis is not conducted by means of classification and categorisation, but in the way of literary texts, by significant juxtaposition and omission, by contrasts of register, by symbolic descriptions, by inconclusive dialogues, by numerous detailed suggestions and implications in phrases and words and by that phased revelation of fictitious incidents and discoveries which constitutes the plot. As such, of course, the analysis is not conducted by Strether, but by the novel. Strether conducts an analysis of his own, as he records and even discovers his own feelings and attitudes with an amusing admixture of surprise and acknowledgement of the need for revision. But, although the dramatisation of Strether's consciousness takes up, apart from the direct speech of other characters and a small number of comments attributable unambiguously to the author, the whole novel, it does not fully interpret itself. It is too erratic to do that. It is only a factor in the meaning of the novel. The novel includes Strether in its significance. He is in fact the central American type which it presents, unreliable in judgement yet penetratingly intelligent, and especially prone to underestimate himself. Strether's characteristically unbrash modesty enhances him for us in spite of himself. The novel endorses our esteem for him over against his own low opinion of himself.

One of the most dramatic examples of a check to Strether's self-deprecation occurs just after his speech in Gloriani's garden in which he urges Little Bilham to live all he can and do what he likes in order to obtain the illusion of freedom: 'don't be, like me, without the memory of that illusion' (ch. XI). Little Bilham is shown to be too amused and too tactful to point out that Strether is going too far in reaction against his New England Puritan inheritance. He is content to say, 'Oh, but I don't know that I want to be, at your age, too different from you!' Strether is too depressed by his sense of having missed out on life to appreciate Little Bilham's compliment. He sees himself as a priceless 'character' who is distinctly unamusing to himself. But the novel presents Strether in a perspective nearer to Little Bilham's than his own here. He is one whose impressionability and critical openmindedness yield him, despite his mistakes, a quality of living far superior to hedonistic intensity or liberated indiscriminateness. But it is still not a full life. When Stephen Spender argues that by the end of the novel 'it is Strether himself, and not Chad, who has, during this amazing six months, lived' (*The Destructive Element* (1935) p. 79), we can accept that Strether has had an emotional adventure and has learned a lot. But as an account of the positive quality of *The Ambassadors* Spender's conclusion seems too paradoxical; for, after all, Strether is on the way downhill – he has been snubbed and he is to go home without wife, status or money, convinced of his own failure. Strether's comic flaw, the flaw of diffidence, is so pervasive that it disqualifies him from having, by the end of the novel, 'lived' in a full sense. That is not to say that *The Ambassadors* lacks life. Relevant here is L. C. Knights's view that James's irony operates to release from a 'sense of suffocation, of being in some way shut off from the free enjoyment of living', a corresponding 'sense of life' (see his 'Henry James and the trapped spectator' (1939), pp. 604 and 607). In that case it is the whole novel that has lived, lived by an interplay of wit and irony in which Strether's consciousness is finely contained.

The most salient area of intellectual interest in *The Ambassadors* is Strether's disillusionment with the narrow, smug ethic associated with Mrs Newsome and Woollett, Massachusetts. Directly related to that is the second theme, the curious spell exercised by French manners and customs upon those Americans who stay in France for any length of time. A less prominent, but in some ways more decisive, issue is the reaction of young people exposed to these contrasting conditions and, in particular, their favourable evaluation of Strether. Strether's own representative value is the fourth theme. These points may be summed up under the heading of Difference, which covers not only the difference between Chad's actual life in France from the moral squalor which it had been assumed by his relatives in Woollett to be, but also the difference between Strether himself as he assimilates this truth and those

Americans who do not assimilate it, either because of moral prejudice or because of absence of moral sense altogether. As soon as he arrives in Paris, Strether feels 'the difference of being just where he was and *as* he was' and feels it to be unexpectedly great (ch. V). In the 1900 scenario James had discussed Strether's return to America at the end of the novel also in terms of Difference; Strether expects to go back 'to other things', to 'the big Difference' in America, which we can apply to the novel as referring not only to the distance which Strether's behaviour had put between himself and the offended Mrs Newsome, but also to divisions in America, between the hidebound and the liberal, the inexperienced and the culturally open, the old and the young. From the viewpoint of sexual romance, Strether's return may be a disappointment, but in terms of the international theme it is a positive, if muted, step. It is a matter of American self-respect. The independence of America from its socially more conventional European progenitors is one of the values which *The Ambassadors* contains. It is embodied not only in Waymarsh's recurrent bouts of 'sacred rage', that is, the rage for freedom of the purest American sort, but also in Strether's pragmatic approach. The idea of American independence which emerges from *The Ambassadors* by implication is remarkably steady; it is of an attitude quite different from neglect of older cultures and from eccentric, homespun isolationism, but, rather an attitude which allows for Americans to be receptive to authentic influence and to be curious for knowledge, yet which ultimately preserves their otherness. They must remain ultimately unseduced by mannered European glamour. Strether is the unseduced American francophile. It is true that he comes as close to seduction as can be imagined, but he retains his integrity. Maria Gostrey is proved right in having paid tribute to Strether's supreme power of discrimination: 'Nothing, with you, will ever come to the same thing as anything else' (ch. IV). It is one of Maria's functions to stimulate with refine those powers.

In Waymarsh and Maria Gostrey, James has Strether flanked, right from the outset of his mission, by two counterbalancing figures with equally strong views, but of opposing tendencies. This aspect of the design of the novel is evidently schematic. Both offer him opportunities and reasons for pursuing a line of conduct which would be alternative to the one which, noncommittally and waveringly, he actually preserves. Both bring pressure on him. Both provide him with confidential companionship in Europe, in Waymarsh's case anticipated, in Maria's unanticipated. Both nearly involve him in developments which would exceed what he can conscientiously undertake in loyalty and disloyalty, respectively, to Woollett. Their function is thematic as well as technical, therefore. James uses them not only to convey information about Strether and Chad to the reader through dialogue, but also to clarify the view of America which the novel presents.

This thematic function is ironically apparent at the very start of the novel, when Strether's 'first question' has to be, not about France or about Chad's life there, but about his old-fashioned American friend, Waymarsh. Yet, although he had expected to meet Waymarsh immediately upon arrival in Europe, in fact they miss each other, and Strether meets Maria first instead. Waymarsh's countenance, so characteristically American, would not be the most appropriate object to strike the visitor's sight first in Europe, unless, of course, the traveller from America was destined to see an American pattern abroad, an unexpectedly rearranged pattern. That is Strether's lot. Waymarsh half-looks like an early member of the American House of Representatives. As a lawyer from Milrose, Connecticut, he has emotional links with the professional rather than with the commercial aspect of the American past, the sector which made and defended the Constitution. He is still militant. Of all Strether's acquaintances Waymarsh proves to be 'most in the real tradition' (ch. II) of American culture and pleads for the 'purest veracity'. Uncompromising in his judgements and unimpressed by subtleties, he is still not as narrow in his vision as the Woollett clan with whom he forms an alliance and for whom he soon comes to work. He always acts from consistent motives. The 'sacred rage' repeatedly attributed to him by Strether and his witty friends is no mere patriotic bluster but the genuine impatience of the New World with the Old, with its inefficiency and imperfections. Waymarsh rebels against the sophisticated influence which Maria Gostrey is having on Strether during their cultural pilgrimage in Chester by striking out on his own to buy something expensive at a jeweller's. 'He has struck for freedom,' comments Strether (ch. III). It is a demonstration of independence, the independence that American money can buy. Strether believes Waymarsh to be still making money himself (he is in Europe for health reasons). The 'sacred rage' for freedom of judgement becomes their convenient phrase to describe one of Waymarsh's 'periodical necessities'. Even the aesthetic crowd in Paris recognises Waymarsh's heroic associations; Little Bilham sees him as a 'somehow portable' Moses, and Miss Barrace sees that he will 'last' in Paris as an American when all the other Americans there have been Gallicised. She likens him to 'the Indian chief one reads about, who, when he comes up to Washington to see the Great Father, stands wrapped in his blanket and gives no sign' (ch. X). Strether is embarrassed by the ridicule in these images and regrets that he himself so little resembles 'a really majestic aboriginal' in the way Waymarsh does. And, indeed, Waymarsh is not so backwardly primitive. Many of his observations are uncomfortably near the bone. Strether grows closer to him in his eventual position than he likes to admit. There is generally a valid point in Waymarsh's sweeping judgements. For example, he is noted ironically by Strether as preferring the American bank in Paris to all other places in that city. He regards the bank as a post of superior observation where there are American newspapers to be read and relief to be had for Americans like himself who are confined to a life in Europe and find themselves unhappily dissociated from the 'indispensable knowledge' of what is going on in America. It seems that Europe is rendered bearable to Waymarsh only 'by these occasional stations of relief, traps for the arrest of wandering western airs' (ch. V). In this amusing passage Waymarsh's chronic inability to be at home in Europe, to feel in tune there, is gently ridiculed from Strether's point of view. Waymarsh's superficial role in *The Ambassadors* is to act as a foil to Strether rather as Henrietta Stackpole does to Isabel Archer in *The Portrait of a Lady* by finding everything in Europe less convenient, less efficient, less modern and less democratic than the equivalent in America: he expects hotel rooms in Europe to be 'noisy', he never gets into tune with Europe, and being there is an 'ordeal' which he has to sit through (ch. II). Naturally, Strether reacts unfavourably to this inflexibility, while appreciating the authentic quality in Waymarsh's patriotism. He fears waking a 'spirit so strapped down as Waymarsh's was' to a sense of what it had lost. Yet at a deeper level there are analogies between Waymarsh's habits and Strether's actions, which prove very ironical. Waymarsh's gesture of regularly attending at the American bank in Paris for news is an exterior consultation not unlike Strether's habitual mental reference to Woollett and his inner, unconscious dependence on another, liberal and rational American tradition. Strether also, eventually, feels out of tune with France and needs to go back, not with sentiments identical with Waymarsh's and much less confidently than he does, yet just as decisively. Strether also becomes, in his own way, a dissenter from 'Europe'. In the meantime Waymarsh has betrayed him, by putting moral conscience above personal loyalty in order to save him from himself. There is a devious side to Waymarsh as well as a dyspeptic one (the lower part of his face is 'weak and slightly crooked'). Though he assumes an air of moral superiority which can even be associated by Strether with Jesus ('He met you as if you had knocked and he had bidden you enter', ch. II), he is prepared to play providence behind one's back. As Waymarsh grasps what is happening to Strether in Paris, he elects himself, in effect, as Mrs Newsome's second ambassador and adopts an unofficial responsibility for Strether's behaviour. He takes it upon himself secretly to alert Mrs Newsome to Strether's backslidings, thus precipitating her decision to send out Sarah Pocock after him, and he gives Sarah his full support when she comes. Waymarsh's impertinent intervention here arises, as Strether humorously concedes, from a 'depth of good conscience'; and so, as 'the pilgrim from Milrose', he knows himself to be 'more than ever in the right' (ch. XIX). The incident forces Strether from his sense of obligation to his friend, but its conspiratorial quality is in line with the more active, rebellious knot-cutting element in the American tradition which Strether cannot in the end entirely repudiate, either.

Woollett, the milieu of Mrs Newsome, is the central subject of *The Ambassadors*. Given James's predilection for indirect methods of presentation, as discussed in Chapter 4 above, the fact that no scene in the novel is set in Woollett only confirms this deduction. The fact also that Mrs Newsome has an absent, non-speaking role leads to the same conclusion. It is remarkable how quickly Strether's perceptions of the Woollett clan become articulate as soon as he is in Europe. Especially under the stimulation of the vivacious Maria Gostrey, whose function, according to the preface, is to distil for the reader 'the complex forces' that have propelled Strether (Blackmur, p. 322), he makes a candid analysis of the factors which underlie the situation at home. He is clear about the financial basis. He accepts that the Newsome family firm, engaged in the business of manufacturing the common article which Strether is too refined, teasingly, to name for Miss Gostrey, had originally been based on practices which were no better than swindling or which were infamies. Yet this corrupt foundation is overlooked or only tacitly expiated by Mrs Newsome in her activities as the leader of Woollett society. It does not prevent her from acting, in Maria's phrase, as 'a moral swell' (ch. IV), in providing, for example, the money for the review which Strether edits, her 'tribute to the ideal'. Mrs Newsome has no scruple in using Strether in her plan to recall Chad from the influence of his putative French mistress to take advantage of a very profitable opening for himself in the family firm. She finances Strether's trip to Europe, and on its successful outcome expects to marry him. Yet these disclosures seem to Strether like the secrets 'of the prison-house' – an allusion to Wordsworth's 'Immortality' ode – which associates Woollett, not with innocence, but with the drab routines of adult experience. Chad's rather hard comment on his relatives, 'They're children; they play at life!' (ch. XIX), is, then, not especially perceptive. Woollett is the unimaginative, unimportant American provincial centre, developing commercially, but limited in ideas, protected 'from life'. Its review, devoted principally to economic matters, does not sell well. And Strether's own contribution to the expansion of Woollett's culture has been undistinguished. It could hardly have been otherwise. He recalls the 'meagreness' of this effort when he is reminded of his one previous trip to Paris, undertaken in the 1860s with a view to his forming a relation 'with the higher culture' there. The result had been 'a meagreness that sprawled, in this retrospect, vague and comprehensive, stretching back like some unmapped hinterland from a rough coast-settlement' (ch. V) – a brilliant comparison of Strether's personal achievements with the geographical nature of his country. The shortcomings of intellectual life in Woollett are a constant theme in *The Ambassadors*: 'our funny ignorance, our funny misconceptions and confusions' (ch. XXVII). It appeared there was no variety of type of people there, except the male and the female (ch. IV). Then, the subjects on which these people held opinions were confined to 'three or four' (ch. XXVII). People in Woollett were shy, almost ashamed, of airing their disagreements in discussions, so that the main social aim, which was 'to promote intercourse', overrode the development of genuine dialogue and destroyed 'the taste of talk'. The sheltered and narrow approach of Woollett to experience derives from a basic dullness and diffidence and amounts to a kind of deprivation. The general feature of life there, as Strether admits to Maria Gostrey early on, is its failure to enjoy: 'Woollett isn't sure it ought to enjoy. If it were it would. But it hasn't . . . anyone to show it how' (ch. I). The apparent detachment in this remark marks Strether off as one more open to hedonism, if he is given a lead, than those whom he has left behind, but in fact Strether participates in the guilt and doubt which he treats so urbanely in conversation. He is very unwilling to transgress the New England moral code. It is to this strictness that he refers when he exclaims to Maria Gostrey during the same conversation: 'The obsession of the other thing is the terror.' This 'other thing', the principle of rectitude, seems embodied in the figure of Mrs Newsome. She has applied her moral sense oppressively and negatively. She has sustained the 'high' merit of never lying (ch. V). Her moral restrictiveness is symbolised in her dress, which is never in any degree 'cut down' (ch. IV). Reading her letters in Paris, Strether becomes acutely aware how big a strain, what a 'long ache', his existence with her in America had been. He had come away from her tired, fatigued, 'done for and finished', 'distinctly fagged out' (ch. V). The American informality of these phrases which express Strether's disenchantment with Woollett suggests that this process does not originate from his experience of Europe but gathers momentum there. Indeed, we understand that the strain of living with Mrs Newsome had originated in the Puritan struggle for moral perfection; there was the continual tension of failing to take things as they came and, instead, actively appreciating 'the way they didn't come'. Released from her immediate influence, Strether still has her standards at the back of his mind. He surprises himself with 'those frequent phenomena of mental reference' to her (ch. VII), even though he has to give up explaining his decisions in Paris to her in his letters as pointless. Mrs Newsome is guilty of taking it for granted that she can impose her views, and, as his personal loyalty to her weakens, Strether realises that his friendship with her was defective as a personal relationship. 'A personal relation was a relation only so long as people perfectly understood, or, better still, didn't care if they didn't.' When she sends the Pococks to follow Strether to France and do his work more efficiently, she deliberately alienates him further. The fact that Mrs Newsome is evidently blind to the major moral defects of her daughter and son-in-law – hardness and carelessness, respectively – confirms that she is really unqualified to be Strether's moral mentor. The main gain, therefore, for Strether during his stay in France is this gradual emancipation of himself from Mrs Newsome's influence, his seeing her for what in herself she really is. Certainly, here Strether develops his Arnoldian faculty of 'seeing things' as they are (ch. VI). Mrs Newsome meanwhile emerges, through the indirect method of presentation, as the most impressive absent character in James's fiction. She is alarmingly present to Strether's consciousness; all the time he is in France he is preoccupied with her possible reactions to everything there. This almost preternatural consultation continues unabated after the abrupt cessation of their voluminous correspondence; 'he had never so lived with her' (ch. XVIII) as after she had stopped trusting him. He still keenly feels her qualities of high austerity and sensitive nobility. 'I've been interested *only* in her seeing what I've seen,' Strether tells Maria Gostrey (ch. XXIX). Yet, despite his attempt to translate his findings in Europe into terms acceptable to Mrs Newsome, she has remained uncompromising. He comes to realise that her negative features are too dominant. She is 'all . . . fine cold thought', calculating and authoritarian in approach, a 'whole moral and intellectual being or block', which is a barrier to the appreciation of other national customs. She does not admit surprises and will not adapt. She stays unbudging and imperceptive. In eventually rejecting her, Strether is distancing himself from more than a single personality. Mrs Newsome represents and embodies a whole calculating, prejudging system, which leaves no margin for alteration, but is 'filled as full, packed as tight, as she'll hold'; so the depersonalising image, 'block', which Strether unflatteringly applies to her, serves to signify the defects of a whole strand in the American tradition. Instead of exercising her moral imagination with regard to her son's exposure to damaging influences in France, Mrs Newsome has stupidly and meanly indulged a conventional fancy and allowed a natural anxiety to fuel the conviction that Chad's affair with a Frenchwoman must be permeated by horrors and evils. Fear has got the better of her. She has evinced 'intensity with ignorance – what do you want worse?' as Strether asks Maria. The whole *exposé* of Mrs Newsome is conducted by James in Arnoldian terms; she sounds through her daughter the 'note of home' (ch. XXIII), whereas 'the note of Europe' which Strether begins to 'prove' as soon as he arrives in England (ch. I) turns out to be the note of freedom from what *she* stands for. The 'proof of his freedom' (ch. XXV) is his ability to visit Madame de Vionnet on his own spontaneously and frequently, thus sacrificing the 'armful of high interests' which he now associates humorously with Mrs Newsome. Mrs Newsome's restrictive disapproval is itself judged as harmful. Strether has had in the end, 'morally and intellectually, to get rid of her' (ch. XXIX), a necessity of which 'somehow over there', back in the States, he was not quite conscious, a conclusion which registers one of the main points which *The Ambassadors* has to make.

The revelation of Mrs Newsome's limitations is facilitated by the self-dramatising role of her daughter. Sarah Pocock takes on her ambassadorial role consciously and literally. Without hardly ever mentioning her mother, she represents her uncannily, as both Strether and Chad recognise to their alarm. Chad comes to see that his mother and sister are in the same boat, since Sarah represents their mother's views perfectly: 'Yes – mother. We called it Sarah, but it comes to the same thing' (ch. XXVIII). And Strether adds the inference that Sarah's hatred of personalities in Paris, including his own, also represents Mrs Newsome's feelings perfectly. For all that, Sarah is in no sense her mother's double. Her representation of her mother's views is an act of will and an exploration of social advantage which is particularly her own and which Mrs Newsome herself would not do on behalf of another. Sarah is an especially aggressive and active proponent of Woollett principles; she embodies the executive rather than the theoretical element. Sarah is a recognised and developed Woollett type, we learn from Strether, and she expresses her attitudes 'with a dry glitter that recalled to him a fine Woollett winter morning' (ch. XXI). She is typical of American women in her social sphere who get what they want and manipulate things behind the armour of moral self-justification. She is intense, simplistic, but also brilliant in style of speech and appearance, while being quite without charm. Her two scornful scenes with Strether (chs. XXI and XXVII) are not mere comic episodes relieving the involuted minutiae of his impression of France, but the true twin climaxes of the novel. They are dramatic deposition scenes presenting a transfer of power, as one ambassador is replaced by another and a new realignment of forces proceeds. Sarah can only defeat Strether by exposing herself and precipitating thus a critical counteraction. He has already noted unfavourable physical signs of her determination, 'the penetration of her voice to a distance' and her thin-lipped smile, which is 'as prompt to act as the scrape of a safety-match' (ch. XX). When she becomes combatant, James underscores these external marks of Sarah's singlemindedness by interleaving her speeches wittily with Strether's exegetical comments:

'. . . We've plenty of reasons', Sarah pursued a little piercingly, 'for everything we do', and in short she wouldn't give herself the least little scrap away. But she added as one who was always bland and who could afford a concession, 'I've come because – well, because we do come.'

Strether's ironic elucidation of her tactics and defences is all the more fascinating because he is at such a disadvantage when it comes to discussing the points raised. Sarah is the only character in the novel to treat Strether rudely to his face as though he were a figure of no consequence. In drawing attention to his lack of distinction, she in effect encourages a kind of recklessness in him which is a by-product of lack of confidence and intermittently represents his new independence in its worst form. But, while snubbing him, she manages to stay polite to his friends – just; 'the privilege of his society is not a thing I shall quarrel about with anyone,' she says (ch. XXI). She makes it clear that from her point of view his standards are hopelessly compromised. In response to Strether's attribution of a 'high rarity', a 'distinction of every sort' to Madame de Vionnet (ch. XXVII), Sarah at once regards such praise as an insult to Mrs Newsome; she calls it an incredible comparison with 'the most distinguished woman we shall either of us have seen in this world', her mother and Strether's betrothed. Strether had not intended the comparison, but Sarah wants to make explicit the irregularity of Madame de Vionnet's sexual conduct. She rams home what is to her an obvious fact, though it is still not accepted as one by Strether, that Madame de Vionnet is Chad's mistress, which she considers a 'hideous' development, irrespective of any 'fortunate development' in Chad which the lady's company may have caused. Strether lightly considers the sexual aspect of the relationship as none of his business. But Sarah, while exaggerating the moral difficulty of Chad's position and exposing her own attitude as rigidly censorious, still has the advantage over Strether in candour and honesty here. It is Sarah's lack of sympathetic understanding for the parties involved which rightly provokes his dissociation from her and from the Woollett matriarch whose hard line she propounds. Sarah makes no concessions; even though she finds her curiosity with regard to Chad's mistress not 'so successfully met' when she discovers she is a charming comtesse (ch. XXI), her mind can make quick 'private adjustments'. She is not to be deflected by Parisian manners. Her new acquaintances in Paris only, as Miss Barrace wittily puts it, 'build her out' and brick her up 'in splendid isolation', so that she is alive and breathing, as it were, merely from the chin up, buried alive in prejudice – a grotesque, depersonalising image which associates Sarah with her mother, the 'block'. But, for Strether, Sarah's respiration drowns 'every other' sound of their 'revel' in Paris (ch. XXV), so portentous is her insistence upon her convictions. When the Pococks had first arrived in Paris to take up the narrowly moral mission which Strether was letting drop, he had asked himself whether they weren't more realistic in their judgement of Chad than he had been. Were perhaps, it is implied, the confident 'Boston "reallys"' about which Miss Barrace had once patronised Strether (ch. X) so superficial after all? Did Strether now (ch. XX) live 'in a false world'? Did Sarah Pocock bring 'the touch of the real' to menace his imaginary structure of values by reducing Chad to plain terms, while Strether had been silly in exaggerating the degree of the change in Chad from an American youth to a cultured gentleman groomed by Madame de Vionnet? Strether rejects Sarah's simplification, but her forcefulness cannot be ignored. Her pronouncements are memorable and open his eyes to the state of conflict which exists between her way of thinking and his. It is to the clarification of this perception that his whole experience in Europe has contributed most. This point is made by Strether in answer to a complimentary remark of Madame de Vionnet's on his success in having come to know Parisians well. He rejoins that on the contrary it is the Pococks whom he has come to know well in Paris: '. . . it's *we* that I know. I know Sarah – it's perhaps on that ground only that my feet are firm' (ch. XXII). The touch of realism which Sarah brings to Strether's appreciation of Chad's life in France is, then, so cuttingly exercised by her that the main effect of the clarification of his vision which ensues appertains to her rather than to Chad. The point is confirmed by James when Strether puts it to Chad that for him, too, the supreme outcome of the Pococks' visit to France has been his 'having seen them for' himself, an insight which he shares with and owes to Strether (ch. XXVIII). Chad responds by giving evidence of the development of his understanding of his sister. He analyses her underlying feelings:

> Because when you hate you want to triumph; and if she should get me neatly stuck there she *would* triumph . . . she can bear *me* – could bear me, at least, at home. It's my being there that would be her triumph. She hates me in Paris.

Although Sarah does in the event get Chad back to America, her triumph is not certain. She does not necessarily achieve a replacement of the detested Madame de Vionnet's influence upon Chad with her own. Chad does not intend, in Sarah's sense, to be 'neatly stuck there'. But he finds the prospect of employment held out by his mother difficult to resist.

One avoidable fate which the novel holds out for Chad is that, on his return to America, he should grow to resemble Sarah's husband, Jim Pocock. Jim represents not so much a definite Woollett type, in Strether's view, as a 'failure of type', the managed husband who falls into conventional patterns of minor infidelity. He comes to Paris 'for a good time', in the vulgar sense, and as much of it as possible is to be spent away from his wife's company. 'Small and fat and constantly facetious, straw-coloured and destitute of marks, he would have been practically indistinguishable had not his constant preference for light-gray clothes, for white hats, for very big cigars and very little stories, done what it could for his identity' (ch. XX). He is even favourable to Chad's staying on in France ('*I* don't mean to persecute him; I couldn't in conscience'), but he has no power, 'leaving all analysis of their question to the ladies alone'. James uses this caricature of the American husband and tourist ('We haven't all the same at Woollett got anything like this') not only as a foil to Strether but also as a cautionary prefiguration of things to come for the unredeemed provincial. Jim sounds 'the note of the home . . . of the business' (ch.XXIII). Chad admits that Jim '*is* a damned dose' (ch. XXVIII), and it is as well he does since Strether wonders 'if what Sally wanted her brother to go back for was to become like her husband'. The presence of Jim in Sarah's entourage displays the weak underside of Woollett's Puritanism; the element of female dominance in the custodianship of its morals results in a convention of indulgence for its redundant married males, who permit themselves bouts of insipid peccadilloes, in Paris and elsewhere, and never seem more deprived than when they are taking their pleasures 'extravagantly common', as Strether puts it. When Jim gives Strether the little thrust which indicates the punitive dressing-down which Mrs Newsome is preparing for her first ambassador on his return (she is 'sitting up' all night '. . . my boy – for *you*!'), Strether feels that 'this *was* the real word from Woollett', censorious, self-deceived, blind to complexities and incapable of taking into account the change which had occurred in Chad. So that Jim Pocock, for all his good humour, also represents 'what Mrs Newsome wouldn't see', and is in his way as authentic a carrier of Woollett's blindspots as his wife is in hers.

For all that, the clarity of vision which both Strether and Chad attain with regard to Woollett does not in the end keep them away from the place. The second of Jim's thrusts at Strether – 'So don't you go home!' – does not convince him as being 'the real word' from Woollett with the same force as the first had done (ch. XX). Woollett's faults are not such as to make Joycean exiles of its favourite sons. The Jamesian observer has no alternative to continuing observation; his detachment is a form of close criticism which may benefit from temporary absence but which in the end requires presence and the sacrifice that presence often entails. Strether's loss of Mrs Newsome's favour and hand only makes his return home more probable. Home may well prove for him personally to be a sunless sea to which he will float, 'doubtless, duly, through those caverns of Kubla Khan' (ch. XXXIV); the Coleridgean allusion suggests Strether's abandonment of his manageable illusions of a French paradise for a grimmer acknowledgement of deeper, ancestral forces. Home's power of recall becomes unmistakable. It is a reckoning that beckons Strether, not in the sense of a dressing-down at the hands of Mrs Newsome, but in the sense of a confrontation with America as it is:

> It was really behind everything; it hadn't merged in what he had done; his final appreciation of what he had done – his appreciation on the spot – would provide it with its main sharpness. The spot, so focussed, was of course Woollett, and he was to see, at the best, what Woollett would be with everything there changed for him. Wouldn't *that* revelation practically amount to the wind-up of his career? Well, the summer's end would show . . .

Strether's self-criticism will attain its final clarity in Woollett, from where he can assess what he has done in France, but this return to base is not a 'reapproximation to Mrs Newsome' or a 'revulsion in favour of the principles of Woollett'. The wind-up of his career as her ambassador is not mere retirement, nor a futile abandonment of European pleasures. The return to pastures old is to result in his acquisition of a new sharpness of vision. America itself is changing, as Strether had already recognised when he explained to Maria Gostrey that the spirit of the age there was taking the form of an 'increasing mildness' which was propelling American young men to Paris (ch. IV), so that even his own mission to recall Chad before he was lost to Europe altogether had a social significance: 'Everything changes, and I hold that our situation precisely marks a date.' That was said before Strether had met Chad in Paris. It is the prospect of appreciating Woollett again 'with everything there changed for him', and not only through his own altered viewpoint but also because it is capable of change, especially in the persons of its young people, that marks another date for Strether. It is this prospect which makes it 'right' for Strether to go back, and this is the consideration as to which he has, in Maria's protesting words, the 'horrible sharp eye for what makes' him right (ch. XXXVI). Out of tactful concern for her at the end of the novel, Strether mentions only the renunciatory aspect of his return and its service to symmetry, but the positive implications contribute equally to our sense of paradox.

Maria Gostrey's claim on Strether is an emotional complication, but it reinforces the novel's theme. She can offer him only love-in-exile and, though his disentanglement from her companionship is embarrassing, it is inevitable. Maria's weakness is the opposite of Waymarsh's; she has cut herself off too drastically from the homeland. She evinces a novel American trait, a neo-dependence on Europe which is historically undignified. She is the most 'thoroughly civilised' American conceivable, but she has got there by unlearning. Her emancipation from her roots is so self-conscious that we are more aware of the emancipation than the roots, or indeed its ultimate destination. Maria's 'expansive subdued suitability' (ch. I) is something quite new to Strether. Her work as a high-class private courier seems to be directed more against her compatriots than towards their enlightenment, since she has no faith in their power to benefit from their experiences in Europe. When she explains that her system for pulling American visitors quickly through Europe effectively enables her to function as 'an agent for repatriation' (ch. III), sending them back 'spent' so that they do not repeat the trip, Strether is exhilarated by her 'strange and cynical wit', yet he also says that he does not want her 'formula' for himself; 'if that's how you're arranging so subtly to send me', he thanks her for the warning. But, against her will, Maria's guidance of Strether through Europe does in fact lead to his repatriation, 'spent' as she puts it, and with a much deeper exercise of his powers of analysis than she could manage for herself. Maria's technical function as a *ficelle* in the novel, which is to draw out the implications of Strether's mission to Europe without necessarily correcting them all, coincides happily with her more vulnerable representative role, and makes her one of the most lovable, amusing and human of James's women characters. It is, however, difficult to apply her astonishing knowingness about American types positively. It is she who first guesses that life in Paris may have in fact helped to refine Chad, not lowered him, but she does not think this insight through to a critical analysis of his situation, which she sees in terms of style rather than of morality. Again, Maria Gostrey suspects, wrongly, that Mamie Pocock lacks culture: she knows what American girls like Mamie '*can* be' and she knows what American men 'sometimes miss' in them. Such conversation is highly diverting, but not always to the point. Though Strether's imagination owes much to Maria's 'free handling of the subject' (ch. IV) of Chad's development of personality in France, he cannot shake off his original New England gravity in the way that she has done. She ignores certain of the most unpleasant moral implications of freedom of action. Maria's freedom is, actually, as Strether notes, more expensive than Waymarsh's. Waymarsh's is based on financial independence and is confined to commercial practice and legal usage, but Maria's is aesthetic and rarefied. It is freedom from the vulgar and the sordid; freedom from contact with the lower classes and the competitive, materialistic basis of the life of tourism and 'being abroad'. The unreality and the dizzying, tempting irresponsibility of this refined freedom are conveyed in her acquiescing in Strether's refusal to identify the common object of manufacture on which the Newsome financial fortune is built. Maria is a destabilising influence on Strether. In their stroll round the Chester shops with Waymarsh he feels presentiments of his future 'collapses' of restraint; a frivolity seizes him which makes him 'want more wants', as he finds himself flaunting 'an affinity with the dealers in stamped letter-paper and in neckties' (ch. III). This is the world of luxurious consumption in which Maria discriminatingly, yet too uncritically, condoningly, lives. She seems to him 'a woman of fashion' floating him into 'society' and disposing him 'to talk as "society" talked', without regard to a finer ethical dimension; for example, she disposes Strether to talk freely, disloyally really, about Waymarsh, to analyse him remorselessly, which strikes Strether momentarily as being 'rather base'. The paradox is that, since both Maria and Strether are, from the point of view of careers, 'perfectly equipped' failures and so 'out of it', they lack the money to do anything influential with their superiority. They are 'beaten brothers in arms', claims Maria, refugees from the hideousness of contemporary 'successes'. She adheres to their relationship almost desperately, but his allegiance is provisional. Thus, when he enters Maria's apartment in Paris, he evaluates it as a 'temple' devoted to the lust of the eyes and to the 'pride of life'. He is not put off by Maria's little world, but he has mixed feelings with regard to it; it is both a circle 'warm with life' and also 'a pirate's cave'. Strether's reaction to 'the empire of "things"' (ch. VII) with which Maria surrounds herself has a comic sureness which reveals the American critical of a fellow-American, sympathetic, committed, but self-reliant. He is aware that Maria's is a life 'more charged with possession' than that of other American residents in Paris, Chad or Miss Barrace. 'Wherever he looked he saw an old ivory or an old brocade, and he scarce knew where to sit for fear of a misappliance.' The idea that Strether has no place in her 'little museum of bargains' (ch. XIII) comes across lightly but decisively. Maria's 'supreme general adjustment to opportunities and conditions', as represented in her 'museum', is too negative a serviceability to stimulate Strether to an offer of partnership. And her conditions themselves are too detached for him to rest in them permanently. Though she accompanies him on his journey of discovery in France she cannot herself be the object of it. In conducting Strether to his experience of Madame de Vionnet, Maria puts herself at a personal disadvantage which no amount of affectionate gratitude can cancel out. The contrast does not invalidate Maria's perceptions of French life. She remains a very reliable guide in several respects. But she has to make way in Strether's attentiveness for the thing itself.

Maria's own delicate tolerance of the thing itself, her sense of being in harmony with French life and dedicated to its appreciation, associates her closely with the set of 'intense Americans' (ch. VII), whom Strether indulgently admires during his first days in France. This group, not all differentiated, but apparently consisting mainly of artists *manqués* who twang 'with a vengeance the aesthetic lyre', forms a background for Chad in Paris, though Strether meets them before

Chad appears on the scene and we are not shown Chad much in their midst. The types seem to have been regarded by James as sufficiently familiar to require no more than a briefly picturesque and tolerant presentation through the enthusiastic eyes of Strether during his initial stage of enchantment with the Parisian scene. He 'unreservedly' surrenders to the spell of their 'faraway makeshift life', reading into the scene 'the legend of good-humoured poverty'. At times the moral bearings of the group, of whom Little Bilham and Miss Barrace are the only definite – if also somewhat peripheral – representatives, are more sharply questioned. The set seemed 'cynically clustered' round 'the fundamental impropriety of Chad's situation' (ch. VI), Bilham is roundly condemned by Waymarsh for acting as a 'door-keeper' for Chad and his putative mistress, and Strether himself sees that Bilham's occupation amounts only to 'an occupation declined' (ch. VII), whereas Miss Barrace, for all her witty and outrageous accentuation of the unconventional *mores* in operation there, sounds for Strether 'the note of a "trap"', the trap of intellectual superficiality, 'the most baited, the most gilded of traps'. Strether oscillates between these unfavourable judgements of the American exiles and Maria Gostrey's firm approval of Bilham as 'one of us', whom she just wishes to stop in his tracks and appreciate: 'he's so exactly right as he is'. This quasi-literary appreciation of Bilham as a type is unsatisfactory when set beside Strether's later concern that Bilham should 'live' and his attempts to connect Bilham emotionally with Jeanne and with Mamie in turn. But it confirms that these minor characters have no special significance in the novel; no great cultural weight attaches to the artistic American colony in Paris. It marks a certain limit to the American tradition, not necessarily without potential, but in fact so *déraciné* as to be frivolous. Its main function in the novel, apart from adding touches of authentic colour, is to provide Strether with a couple of additional interlocutors, who can be both comically shocking to him and genuinely friendly.

PRESENTATION OF FRANCE IN *THE AMBASSADORS:* CHARM, CONVENTIONS, HARDNESS AND DECEPTIVENESS

There is no warrant for supposing that James was attempting to present the essence, or even the leading features, of French life in *The Ambassadors*. There is, on the contrary, an obvious absence of French characters and of dialogues with Frenchmen. The narrative exposes a series of evaluative phases in Strether's consciousness as he responds to French scenes and manners, but this commentary, though perceptive, is not very original, appertaining rather to the delights and shocks of the curious and sympathetic visitor than to the serious foreign analyst of French affairs. The novel does not offer a balanced contrast between two cultures, but studies one culture, the American, at a distance, in the light of another. Such subjects as French intellectual life, topical ideas, political developments, would have needed a differently structured novel. At most, through Strether, James opens an American perspective on France which is tentative, unassured and subject to marked changes of emphasis. Strether's main concern is France's effect on Chad, and the dramatic revisions of opinion with regard to Chad reflect indirectly the variations in Strether's selection of emphases from his impressions of France. The personal relationship between the older and the younger American is in the foreground. When briefly, just before the Pococks arrive, Strether takes time off from the consuming process of analysing this relationship to do a spot of sightseeing on his own account to absorb impressions of the surrounding scene directly, James's prose is significantly bored and perfunctory in tone:

> He himself did what he had not done before; he took two or three times whole days off – irrespective of others, two or three that he took with Miss Gostrey, two or three that he took with Little Bilham. He went to Chartres and cultivated before the front of the cathedral a general easy beatitude; he went to Fontainebleau and imagined himself on the way to Italy; he went to Rouen with a little handbag and inordinately spent the night. (ch. XIX)

The Ambassadors is not travel-writing, but a novel. Little is to be expected of Strether *qua* tourist (he is likely to imagine himself somewhere else, or to pay too much for his accommodation). The people with whom he is involved interest him so much that they pre-empt his appreciation of the French scene. Indeed, they lend ironic meaning to it. *The Ambassadors* is full of episodes in which Strether's visual pleasure is, if not spoiled, at least complicated by the irruption of personal factors. Thus, when he drops 'his problem at the door' of Notre-Dame and wishes he were free to be like 'a student under the charm of a museum', he soon comes upon Madame de Vionnet inside, gazing before her (ch. XVI). James closely entwines Strether's examination of his personal predicament with his visual impressions of France, and this method results in the continual drawing of contrasts between France and America.

This interconnection is obvious from the first, when Strether receives his impressions of Paris while looking round for 'the best place of all for settling down with his chief correspondent', Mrs Newsome. The very voluminousness of the letters from Woollett comically ensures the circumstance which she wishes Strether to avoid: leisure in Paris. He must have leisure to read them and to compose replies, and all that is time stolen from the task of harrying Chad. The Parisian air enables

Strether to judge the letters more critically than he might have
expected. Mrs Newsome is, therefore, responsible for his present image
of himself, thankful for breathing-time, 'poor Lambert Strether
washed up on the sunny strand . . . by the waves of a single day'
(ch. V). This image associates Strether's Parisian experience with the
hedonistic and aesthetic view of life. The artistic element which Paris
admixes with nature in its figures, colours and character, 'all sunnily
"composed" together', is so different from his memory of Woollett that
he gets a sense of freedom from the life of moral effort. He begins to
suspend acting on behalf of his mission. He develops a 'scruple' about
interfering in Chad's private life, a scruple which is aesthetic, or
Paterian, in origin, not moral. He soon accepts that Chad's acquisition
of personal polish and sophistication has been the work of Paris. The
process of Chad's having been 'made over' in this way Strether judges
to be 'perhaps a speciality of Paris' (ch. VIII). He wonders if Chad's
development into 'being a man of the world' through 'having learned to
be a gentleman' is only a 'forced maturity' asserted by his own
'crammed consciousness of Paris' (ch. VII), but when Chad himself
insists how much he likes Paris and how 'one's kept' there not only by
women but also, by implication, by Paris itself Strether feels guilty
about his doubts (as to the depth of the change in Chad), which were
an example of Strether's sharing in the 'low mind' of Woollett. From
then on Strether confidently gives Paris the credit for transform-
ing his friend. And that in turn allows Strether to try to absorb the
influence of Paris upon himself at leisure. Undoubtedly he wants
simply to surrender to its charm. At least this mood of appreciation
is his initial reaction, and it is intermittently renewed throughout his
stay.

It also takes the form of an over-reaction, impelled by the sense of
release from home restraints. Strether's immense feel for what Chad
calls 'the charm of life over here' seems at times to dominate everything
else. It grows to what Strether foolishly calls 'a certitude that has been
tested – that has passed through the fire' (ch. XVII), using a word
associated with religious commitment, 'certitude', a word featured
prominently in J. H. Newman's *An Essay in Aid of a Grammar of Assent*
(1870), and an image suggesting suffering and self-sacrifice. In the light
of James's ideal of objectivity in judging different national cultures,
Strether's partiality towards France appears at times like an extravagant
declaration of love by a man with a ruling passion. Indeed, the speed
with which he reacts approvingly to the indolent life of the American
expatriates in Paris is a fault in an attractive personality – a venial and
understandable fault, of course. 'Wherever one paused in Paris the
imagination, before one could stop it, reacted,' he half-complains, half-
rejoices (ch. V). There were to be had there 'shining hours to use

absolutely as he liked' (ch. VI). There is plenty of such aesthetic impressionism, recreational in mood, but it also can modulate into more serious and exploratory observations. An example occurs in the garden of the Tuileries where Strether looks at the French people, bare-headed girls, a priest, a soldier, 'little brisk figures', the 'ancient thrifty persons', the 'humble rakers and scrapers'. The sketching of character-istic types leads into deeper intimations:

> The palace was gone; Strether remembered the palace; and when he gazed into the irremediable void of its site the historic sense in him might have been freely at play – the play under which in Paris indeed it so often winces like a touched nerve. He filled out spaces with dim symbols of scenes . . . (ch. V)

The point here seems to be the lack of specificity in Strether's political concepts. It is an American consciousness disturbed by a reminder of extreme political violence, and it chooses to protect itself with vague-ness. T. S. Eliot denies that James possessed the historic sense. But it may not be so at all (see my '*The Sense of the Past*: the backward vision', (1981)). For an awareness of the strength of the democratic passion in France, and a wry contrasting of its manifestations with the cor-responding signs of freedom in America, recurs in unexpected places in *The Ambassadors*. An instance comes during the hotel dinner, when Strether confesses to Waymarsh that he has been 'captured' by Little Bilham and then finds that everything to do with their meal is 'congruous with his confession'; the sociable dining-room, the taste of the soup, bread and wine, 'the high-shouldered *patronne*', but more significantly the fact that the waiter, 'François, dancing over it, all smiles, was a man and a brother' (ch. VI). The reference to equality and fraternity in the context of hotel service is a striking example of the combination of sensual and political motifs and reflects back on American inadequacies. For everything was right for the occasion, except 'what Waymarsh might give'. Waymarsh lacks true fraternity, nor could he ever dance in the service of others; his culture suffers from a repressive moralism. Though Waymarsh's impatience with Strether's dallying with sensuality is justified, his own idea of the good life is impoverished and biased, whereas James's prose here celebrates the French art of life with delicate perceptiveness.

In the scene in Gloriani's garden there are yet more and more per-ceptions recorded. The people there bring to Strether's mind the other of the three revolutionary watchwords, liberty. The French form of freedom, so different from the American form of freedom represented by Waymarsh's 'sacred rage', his insistence on the right to be un-restricted by social conventions, to be free to compete for his own success and establish himself as self-reliantly professional, is now defined by Strether with precision. It is the freedom of people to be as they are within the framework of a 'strong, indifferent, persistent order' (ch. X), an order embodying Catholic and aristocratic values. It is true that Strether's positive rejoicing in these people's form of liberty and 'their conditions at large' is premature, in that there is a contradiction as well as an interdependence between the Parisians' relaxed identities and the social conventions to which they submit, as will become clearer to him later, but what is important to stress is that Strether's yielding to the beauty of the scene in the garden is accompanied by an attempt on his part to understand the basis of its cultural distinctiveness. The garden is a 'remnant' of an old aristocratic way of life, an enclave within 'the immeasurable town', its trees and walls speaking of 'survival, transmission, association'. It suggests to Strether a convent, 'a nursery of young priests' – priests of the cultured life, it is implied. Strether's surrender to the full assault of images in this place is so heady that the sculptor Gloriani, having turned upon him 'the most special flare, unequalled, supreme, of the aesthetic torch', rejects him as a subject for his art, Strether having been at that moment too seduced by Paris to serve as a representative American model, no doubt. Strether is particularly enraptured by the aesthetic effect of the women there, while being 'aware of fearing closer quarters'. However, when Little Bilham makes more explicit the aesthetic values of the set which adheres to Gloriani, Strether experiences a recoil. The charm extends beyond these people's appearance to their conversation: 'That's half the battle here – that you can never hear politics. We don't talk them.' Strether accepts from Little Bilham that he may not 'talk politics' among Gloriani's friends, but he is not entirely won over. Strether suspects 'a Pole or two' among the company, some of their faces appearing 'only strange' rather than 'charming'. Strether wavers between an incipient Arnoldian curiosity about suppressed political issues, such as the amount of support for Polish liberty, and a more sensuous, Paterian appreciation of the fluctuating surface of things. Little Bilham advocates the latter approach, as is underlined when Strether presses him about 'the virtuous attachment' which, as Little Bilham has given Strether to believe, Chad has to certain French ladies, a mother and a daughter. Bilham equivocates:

'I can only tell you that it's what they pass for. But isn't that enough? What more than a vain appearance does the wisest of us know? I commend you', the young man declared with a pleasant emphasis, 'the vain appearance.'

The allusion to Pater's 'conclusion' (first published as part of 'Poems by

William Morris' in the *Westminster Review* in 1868), to *Studies in the History of the Renaissance* (1873) in the phrase 'the wisest' makes a link between sexual irregularity and aesthetic incuriosity. According to Pater, the 'wisest' were supposed to spend their days in 'art and song' rather than in 'listlessness' or in 'high passions'. Strether cannot rest content for ever with 'the vain appearance' of things, however charming that they may be in France. He has too developed an interest in human cases for that, and finds French arrangements with regard to marriage and adultery thrust upon his notice.

This particular issue bears directly upon his mission, which depends upon his discovering the true nature of Chad's 'virtuous attachment'. It is in Gloriani's garden that Strether first meets the object of that attachment, Madame de Vionnet. She rapidly comes to embody for Strether the essence of French charm, culture and good taste. It is still significant that there are two humorous references to her not being a Pole at the very moment of introduction, showing the vague hovering presence in Strether's consciousness of political issues and also alluding to the belief of the Woollett ladies, Mrs Newsome and Sarah Pocock, that Polish or other 'more vividly alien' women were excessively passionate and possessive. During this scene of introduction, as Oscar Cargill points out, Strether's preoccupation with making connections between Paris and Woollett diverts his attention from the status of Madame de Vionnet's flamboyant friends, 'the brilliant strangers', to whom she does not introduce him and one of whom gains her undivided attention by a trick of 'social art' that is beyond Strether's own capacity (ch. XI). Strether's notation of the scene allows the reader to draw conclusions which are not uppermost in Strether's own mind. 'Strether attributes Maria's failure to introduce her friends to differences between the customs of Woollett and Paris, while the reader should wonder why she has such friends' (Cargill, p. 311). During the period of Strether's initial enchantment with Madame de Vionnet's 'feminine fairness', many minor observations of his have an ironic importance in view of later developments. This technique is especially highly developed in *The Ambassadors*. A surprising element in Strether's first impression of Madame de Vionnet is his sense of her 'common humanity'; he notes that she '*differed* less' from the ladies of Woollett than he had expected and might even have reminded Chad *of* them. The suggestion is there primarily to dispel any idea that Madame de Vionnet is an obvious seductress or woman of immodest behaviour, but it also alerts us to the point that her particular personal problems are of as much interest to Strether, and to the novel, as is her representative value as a carrier of French value and charm. Much of her impact is physical, indeed sexual, rather than intellectual. Although her social position indicates, for James, the French capacity to accommodate sexuality within a rational framework of conventions, at a price, and is, to that extent, culturally significant, she is not presented by James purely as a national type as are the American characters, but principally as an example of the transience of the sensual life. Hence the aura of romance which surrounds Madame de Vionnet. Although her career, her tastes and her deft handling of personal relations are, arguably, all characteristically French, the novel's main tactic is to catch her in a melancholy light, a beauty of 38, on the point of decline. Indeed, she shares with Strether, across the age-gap, the quality of pathos in the face of imminent superannuation, and she has even less to acquire than he has.

Maria Gostrey, in the carefully selected information which she gives about Madame de Vionnet's early life, stresses that it was marriage which had moulded her into French ways. Her origins were more cosmopolitan. Her mother had been a selfish adventuress, and English. Her father, 'a Frenchman with a name that "sounded"' (ch. XII), had left her 'an assured little fortune'. At school, in Protestant Geneva, she had been a 'small child of nature' and had won the best parts in the dramatic productions, but no academic prizes. She had been 'dazzlingly, though quite booklessly clever', an instance when Maria's own language of analysis is cleverer than the cleverness which she is analysing. Marriage to the Comte de Vionnet had, however, quite changed her; she had been 'quite made over – as foreign women *were*, compared with American – by marriage'. The phrase 'made over', repeating the one chosen by Strether to characterise Chad's conversion to French ways (ch. VIII), indicates the strength of social conventions among the upper classes in France. They are a people who think it vulgar and impious to divorce, to emigrate or to abjure, Strether learns. Madame de Vionnet has, however, obtained a 'judicial separation' from the comte, having been quite 'faultless' in the affair of the breakdown of the marriage, though Maria adds somewhat ominously that there 'were doubtless depths in her'. In particular, Madame de Vionnet acts conventionally towards her daughter Jeanne: 'as a mother she's French'. The full implications of these *aperçus* of Maria Gostrey's are not immediately apparent to Strether. There are contradictions in Madame de Vionnet's situation which make her devotion to her own interests hard to discuss. Strether takes time to work out what she is planning. He chooses rather to sympathise with her as one disinterestedly devoted to Chad's interests, for he assumes idealistically that her view of Chad's interests coincides with Chad's own, namely that he should remain indefinitely in the civilising *ambience* of Paris, vaguely occupied in cultivating this personal relationship and others. Strether begins to see his own interests as themselves coinciding with this *status quo* since he would enrich himself as a benevolent observer. Much of what Strether perceives of Madame de Vionnet fits in conveniently with this view rather than the sharper discriminations made by Maria Gostrey. During this phase of growing admiration, Strether keeps his critical armoury pointed towards America rather than towards France, but we are kept aware of an undertow which will eventually swing it back to cover a broader arc of targets. The predominant associations of Madame de Vionnet's way of life are at first romantic and aesthetic. Strether approves of her furniture and possessions in her drawing-room as being, not a collection like Chad's or Maria Gostrey's, but an inheritance. These objects, bought perhaps as substitutes to relieve the 'pressure of want' in an old noble family, connect her with 'the ancient Paris that he was always looking for'. Strether attributes to her personal surroundings an 'air of supreme respectability, the consciousness, small, still, reserved, but none the less distinct and diffused, of private honour' (ch. XIII), not, perhaps, the qualities which really distinguish Madame de Vionnet, but Strether is in a mood to let impressionism have full rein. He feels that their 'relation profited by a mass of things that were not, strictly, in it or of it . . . by the first Empire and the relics in the stiff cabinets', as well as by the lady's natural expression and 'the unbroken clasp of her hands in her lap'. In this Paterian catalogue the physical aspect is predominant, with historical nostalgia and aesthetic appeal as associational supports. So various are these associations for Strether that he is able to compare Madame de Vionnet in Chad's 'lovely home' with Cleopatra. Not only is she one of the finest developments of the type of the *femme du monde*; she is also 'a woman of genius' (ch. XV), whom a poet, presumably a Paterian prose-poet, could have compared 'to a goddess still partly engaged in a morning cloud, or a sea-nymph waist-high in the summer surge'. Such pagan imagery, as well as the stress on gems, satin and embroidery, points in the direction of aestheticism, as does the comparison of her head with an old coin; it was 'like a happy fancy, a notion of the antique, of an old, precious medal, some silver coin of the Renaissance'. This response corresponds closely to the manner in which Pater in the conclusion to *Studies in the History of the Renaissance* recommends one to appreciate 'the face of one's friend'; the critical terminology used by Strether, culled from the pejorative half of the Coleridgean polarities, imagination and fancy, idea and notion (as developed by Newman, too), leaves his fascination with the lady counting as less than serious. Strether's more strenuous mental faculties are not engaged here. The main effect of Madame de Vionnet on Strether's visual sense is to activate his fancy – a process which culminates, and is also superseded, in his train of thought when he comes across her in Notre-Dame Cathedral. James distances himself from these imaginings of Strether by referring to him as 'our friend' at this point. Madame de Vionnet appears there as a dim still figure, reminding 'our friend – since it was the way of nine-tenths of his current impressions to act as recalls of things imagined – of some fine, firm, concentrated heroine of an old story' (ch. XVI). He contrasts the tasteful vagueness and apparent patience of this 'lurking figure of the dim chapel' with his own present uneasy irresponsibility and want of colour. As they leave the cathedral he conceives of her as being 'on her own ground', conscious of her roots:

> When people were so completely in possession they could be extra-ordinarily civil; and our friend indeed, at this hour, had a kind of revelation of her heritage. She was romantic for him far beyond what she could have guessed . . .

This particular setting, however, stimulates Strether's imagination to insights that are more admirable than mere enthusiasm for French cultural colouring. The whole sequence in which Strether responds to Notre-Dame shows James's prose at its most sensitive and alert; again it is more in the style of Matthew Arnold than of Pater. Strether, as an agnostic for whom the cathedral has 'no altar for his worship, no direct voice for his soul', nevertheless feels the need for its 'beneficent action on his nerves'. His main deduction is magisterial, subtly critical, yet not disapproving; he remarks that both justice and injustice, which had been so palpably present 'outside in the hard light' of the city, were equally absent inside, in the protection of the Catholic tradition and order. This moral discontinuity between the religious and the secular worlds is alien to Strether, but he sees its advantage. Madame de Vionnet, on the other hand, professes that the history and beauty of the cathedral 'came to her most in the other, the outer view'. At one level this response is valid; the exterior of Notre-Dame is more impressive as a Gothic edifice than the interior, much of whose appurtenances are too petty, emotionally, for the purport of the whole. But it is primarily an aesthetic reaction. This time Strether penetrates to a deeper, social and ethical level. Yet he still idealises her conduct with Chad. Possibly, Madame de Vionnet's preference for the outer rather than the inner view of the cathedral should be suspect in one who had just placed her-self, as Strether never does, 'within the focus of the shrine' and might have provided a clue to the fact that her standards were not his. But Strether concludes that her relationship with Chad is now demonstrably innocent. 'Unassailably innocent was a relation that could make one of the parties to it so carry herself. If it wasn't innocent, why did she haunt the churches?' (ch. XVI). Strether's argument here has the tendentiousness of special pleading; the legal phrasing recalls Waymarsh for an instant. By 'innocent' Strether can only mean

'Platonic' or 'free from physical contact'. The alternation between perceptiveness and misjudgement is precisely what gives the account of Strether's experiences in France its convincing authenticity and fascinating textual density. James seems to applaud himself for a moment when he intervenes authorially to remark that Strether's 'reading of such matters' as Madame de Vionnet's motivation in coming to Notre-Dame Cathedral was, 'it must be owned, confused'. Her true motive is to face the end which she foresees for herself, the same end as that of the 'old women who live in' churches, and to achieve resignation in the face of inevitable desertion and deterioration.

In this habit of the old women Madame de Vionnet finds an element that is 'terrible', but it is at least hard and unalterable, and it can be found in Madame de Vionnet's habits, too. Strether takes time to come to terms with this element of hardness in her, which is also characteristically French. She has in fact already exercised this hardness upon him once at this point in the novel and is about to do so again. Strether uses the metaphor of her driving in the 'little golden nail' for this process of securing his obligation to her. She had got Strether to agree to find out if her daughter Jeanne really loved Chad, not, as Strether believed, to facilitate a match beween the two, but to take action to prevent one if it were likely. Strether, however, having seen Jeanne, asks Madame de Vionnet, as a favour to himself, to cease from prying into Jeanne's feelings. Madame de Vionnet, 'with her subtlety sensitive, on the spot, to an advantage' (ch. XV), agrees not to interfere in her daughter's feelings, thus putting Strether under an obligation. Actually, it transpires that she is so incurious about Jeanne's feelings that she is perfectly ready to hand her over to someone whom she hardly knows, a Frenchman, in an arranged marriage. So she uses Strether's scrupulous concern for her daughter's independence to her own ends without respecting it in the least. And she builds on her advantage with Strether to extract a second undertaking from him, after the visit to Notre-Dame Cathedral, this time, more generally, to see her 'through' (ch. XVI). This demanding commitment Strether makes out of honourable concern, but he is aware that the golden nail pierced 'a good inch deeper' this time. He is aware of Madame de Vionnet's determination in imaginative terms, but as to the exact bearing of her tactics he is quite deceived. When he revisits her apartment he is aware of something full of 'faint far-away cannon-roar' from Napoleonic times. It is a sinister omen, since he is soon to sustain the shock of learning that Jeanne's marriage has been arranged. Strether had been allowing his mind to dwell on improbable developments like a marriage between Jeanne and Chad or even one between Jeanne and Little Bilham. Despite warnings about French parents' requirements and providential attitudes in such matters, from Little Bilham and Maria Gostrey, Strether is still unprepared. He is not even alerted to what is in the wind when Madame de Vionnet asks him to give her his word of honour that, if she releases Chad to return to America, his mother 'won't do her best to marry him' (ch. XVI). This anxiety stems from a French view of a mother's role in matchmaking, where it is taken for granted that an arranged marriage is acceptable. For once Strether avoids making the comparison between American and French customs. But it is prominent in the novel. Indeed, James stresses that Madame de Vionnet's own failed marriage had been an arranged one, primarily to show her hardness in her attachment to French conventions in that, despite her own pitiable experience, she is willing to do the same thing to her daughter, and to treat with her estranged husband to effect it, into the bargain. Christof Wegelin argues, in *The Image of Europe in Henry James* (1958), that the main point of Madame de Vionnet's own arranged marriage is to render her relationship with Chad merely 'technically adulterous', which frees Strether to appreciate her virtues, which are proved in the beauty which she salvages from the wreck of life (pp. 100–1). Yet Miss Barrace is not certain that Madame de Vionnet did not contribute to the failure of her own marriage (ch. XIV). Strether is not freed from the possibility of criticising Madame de Vionnet before he can appreciate her virtues. A mixed attitude remains possible, probably desirable. Strether finds it hard not to regard the arranged marriage of Jeanne with alarm. The Monsieur de Montbron, who is the husband chosen by the Vionnets for Jeanne, is the most significant mute in *The Ambassadors*. Strether has to learn his identity much later than he learns the fact of his having been selected. He learns it from Maria Gostrey (ch. XXIII) and again from Mamie Pocock (ch. XXIV). Monsieur de Montbron's totally unexpected emergence among the objects of Strether's consciousness, though the same gentleman had 'for some time past occupied' Madame de Vionnet's consciousness and also Chad's (ch. XXII), confirms a darker interpretation of French life which Strether's intuitions had sometimes supported.

In this darker mood, which occurs at first only rarely, Paris strikes Strether not as a temple of civilisation, but as a 'vast Babylon' resembling 'a jewel brilliant and hard', a place in which 'what seemed all surface one moment seemed all depth the next' (ch. V). The assessment of Paris as a place whose seductiveness is no guarantee of intrinsic worth, so that almost any acceptance of it 'might give one's authority away' and one might love it 'too much' for one's own peace of mind, indicates the deep Hebraic earnestness always available in Strether's critical equipment. The vocabulary links Strether with Waymarsh or even with that 'grand old American' type, the 'Hebrew prophet, Ezekiel, Jeremiah', who used to visit Miss Barrace's father when she was a little girl in the rue Montaigne 'and who was usually the

American Minister to the Tuileries or some other court' (ch. VI), an ambassadorial prototype. In this censorious light Paris becomes for Strether 'the great ironic city', with windows 'open to the violet air' (ch. V), a phrase taken up by T. S. Eliot in 1922 to characterise the atmosphere of his 'Unreal City' in *The Waste Land* (line 372). Miss Barrace is an experienced guide to this imaginative underworld, where 'the light of Paris seems always to show' what things unexpectedly resemble. Though a cynic, for whom it is a joke that Strether 'should be serious about anything', or so he wonders, Miss Barrace defends her preference for the visual sense over the moral sense as being the finer penetrating instrument of the two into the true hardness of French life. She knows 'strange people', she confesses, and the unflattering resemblances which the Parisian air reveals may 'sometimes – yes' be close to reality. Her idea that the French are 'savages' underneath and 'simply convert' those idealistic Americans like Strether who come over hoping to convert them is taken comically further by Little Bilham, when he designates the French as 'cannibals' who have converted him 'into food' (ch. X). The main thrust of these exaggerations is to alert Strether mockingly to the irresistible allurement of French *mœurs*, but the secondary meaning, that there is a primitive, sacrificial element in French society, is not so far-fetched. At this stage Strether is merely excited by such audacious remarks, but after his visit to Notre-Dame Cathedral, when he takes Madame de Vionnet to lunch in the restaurant overlooking the commercial life of the Seine's quays and barges, he himself feels converted and demoralised. On this occasion the excellent French meal and wine conduce to a mood of fatalism, in which he feels he touches 'bottom' and his reservations go 'smash' as their human questions multiply for them. Probably somewhat drunk, Strether now experiences 'the appearance of collapse and cynicism' as acceptably easy for himself (ch. XVI). He has gone so far now in acceptance of Madame de Vionnet as to have written to Mrs Newsome with the news that Chad's lady-friend is worth saving. Madame de Vionnet asks Strether how she can thank him enough. James himself intervenes to comment that Strether 'couldn't tell her that, however', implying surely that an offer of physical recompense was on the cards. Madame de Vionnet extricates herself quickly from this indelicacy, but the glimpse of her mercenary streak, so much at odds with Strether's romanticising images of her in the cathedral, is striking. Strether's conversion, at the hands of Madame de Vionnet, is in fact only provisional.

From this point onwards, Strether repeatedly feels that, she having succeeded in securing his support, Madame de Vionnet and himself are together in the same boat. The 'boat' metaphor has an obvious structural irony in view of the coming denouement scene, in which Madame de Vionnet is found in the same boat, literally, as Chad, and finally compromised, a boat from which Strether is symbolically excluded, but the bearing of the metaphor on some of the intervening episodes is somewhat obscure. It is not entirely clear what Madame de Vionnet hopes to gain from the alliance with Strether. She presses Sarah Pocock for a meeting between Jeanne and Mamie, of which Strether says 'something *shall* come', declaring an interest in the furtherance of the proposal (ch. XXI). What that 'something' is that will come of it it is hard to see. Sarah Pocock is not likely to re-assess Madame de Vionnet's respectability, simply through an appreciation of her by her daughter. Neither Mamie nor Strether himself is an effective advocate of anything, as far as Sarah Pocock is concerned. Madame de Vionnet is not likely to have had *her daughter's* interests primarily in view in working for this meeting, since she later admits her fear that Mamie might hate Jeanne (ch. XXII). Yet it is Strether's bemused assent to the suggestion of the meeting which, he feels, puts him in Madame de Vionnet's boat. 'They were in it together.' He is now seen openly by the Pococks as the lady's ally. Whatever the object of Madame de Vionnet's plan (it may amount to no more than a rearguard action to retain Chad, though she also toys with the idea of returning with him to America), she at least avoids alienating Strether's sympathy by obvious scheming. Indeed, he is very vague about the character and moral nature of his new companion, who speaks 'now as if her art were all an innocence, and then again as if her innocence were all an art' (ch. XXII). The latter would seem to be the more plausible interpretation. It might at least do as a working hypothesis. But Strether reserves his judgement. For example, when, in response to his confession that he thinks of so many possibilities in any situation that he can be tormented by them, she says, 'Ah, one must never do that. One must think of as few things as possible,' he does not blench. He picks up from this witty statement no implications of indifferentism. Madame de Vionnet's words could indicate, ambiguously, a recommendation for patience and calmness of mind, or an underlying hardness, even a limiting meanness.

It would seem to be, indeed, the philosophy which underlies the arrangement of Jeanne's marriage. Madame de Vionnet's announcement of this *fait accompli* seriously jolts Strether. He reacts to it instinctively coldly; it affects him 'on the spot as a move in a game'. His critical sense is at last actively aroused, 'the sense that this wasn't the way Jeanne should be married'. Indeed, the peculiar grammatical usage, taking the verb 'to marry' transitively and actively to mean 'to arrange a marriage for', is itself disturbing, the kind of brevity that covers a multitude of sins. What 'vaguely and confusedly' troubles Strether is the way in which Jeanne's consent is just fitted into the pattern of the decision. It is the real old France working through

Madame de Vionnet's will, 'through something ancient and cold in it'. There is a paradox in their relationship, their personal *rapport* in the form of manners versus their cultural differences: she is one with whom he stands 'so easily in these cold chambers of the past' (ch. XXII). Her explanatory reference to the 'strange' ways of the French in arranging marriages ('one has to accept one's conditions') has an alienating effect upon him. 'He had allowed for depths, but these were greater', and the result is that it makes him want to get away. His distress is all the more sharp because he had got the impression from Jeanne herself that her mother had wanted her to be like American girls at least in respect of the degree of freedom which she was allowed: 'She had been free, as she knew freedom, partly to show him that . . . she had imbibed that ideal' (ch. XIV). Strether had regarded her as 'an exquisite case, of education', received at her mother's hands, but Jeanne's disposal seems to make a mockery of all that. He is oppressed by the hardness of French conventions. He has come up against 'the real thing', finding that Madame de Vionnet is exercising 'something exquisitely remorseless' as she presses him farther 'in' to French ways. But the effect of the episode of the arrangement of Jeanne's marriage is to replace surrender to French charm in Strether by resistance. The fact that Chad has partly initiated and certainly endorsed the scheme increases Strether's desire to 'get off'. It appears to prove that Madame de Vionnet's hold on Chad is so tight that Chad has 'ceased squirming' (ch. XXIII). Strether does not see that Chad's involvement in the arranged marriage makes it easier for his conscience to accept abandoning her since he would leave her with an interest and a new place in French society. He is convinced now that Chad's attachment to Madame de Vionnet, which he still believes is a 'virtuous attachment', is too deep for it to allow Chad to make another attachment, for example, to Mamie Pocock. So certain is Strether of this immobility in Chad that he now even advises Little Bilham to propose marriage to Mamie Pocock. Strether explains his unexpected fertility of ideas as a matchmaker here as a form of expiation on his part, as a return to American ways. 'I've been so sacrificing to strange gods that I feel I want to put on record somehow my fidelity – fundamentally unchanged after all – to our own. I feel as if my hands were imbued with the blood of monstrous alien altars – of another faith altogether.' Strether's disillusionment with French life is well under way here. The tone is not bitter – indeed, the criticism is reluctant. But the honeymoon period is over. The episode of Madame de Vionnet's handling of her daughter is not dramatised for its own sake with any marked specificity. Its function in *The Ambassadors* is indirect: to alert Strether again to one of the positive elements in the American tradition, the high evaluation of individual freedom, the principle to which his allegiance is unchanged. He sees, of course, that to compare two traditions is not to advocate transplanting elements of either in the other. Neither the negative nor the positive aspects of French civilisation could be transferred to America. Chad would not move 'the whole show' of his improved and yet compromised social life back to America. Strether at last articulates his insights as follows: the people of both cultures are all right, but a social occasion isn't the people; 'It's what has made the people possible'. James's international theme is finely embodied in the account of Strether's recoil from the arranged marriage. What is important in assessing and comparing social forms in two countries is not so much personal types as the conditions behind them. So, in urging Little Bilham to marry Mamie Pocock, Strether has come a long way from his earlier, enthusiastic, admonishing mood in which he told the same listener to live all he could, to follow Chad's example and cherish the illusion of freedom in Paris. Marriage to Mamie Pocock represents a novel, viable alternative, with its own attractions.

Yet still Strether's perception of the nature of Chad's relationship with Madame de Vionnet remains problematic and unclarified. This difficulty leaves the bearings of his judgement still basically loose. After all, he lapses into the comforting sense 'that he himself was free to believe in anything that, from hour to hour, kept him going. He had positively motions and flutters of this conscious hour-to-hour kind, temporary surrenders to irony, to fancy, frequent instinctive snatches at the growing rose of observation' (ch. XXV). This passage may provide evidence of the continuing relativism and pragmatising indeterminacy of Strether's consciousness. R. A. Hocks, in *Henry James and Pragmatistic Thought* (1975), argues that Strether embodies William James's ideas of the pragmatist who is remoulded every moment by experience, ambulating between the polarities of freedom and determinism and refusing to distinguish the confluently related elements of a pluralistic universe (p. 181). Yet some distinguishing must be going on. The final, complex image used by Strether, 'frequent instinctive snatches at the growing rose of observation . . . in which he could bury his nose even to wantonness', suggests a comic, painful, erratic but developing awareness; not yet a blossoming one, admittedly. Arguably, the fluidity of Strether's reactions to the situation at this late stage is less a sign of the sensitive, if inept, open mind than a sign of ominously bewildered misgivings during the wait for a revelation. This revelation comes, characteristically, when Strether realises that Madame de Vionnet and Chad have actually been deceiving him about their relationship by fostering a false impression.

The discovery that Madame de Vionnet is Chad's mistress disconcerts Strether so painfully, not primarily because he is offended by an instance of sexual irregularity, nor because he had maintained so implausibly to Sarah Pocock that their relationship was virtuous, but because he realises he has been the victim of deception on their part. Strether's own scrupulosity in not deceiving Mrs Newsome about his favourable impression of Madame de Vionnet makes the recognition of this deceptiveness all the more shocking. Strether had been cultivating his new freedom from Mrs Newsome by paying frequent visits to Madame de Vionnet. Yet he had been 'careful' (ch. XXX); he hadn't fallen in love with her or been converted to total submission. Strether had wanted her to feel that she should be as disinterested in their friendship as he was. Her 'new tone' had acknowledged that this disinterestedness was what he wanted in her, but it had not conceded it. James shows Strether here as being too concerned over his own possible lapses from good faith in her company by, say, dwelling too much on Chad to notice hers. But she has been leading him along. The whole episode of Strether's visit to the Cheval Blanc inn in the country is pointed up as his final, yet chastened, flirtation with French charm before the truth about Madame de Vionnet breaks unmistakably. Metaphors from the visual arts underline the fictive elements in Strether's experience as the bemused francophile; for instance, 'The frame had drawn itself out for him as much as you please' (ch. XXX). But more significant in view of the recognition scene which just awaits him is Strether's ironic selection of metaphors from the drama. Seeing, for example, the worldly rustics of the French landscape and the hostess of the inn receiving him with characteristic aplomb, he feels that the scene and the stage become one, 'the picture and the play . . . supremely melt together'. For 'the conditions' of French life which he has come to understand make this play and the characters inevitable and nowhere so assert 'their difference from those of Woollett' as here at the Cheval Blanc, where he arranges with his hostess 'for a comfortable climax'. Nothing sexual is meant for him, only a meal, but the actual uncomfortable climax of his trip to Europe occurs before he can eat it, when he finds that something definitely sexual is meant for Madame de Vionnet and Chad, who are revealed in their intimacy. The language drawn from the drama then becomes unpleasantly appropriate, as Strether glimpses a darker vision of plotting and even violence, with Chad acting facilely and Madame de Vionnet, nervously speaking in French, 'fairly veiling her identity, shifting her back into the mere voluble class or race' (ch. XXXI). On reflection, he becomes aware of the lie and the performance, at which he has been a spectator, 'the essence of her comedy'; and he is forced to admit that his long labour of trying to suppose nothing about those two has been labour 'lost'; delicacy's labour's lost, his comedy might be called.

There is, then, this dark element in Strether's comic humiliation. It is the fact of their having played him along for so long that 'finishes' Strether with them, a fact so evident at the inn in their need to improvise, especially Chad's, so as to avoid apology. Afterwards, Chad simply fails to turn up to explain. Madame de Vionnet writes to Strether to make a request for a meeting, which Strether grants quickly in case he should be off (without seeing her again) if he thought about it a bit. And now the atmosphere of the Postes et Télégraphes, where he dispatches his acceptance, has desolating associations for Strether. The public pens wielded there by 'little prompt Paris women' symbolise for him 'something more acute in manner, more sinister in morals, more fierce in the national life', than he had been assuming in his association with Madame de Vionnet, and he feels now that he is 'mixed up with the typical tale of Paris', a tale, no doubt, of disloyalty and deceit (ch. XXXII). He prefers, for his last rendezvous with Madame de Vionnet, a setting that will suggest 'some form of discipline'. He needs, guiltily, to sense that someone is paying some-how for the mistakes, 'that they were at least not all floating together on the silver stream of impunity'. In this wish for 'the penal form', as James wittily, almost wickedly, terms it, Strether's American con-science reasserts itself with embarrassing strength. The shudder is almost palpable in the brilliant prose as Strether, naturally enough, over-reacts against France. Indeed, from the open windows of Madame de Vionnet's apartment, where he visits her for the last time, come alarming suggestions of 'the vague voice of Paris', intensified by Strether's historic sense again. This time the intimations of the violence of the past are less vague than they had been when the reminder that the 'palace was gone' had once touched his nerve (ch. V). The sounds he hears now, he thinks, are similar to sounds that had come in through apartment-windows during the French Revolution, 'the omens, the beginnings broken out. They were the smell of revolution, the smell of the public temper – or perhaps simply the smell of blood.' It is a tribute to James's critical poise that this lurid passage is not felt to be out of character any more than is the comparison with which Strether follows it, the comparison of Madame de Vionnet's dress to that worn by Madame Roland on the scaffold, a dress 'for thunderous times' (ch. XXXII). The allusion may well be, as Oscar Cargill suggests, to Madame Roland's utterance, 'O Liberty! what sins are committed in thy name!' If so, it is, as he says, 'a thought that delimits "living" in the Parisian sense as swiftly as possible' (Cargill, p. 318). Strether has, of course, swung too far into moral revulsion in evoking the Terror. Madame de Vionnet is skilful enough to reassure him of her goodwill and to reconcile him to her at the level of manners. She subsumes the deceptive element in her relationship with Strether into a general tribute to good taste, which he 'couldn't have wished' otherwise. But this recovery of equanimity does not lead to Strether's staying to enjoy her company, least of all to succeed Chad as her lover. He does not contemplate himself as the recipient of a transferred affection. His confidence has been violated, and her apology for having 'upset everything' in his mind, so much so that she doubts whether he has a spiritual home left, amuses him slightly. He can survive such a disturbance. He is 'conscious of some vague inward irony in the presence of such a fine, free range of bliss and bale' (ch. XXXIII). Strether's reaction to Madame de Vionnet's fondness for extremes points him in the direction of his true spiritual home, America. The rebirth of his 'inward irony' leads to his ultimate detachment from France, his awareness of Madame de Vionnet's 'different world, traditions, associations; her other opportunities, liabilities, standards' (ch. XXXIV). *The Ambassadors*, like *A Passage to India*, ends on a note of respect for difference, for separateness, with a refusal to merge. Strether's reluctance to rear 'anything definite' on the affair between Madame de Vionnet and Chad is, then, a new stance; not an oscillation between disapproval and approval, but an aspect of his sense of the cultural gap between America and France. Strether's detachment is not mere scepticism, but a form of American refinement, which allows him freedom of observation in France but not absorption. Strether is able to consider and reconsider the civilisation from which Madame de Vionnet's charm stems, but it is not clear that that civilisation, or at least those strands in it which he confronts, has the will to reconsider itself. Herein lies the difference, and the American advantage. This sense of difference underlies Strether's decision to reject marriage with Maria Gostrey, too. He explains to her that he is not now 'in real harmony with what surrounds' him in France; he takes it too hard, whereas she does not. She has finished with the products of Woollett, whereas he has not (ch. XXXVI). The rightness which Strether finds in his return to America does not appertain merely to aesthetic patterning or to Puritan self-denial, but also to the deep difference in their outlooks, a difference too abysmal for a shared life in France. The whole tendency, then, of Strether's encounter with France is that it keeps America in view. It is preserved at the level of encounter, and its upshot is a reidentification with America.

STRETHER, 'THE ADDED LINK' BETWEEN AMERICA AND FRANCE: HIS WEAKNESSES AND STRENGTHS

Is it true to say, then, that in *The Ambassadors* Strether comes full circle? In his end is his beginning? Is his last position a reiteration of his 'first question', which was about the obtrusively American countenance of Waymarsh? This is not the case, in spite of the attractions of symmetry, because Waymarsh's subsequent behaviour has enabled Strether to answer that question and because Strether's own participation in the small drama of events which have ensued has altered the course of that drama. Strether's influence upon events is all the more subtle for his own self-deprecating character. His modesty makes him a poor judge of the extent and quality of his own exemplariness. Basically, Strether is conceived by James as an Arnoldian or near-Arnoldian critic of life who has been placed in a false position. The mission entrusted to him by Mrs Newsome prejudges the issue of Chad's future. If she is right about her son's conduct, it is on too narrow grounds or for the wrong reasons. Strether can, therefore, only be true to himself by disentangling himself from his obligation to her. He must reassert his commitment to the American democratic tradition at its most evolved and refined, to the free play of mind on moral issues. At the same time he can take advantage of his detachment to indulge experimentally in an aesthetic appetite for sensuous impressions which are always checkable by Puritan scruples. If Strether reneges on his mission in one sense, he is effective in another. Strether's very scrupulosity and subtlety impress Chad. Strether is a humane man whose imaginativeness leads him into generous mistakes, but does no one a permanent injury. In Strether the intellectual adventure, the understanding of life, always overrides the personal inclination. But the understanding is delayed and tortuous, so that his moral decisions tend to be overtaken by events and result in negative outcomes. He himself is liable to be depressed by his setbacks and narrow escapes.

A key factor in this sense of disappointment is Strether's age. He is too old, really, for the emotional roles into which various characters would push him. His missed opportunities in the past, his failure to 'live' in the sense of the word conveyed by him to Little Bilham, his inadequacy in public life are no guarantee now of success, satisfaction or compensation. Any late consolation other than 'the gifts reserved for age', as detailed in *Little Gidding*, proves delusive, or temporary. A certain simplicity and privacy are associated by James with Strether's time of life, as emerges strikingly in an authorial comment near the denouement. When Strether links the appearance of the pastoral landscape around the Cheval Blanc inn with a Lambinet painting which he had once admired at a Boston art-dealer's, the author comments directly: 'It will be felt of him that he could amuse himself, at his age, with very small things if it be again noted that his appointment was only with a faded Boston enthusiasm' (ch. XXX). Strether's world has its smallness and outdated areas. He is inclined to fall back for his standards and points of comparison on certain limited American experiences. He cannot always keep up the heroic effort of assimilating new insights and making new connections. Like all Americans, it is implied, he is, culturally, young for his years, and he has lapses. So lacking in excitement was his actual youth – 'nothing else ever was' in his youth, he feels, 'somehow at the right time' for it to take shape (ch. XVIII) – for a long time in the novel he believes he is at last achieving a richer youth vicariously, through the experience of others. Chad and Madame de Vionnet 'are' his youth for him now, in that they give him the sense of youth. His staying on in Paris with them is his tribute to youth. He even says he got the first benefit of youth when he met Maria Gostrey in Chester and he is making up late for what he did not have early: 'I cultivate my little benefit in my own little way.' A romantic attachment to youth is not unusual in one in Strether's circumstances, without a family, but in his case the experience has a reductive, private tendency which contributes to a lack of realism. Strether's tributes to youth tend to exaggerate Madame de Vionnet's freshness and to overstress his own inexperience. Maria Gostrey keeps in view the idea that the American tradition is a younger, fresher one than the French when she reminds Strether that his 'particular charm' just is that he *is*, 'at this time of day, youth'. In such interchanges 'youth' and 'age' both have ambiguous connotations; both are attractive qualities in Strether, but their co-presence, as it were, militates against his making mature judgements swiftly. He remains 'the friend of fifty-five' (ch. XIX).

A feature of Strether's visit to Europe which is undoubtedly connected with his age is his desire to relax his moral attitudes. He starts off in holiday mood, and he undertakes many circuitous diversions before he feels worried at all. James stresses Strether's unguardedness right at the beginning when it is stated that for Strether 'the note of Europe' was 'such a consciousness of personal freedom' as he had not known for years, this freedom consisting in his 'having . . . nobody and nothing to consider', in a break from responsibilities and ties. This 'note of Europe' is, of course, out of harmony with the dominant note of America, which is his consciousness of Mrs Newsome's alarm over Chad. The conflict in Strether's consciousness is left unresolved in the earlier part of *The Ambassadors*, until his critical awareness is heightened by turns. Strether's relaxed mood at first tends to disarm his faculty of moral censorship, inclining him, for example, to a romantic view of the American aesthetes in Paris. He suspends his judgement and his ironic sense, though reminding himself of the need not to 'dispossess himself of the faculty of seeing things as they were' (ch. VI), as if to reassure himself that he still has an Arnoldian critical power in reserve. Strether's 'seeing things as they were' echoes Matthew Arnold's definition of the first function of criticism, 'To see the object as in itself it really is', first used in *On Translating Homer* (1861), itself echoing a phrase in Wordsworth's 1800 preface to *Lyrical Ballads* (see Super, Vol. 1, p. 140). So Strether never really acts as a hedonist himself, but, feeling that in France he is 'in the presence of new measures, other standards, a different scale of relations', he enjoys fanciful mental pleasures, allowing himself a run of overhasty acts of approval cf others. That James wants the reader to be on the alert for Strether's mistakes is clear from his occasional application of the epithet 'poor' to his hero, as when he is contemplating Chad's balcony: 'Poor Strether had at this very moment to recognise the truth that, wherever one paused in Paris, the imagination . . . reacted' (ch. V). We know Strether's overactive imagination builds up models of behaviour which are more desirable than probable. Having decided that Chad is not a mere sensualist in danger from his mistresses, he imagines that Chad wants to marry Jeanne de Vionnet and that his relationship with her mother is purely loyal and protective. Strether's values are humane, but his perceptions are sometimes erratic and incautious. His liberal appreciation of the situation is incomplete. Thus, when Strether expresses the desire to have *lived*, he has in mind some ideal combination of full experience, care for and goodwill towards others, intelligent understanding of culture, development through personal relationships and various harmless excitements which he attributes to a putative Chad, 'that rare youth he should have enjoyed being "like"' (ch. XI), without too much concern for the disadvantages of Chad's actual position. Strether's synthesised idea of life is not invalid in itself; he errs only in identifying someone as being well on the way to achieving it. Hence it is so easy for Strether to let truth spread 'like a flood' and to accumulate an excess of internal experience. He becomes the man, 'such a man as he', who has 'an amount of experience out of any proportion to his adventures' (ch. XII). It is Chad himself whom James has point out this imbalance in Strether's mentality when he accuses him of having 'rather too much' imagination (ch. XXVIII) and later explains to him his own reticence over the exact nature of his relationship with Madame de Vionnet by suggesting that Strether's reaction to truth had not been at all predictable, 'for anything, with you, seemed to be possible' (ch. XXXV); so wide a scope, evidently, does Strether permit himself in interpreting the data of human life. Chad's reproach comes late in the day, but it pinpoints a weakness.

This relaxed mood and the recurrent indeterminacy to which it gives rise do, then, debilitate Strether. They leave him open to psychological pressures of unacknowledged force. There are indications in the text of feelings of sexual unfulfilment in Strether, signs of homoerotic envy of sexually successful youth and of repressed heterosexual need, too – impulses in the early autumn of his life which may disturb his perceptions and colour the language in which they are formulated, but which are never tragically exclusive or intense. Strether's judgement is most open to question during the crucial episode to which in all discussions of *The Ambassadors* one continually returns: the episode in Gloriani's garden when he bursts out to Little Bilham in the long speech about its being a mistake not to 'live'. It occurs just after he has met Madame de Vionnet but before he has met her daughter or considered what may be problematic in their relationship. The speech is concerned with the use of human freedom under the pressure of passing time. Strether says that the 'abundant message' which his 'impressions of Chad and of people I've seen at *his* place' have for him is that one should use that freedom. He urges Little Bilham, almost recklessly, to live life to the full; 'it doesn't so much matter what you do in particular'. He tells him to do what he likes provided he does not make Strether's mistake. The permissive injunction seems irresponsible, even though Strether warns him that his own mood is one of reaction against the narrowing circumstances of his own youth. It is not that the gentlemanly Strether really means to give bad advice, but his feeling gets the better of his skill in controlling his tone. Also, his lack of self-respect at this point makes him inclined to overenthuse over others. He is liable to combine sensual interest with admiration of achievement. He admires and envies Gloriani the sculptor, but in the shape of 'the glossy male tiger, magnificently marked'; and Chad, 'the handsome young man', is 'better still even than Gloriani' (ch. XI). Both enthusiasms are involved with fantasies, 'absurdities of the stirred sense', in Strether's own phrase, for Gloriani is marked more by worldliness than by artistic honour and Chad is using Jeanne to protect himself against Strether's criticism. Indeed, the admiration is not without fear and dislike of something 'covertly tigerish' in the 'great world'. Yet the sensual element suggests an unease in Strether. Occasionally he uses language with sexual overtones with unconscious comedy as when, in analysing the 'beautiful' friendship of Madame de Vionnet and Chad, he insists that she 'keeps *him* up' and they are 'straight, they feel', since she has 'simply given him an immense moral lift' (ch. XV). Strether's range of allusion, from the physical to the ethical, gives the prose of *The Ambassadors* a texture of amusing checks and counterchecks. The odd *risqué* phrase serves to emphasise that Strether can never ultimately let himself go or give himself wholly over to pleasure. He is always making connections, always considering, as he warns Maria Gostrey, something other 'than the thing of the moment' (ch. I). The 'deuce of it' is that he 'never can' give himself up. By his self here Strether means his mental activity, his power of reference to relevant factors. If he does, once or twice, nearly give himself up, there is sure to be a recoil. Indeed, he carries a sense of guilt until there is one, as is made clear when he modifies his previous advice to Little Bilham by suggesting that he marry Jeanne de Vionnet:

'Why don't you go in, Little Bilham?' He remembered the tone into which he had been betrayed on the garden-bench at the sculptor's reception, and this might make up for that by being much more the right sort of thing to say to a young man worthy of any advice at all. 'There *would* be some reason.' (ch. XV)

Here Strether acknowledges to himself certain Pater-like thoughts on the degree of liberation it is wise to recommend to young men (compare the note to the conclusion to the third edition of Pater's *The Renaissance* (1888), explaining why the conclusion had been omitted from the second edition of 1877), while bringing in 'reason' as a criterion for conduct in Paris. Such self-administered checks continue as stages in Strether's adventure. They are not decisive for a while. In general, Strether undervalues his own power of self-correction and readjustment.

Strether's diffidence is at once, by its unusualness, an aspect of his impressiveness as a sensitive and cultivated American and a means subtly deployed by James to underplay it. Strether is a prime example of the unreliable narrator who can nevertheless be relied upon to be always interesting and generally worthy of respect. The steps in Strether's journey as he questions his predetermined aims, as he relaxes, delays, revises his opinions, changes sides, revises his views again, accepts and criticises the role of others and eventually decides to return to America are not meaningless and confused. He abandons moralism for a more refined, rational viewpoint. He asserts, by example, a more cultivated American moral tradition than either Puritanism or aestheticism, a tradition which has affinities with the rationalism and tolerance of Benjamin Franklin, who placed the utmost importance upon '*truth, sincerity* and *integrity* in dealings between man and man' and made it a rule of his club of mutual improvement to ban 'all expressions of positiveness in opinions, or direct contradictions' so as to prevent warmth. Franklin was proud to be nominated as 'merely an honest man, and of no sect at all' (see his *Autobiography, 1771–1789*, ed. D. Welland (1970), pp. 54, 56, and 113). For Joseph Warren Beach to assert, therefore, that Strether moves from a 'starved life' in Woollett to a Paris that is 'physically and socially a seat of great amenity' (introduction to the 1954 reprint of his *The Method of Henry James*, p. xlviii), offering him the social intercourse which is an unattainable ideal in America, is to state a limited truth, but to miss the point of the novel, which is to present Strether's distinction in operation. Strether's lack of spiritual pride and his struggle against bias to make him alert to potentiality in his situation and flexible in his preferences. His slowness to condemn, while it accompanies errors of judgement, is itself an admirable trait. Strether's positive traits derive from America. France is vividly present in its light and shade sufficiently for him to contrast it convincingly with America, but the free play of ideas which he applies to it is his, not France's; it is *an import*. Strether's natural individual superiority is in fact an American contribution; the link, the evaluative contrast between France and America, is what he adds.

Strether would never say that; but James has other persons in *The Ambassadors* paying him tributes and speaking in his favour. To them his superiority is obvious. Maria Gostrey is sure before the event that Strether will have a good effect upon Chad: 'You'll do more – as you're so much better – than all of us put together' (ch. IV). This response is indeed the proper one to Strether. The novel does not question it. The fact that Sarah Pocock is a lone dissenter from this opinion only confirms its authority. Madame de Vionnet's praise of Strether is almost effusive at times, but it can also be coolly incisive, as when she comments, 'we all love Strether: it isn't a merit' (ch. XXI), and notes about Strether's 'success' with everyone, including her daughter, that 'his success is a matter that I'm sure he'll never mention for himself'. She sincerely cares about his opinion of her, what he 'might' think of her and 'perhaps even did' (ch. XXXIII). Strether's good opinion matters, not because he is hard to please, but because he is one on whom in the long run nothing is wasted, because he is an admirable, amiable man, benevolent, sympathetic, fair, sensitive, moderate, conscientious, open-minded, unpretentious – in fact surely the most desirable acquaintance among Americans in fiction.

PRESENTATION OF THE FUTURE IN *THE AMBASSADORS*: THE YOUNG

The problem of Chad is, to a large extent, the problem of *The Ambassadors*. The reader has to accept that the novel presents Chad as a problem. Despite all his sensitivity, Strether always seems to get Chad wrong. We gather that, but, since James does not make Chad particularly articulate, we are not very far ahead of Strether in this regard. Chad remains somewhat opaque as a conception. He is one of those Jamesian characters who are not 'there'. There is usually a reason for such Jamesian self-denial. Partly the effect is to render Strether's difficulty in fixing in his judgement a character who is changing under the impact of that own judgement of his upon him – an impact which Strether tends to discount. Partly the idea is to suggest the quality of unformed youth. Despite his greying hair and his command of the French of Paris, Chad has not yet found his feet. He is impressionable and changeable, and Strether always seems to see him in his previous, not his present, shape. He is, however, consistent in his affectionate disposition towards Strether. He is obviously no deep dissembler, but he is inclined to give Strether the response which he wants. Chad is inclined to take his cue from Strether. At first Strether had been prepared for Chad to hate him, because of his intention of interfering in his private life, but Chad likes him. When Strether impartially conveys to him information about his career prospects in Woollett, Chad inclines 'a critical head to either quarter' (ch. IX), so indicating his sense that he is free to choose and can reflect Strether's objectivity. His attentiveness puts Strether 'a little out of countenance', because Chad's suspension of judgement about his mission to see him is a reflection of Strether's own free play of mind on that topic. It may include, on Chad's part, a form of playing for time, but Strether has a similar preoccupation. Chad, as Strether concludes, certainly has 'a way. The main question was of what it was a way *to*.' This is yet another of Strether's questions and it might also be applied to himself. The questioning of purpose passes from mouth to mouth. Strether fails to register the extent to which Chad's 'way' is dependent on his own 'way'. There is no doubt that Chad looks up to him. Chad's sincerity is certain when he introduces Strether to Jeanne de Vionnet as 'the best man in the world, who has it in his power to do a great deal for us, and whom I want you to like and revere as nearly as possible as much as I do' (ch. XI). Reverence for the power of good in Strether is a romantic, idealistic component in the young, vaguely conceived in Chad, yet persistent. Chad's belief in Strether's influence with his mother fades, but it is influence *on* rather than influence *with* that matters. Chad becomes aware of Strether's role as a catalyst. He regards him as the exemplary American, whom one can introduce to anyone, whose opinion one would respect on anything. He consults him as an authoritative 'observer of manners' who may study in Jeanne de Vionnet the type of the *jeune fille* 'as she actually is' and compare that with the American type at home (ch. XIV). In the course of receiving these compliments Strether dimly feels that he is being 'used' by Chad, but he cannot think 'exactly to what end'. The fact that there can, in Chad's current circumstances, be no satisfactory end eventually worries Strether, but in the meantime Chad welcomes Strether as an asset to everybody. Strether, as Chad tells him just before the Pococks' arrival, has 'done a great deal' for Madame de Vionnet (ch. XIX). Again the benefits are unspecified; they may include cheering her up by providing her with a new interest and diverting her from her bleak personal prospect or simply fortifying her with the acquaintance and example of a man like Strether, who neither hypocritically tolerates her nor condemns her, but displays an American type of goodness, not always realistic but attempting constructiveness. Chad is less self-conscious than Strether and he sees the beneficial psychological and moral effect of Strether's refined scrupulosity and defensive wit upon others. He recognises that Strether's openness to new facts and ideas and his willingness to revise his judgements constitute an approach to experience that is superior to any other, and he tries, perhaps crudely, to imitate them. He is quite prepared for a while to leave Madame de Vionnet in Strether's hands, at once showing an 'unconscious insolence of proprietorship' and waiving the right to require Strether to ask his leave. The mixture of trust and insensitivity is characteristic of Chad. Certainly he can have no complaints about Strether's power of imagination (ch. XXIX) and insight. As Maria Gostrey points out, it would be very ungrateful of him if he had any: 'That's all that would be wanting' – to reduce him to a replica of his mother, is what she implies. The remark registers a criticism of Chad, but it also implies that Strether is doing more for Chad than Strether realises himself. Maria sees that Chad's view of the life that awaits him back in America has been sharply clarified by Strether: Chad now sees that what his mother and relatives want of him there contrasts unfavourably not only, in some respects, with what Madame de Vionnet wants of him but 'most of all' with what *Strether* wants of him. Strether is self-effacing here, remarking that what he wants is a thing he has 'ceased to measure or even to understand'. Strether is too diffident to take Maria Gostrey's point that Chad's return might be to an independence of his relatives' views, to a position different from Jim Pocock's, because Chad has been influenced by the more critical, more tolerant Strether. When she asks Strether, 'Wasn't "your" little Chad just your miracle?' (ch. XXXVI), she is arguing that Strether's contribution to the change in Chad was vital, even if the transformation is different in kind from what at first seemed the case. She sees that Chad's return to America is connected with Strether. There is more to it than money or family loyalty. Strether's developing critical judgements on both America and France rub off on Chad. Madame de Vionnet, too, sees that any deterioration of Chad to Jim Pocock's level is out of the question, owing not only to her own influence on Chad but also to Strether's; Strether is 'better than anything' (ch. XXII), she has to tell Strether when he says 'Everything's comparative'. The capacity to compare is what is superior. No one 'feels' as much as Strether does, she knows. And that feeling has an external effect.

That Chad, from his own perspective, confirms these points made by Maria Gostrey and Madame de Vionnet emerges as he begins to distance himself, emotionally, from Madame de Vionnet. He remarks to Strether that, having tried, with Strether's help, but without success, to learn to dislike Madame de Vionnet in France, he might find out in time if he could dislike her, if he returned to America. Strether, ignoring Chad's irony, steps in to praise Madame de Vionnet's work in effecting the improvement in Chad; more has been done for Chad by her, he gravely affirms, 'than I've ever seen done . . . by one human being for another'. Chad appears to do 'full justice' to that great deal but then points out to Strether: 'And you yourself are adding to it.'

James intervenes to emphasise Strether's modesty: 'It was without heeding this either that his visitor continued' (ch. XXVIII). The authorial underlining of Strether's lack of attention to his own beneficial influence upon Chad is remarkable. The indirect point-of-view method of narrating cannot bring it out. Later Strether does admit that he has 'finished' Madame de Vionnet's work in producing the changed Chad; 'his own high appreciation had, as it were, consecrated her work' (ch. XXXIII). The consecration involves, of course, not a literal depreciation of Madame de Vionnet by Chad, but a respect for Strether's own values. What Chad says sincerely by way of a tribute to Strether is that he had presented Chad's duties to his home to him in a unique way, a way quite distinct from Sarah's. 'No one – with us – will ever take' Strether's place, he assures Strether, since Strether needed no one to make himself better. In correcting the text for the first American edition (November 1903), James emphasised and expanded some of these complimentary phrases, perhaps judging he needed something more explicit, even fulsome. Chad says that Strether could not be improved, and what was so beastly about losing him was that he had spoiled them in France, by making everyone else seem relatively stupid. This compliment is paid by Chad to Strether with 'extreme emphasis' (ch. XXXV). It carried with it 'a protest against doubt and a promise, positively, of performance'. Chad's implicit undertaking to maintain the advantage of Strether's example again combines sincerity with insensitivity, since Strether is now insisting that Chad should stay with Madame de Vionnet. But there is a touch of sentimentality in this latter attitude. At all events Chad continues to find Strether 'exciting' and has a conception of all he is 'worth' to him. He knows that he does not want to lose Strether. Their future relationship in America is left to be worked out. One may say that Chad's vocation in advertising seems unlikely to conduce to its development. But even if they were to have no relationship (and nothing in the novel indicates that definitely) Chad's image of Strether will remain. It is an idea of an independent judgement which is more subtle than his mother's.

Strether himself realises another sense in which his intervention in Chad's affairs has made a difference in them. It has 'absolutely aided and intensified' the intimacy of Chad and Madame de Vionnet. Strether's idealised view of their relationship itself lent it secrecy, excitement and further bonds, so that he became 'almost an added link' and new ground for them to meet upon, not only by driving them to tactics of concealment but also generally by being himself, by interesting them in his complicated reaction, by demonstrating 'the ridiculous mixture, as it must seem to them, of his braveries and his fears, the general spectacle of his art and his innocence' (ch. XXXII). Strether's evaluation of his own variety of response is comically dismissive, but their appreciation of it is quite different. Not only does it temporarily bind them together with a shared experience; in the long run it reflects a critical light upon their own situation. Although at one point Strether had felt 'odiously conscious' of how he might strike Chad and not at all conscious 'of what would have served him' (ch. VII), in fact it is precisely the impression which he makes on Chad that does serve him. Consequently, when Strether mentions to him the 'real right thing' for all of them alike in America, their future there, that does seem a plausible alternative to Chad. Chad has a practical streak, which is different from Strether's tendency to romanticism. Chad is more unembarrassedly aware of the economic basis on which Strether's liberal culture is built than Strether himself is. He thinks of his return to America primarily in terms of a job. Little Bilham had noticed that Chad was not entirely happy with the benefits of Madame de Vionnet's company, but really wants 'to go back and take up a career. He's capable of one, you know, that will improve and enlarge him still more' (ch. IX). This observation is certainly more to the point than Strether's recurrent vision of Chad as a 'happy young Pagan, handsome and hard but oddly indulgent'. Chad shows his bargaining hand on more than one occasion, but most notably when he agrees to return to America provided that Strether takes on Madame de Vionnet himself. This offer is dealt with in Strether's train of thought in commercial terms, with references to a 'bill for expenses', debts, interests, reconstruction, money and change (ch. XII). Later Strether frankly admits that Chad will be the man to take the advertising side of the Newsome family business 'in hand', since his capacity for business has at least not been impaired by his experience in France: he 'has a natural turn for business, an extraordinary head' (ch. XX), and is both his father's and his mother's son. Strether need not, then, have felt so devastated to learn, at the end, that Chad, having learned something of the trade of advertising in London, intends to return to America to practise it on behalf of his family's firm. Chad's decision to attend to the material basis of their exile in Europe is now irrevocable. It appears that he thinks he is doing something intelligent: he has gone one step beyond the critical curiosity advocated by Strether. When at the end Strether is made to ask himself wearily why Chad's destiny should be 'dragging him, at strange hours, up the staircases of the rich' in order that he might be fortified in the 'pleasant practice . . . of finding reassurance in comparisons and contrasts', the ironic allusion to Strether's own Arnoldian critical detachment and its dissociation from material affluence sheds some light on Chad's simple thinking. He has made a comparison, between work and leisure, which Strether leaves somewhat unstressed. For Chad has been stimulated – 'excited', to use his own word – by Strether's quick-wittedness, to relate leisure to economic activity, to use rather than to cultivate his enhanced personality. The enrichments of personal relationships can cloy; if 'one *should* wish to live on one's accumulations', says Chad, referring to his 'finished' self, the joint product of Strether and Madame de Vionnet, 'five times oneself might be enough' (ch. XXXV). He thus turns Strether's advice to Little Bilham on its head; it is not enough to live. One has to live *on* something. Intense self-cultivation has its limits. He has made a connection which shows up Strether's feeling of 're-assurance in comparisons and contrasts' as a bit fastidious and exclusive. Here is the significance of the fact that on two occasions (ch. IV and XXXVI) Strether declines to name to Maria Gostrey the object which is manufactured in the Newsome factory in Woollett. Chad's dedication to the advertisement of that product seems a gesture at the farthest possible remove from Strether's distasteful reserve. The point is that it is more than a gesture. There is some justice in the implicit rebuke for Strether which it represents. It does not, however, offend Strether as much as Chad's tactless and too definite dismissal of the subject of Madame de Vionnet, who had never been anything he 'could call a burden' (ch. XXXV), since he had never been wholly 'stuck'. Chad has certainly not learned tact from Strether. But there is nothing in his decisions at the end that is incompatible with an affectionate regard for what Strether stands for. The true grounds of Chad's change of mind are not available to us in the novel; Chad is not presented to us as a character who judiciously reaches decisions by stages. Obviously, Strether's inadvertent exposure of the sexual element in his relationship with Madame de Vionnet precipitates the crisis in Chad; he feels a need to resume the active life. The text leaves open the exact nature of the urgency: Strether is not curious for facts. The novel makes it clear, however, that one factor in the decision is Chad's favourable response to Strether, a factor which Strether is constitutionally incapable of examining. It is not the case that Chad is simply reabsorbed into the business world of America out of renewed admiration for the Pococks. Alwyn Berland's view, in his *Culture and Conduct in the Novels of Henry James* (1981), that Chad abandons Madame de Vionnet for the 'world of grab', having been 'conditioned by warped values' (p. 205), is itself conditioned by a hostility to commerce which may involve false values, I would argue. Strether's horror is overdone and not tragic. The choice of the advertising sector for Chad's activity is not unexpected and, though it may show excessive self-confidence, it is not a vote for respectability or the excessive prurience which he has repudiated in his mother. It does offer him a credible future. Strether's idea of Chad's future as the protraction of a fading love-affair with an ageing French mistress does not have the moral appeal with which he touchingly invests it. Chad must *un*develop from the *affaire*. Madame de Vionnet, for all her instinctive resistance, does not suppose otherwise.

A more distinct view of the future is provided by the emergence of Mamie Pocock in the novel as a personality of considerable interest. By elaborating her relationship with Strether to an extent not really envisaged in his plans for and comments on the novel, James enlarges the cultural dimension in Strether's embassage and indicates that the implications of Chad's return to America are not mainly negative. Jim Pocock's younger sister turns out to be more than a comic appendage to Sarah's entourage. Mamie is one of the surprises of *The Ambassadors*. Billed as the typical 'American girl' (ch. XXI), a rather brash madam, well turned out and comparatively liberated, but terribly unsubtle, 'the splendid type every one is so agreed that your wonderful country produces', as Madame de Vionnet archly puts it, Mamie in fact shows how very perceptive she is. She is the only one of the Pococks, as Strether belatedly recognises, who can see that Chad's relationship with Madame de Vionnet has improved him and altered him – 'she sees him as different,' a discrimination which makes her, in Strether's eyes, 'a case' in Paris of the kind that he himself had been as soon as he had seen Chad there (ch. XXII). Her observant quality aligns her with Strether. She is another of the subjects on which he has to revise his preconceptions. He had previously thought of this 22-year-old young lady as a person of limited horizons whom Woollett would regard as the last word in representatives. Mamie is more like Strether as an ambassador than that; she is too conscious of fine distinctions to be merely an epitome of narrow virtue. Strether had thought she might be malleable; he expected her to be 'festal', 'bridal', confidently happy with a 'pleasant public familiar radiance' and a rather simple, unmixed, 'empty' consciousness which was capable of receiving ideas (ch. XX). That did not amount to much, but he had also, patronisingly, given her value as 'the symbol of an opposition', a bait to attract Chad to Woollett. He had presumed that Mamie would be 'turned on' by the Pococks to divert Chad, pushed as a rival to Jeanne de Vionnet for Chad's possible affections. The guess is an awry one, but it does lead him to make comparisons between the French and the American girl which are not to the latter's disadvantage. Jeanne has no chance to foster any feeling she may have for Chad, any 'still and shaded flame' (ch. XX), because of her subordination by her mother. Mamie Pocock, by way of contrast, is much freer, more purposive, unruffled and open to enlightenment. The comparison of these two characters works to the advantage of the American social and moral tradition, highlighting its humanity and optimism, and minimising the importance of its failures in decorum and its provinciality of tone. Those civilised and cultured qualities which, as Maria Gostrey knowingly remarked, one does 'sometimes miss' (ch. IV) in pretty American girls like Mamie may be only skin-deep. Mamie is deep, and she is capable of development. She is not only acute; she is also critical.

Her exercise of judgement also aligns her with Strether. She knows the faults of her brother, Jim Pocock, as Strether does, but as Sarah and Mrs Newsome do not. She has decided that Jim is 'extremely awful' and 'impossible' (ch. XXIII). In this connection Strether mentions Mamie to Maria Gostrey as a significant new factor, 'as if there were a good deal' in the distinction between Mamie's judgement and Sarah's, as indeed there is. It says more for her than Maria Gostrey's judgement does for *her*self when she assumes a reckless flirtation to be going on between Mamie and Chad. In fact, when he takes Mamie out and dines alone with her in his home, she merely uses her freedom and moral innocence to impress Chad with her intrinsic worth and the future liberal development of the American tradition for which she stands. Mamie has her feelings under rein. Strether deduces from this self-control that she 'finds she does' care for Chad. It is the kind of negative way basic commitments are communicated in James, not through rhetoric about how to 'live', but tacitly. Then, symbolically, Mamie appears in another role aligned with Strether's. She is the novel's second impassive observer of France. In chapter XXIV, Strether comes upon her unexpectedly in Sarah Pocock's room, studying Paris from the balcony, 'the huge collective life', and he observes her observation. As the inexperienced, emancipated American girl abroad Mamie has her counterparts in James's other novels and short stories, but she has enjoyed an advantage denied to all of them: she has been tutored by Strether. He had almost forgotten it. But he had actually, in 'Mrs Newsome's parlours', been her mentor in English literature. It was a course 're-enforced by exams and teas', but the gently mocking zeugma should not prevent us from connecting it with Mamie's present attitudes. Strether remembers her 'finally, as very much in advance', which is indeed entirely plausible. Strether characteristically under-values his own contribution to this advancement when he finds it strange that she has now 'more to say to him than he had ever dreamed the pretty girl of the moment *could* have'. It is not fair to Mamie to think of her as ephemeral. So much in advance is she that she cannot communicate with her fellow-travellers, but only with Strether, and in Strether's consummately indirect way. By not mentioning Chad at all, she lets Strether know unmistakably that she has taken the measure of the change in Chad. Such silences and omissions are the very high-point in the Jamesian art of signs. We have to take note that Mamie is a worthy pupil of her master, Strether, and well suited as a transmitter of his skills to future generations. As an American type Mamie Pocock is a young and promising learner, quite outside the range of Maria

Gostrey's classification. It was with such stereotyping in mind that Strether had at first tended to notice the 'funny' elements in Mamie's appearance, a certain inappropriateness of dress and manner, and to analyse it in terms of American social pretentiousness, 'her beautiful benevolent patronage' and her 'hint of the polysyllabic', which might turn her into a bore in middle-age. But Mamie is to make more of an impression on him with the non-syllabic than with the polysyllabic, and after ten minutes of her charming company Strether feels in her 'a quiet dignity that pulled things bravely together'. The value of her society now, surprisingly, makes Strether actually homesick for the first time and 'freshly restless' as though under 'the breath of some vague western whiff'. He has such a revulsion in her favour 'as might have come from remorse at some early injustice'. He does her justice now. He appreciates not only the insight which she shows in personal relationships, but also her positive moral intelligence akin to his own. It was this faculty which Mamie had exercised when she called on Madame and Jeanne de Vionnet. She like them both as a result. Strether registers the 'true inwardness' (an Arnoldian term of approval; see Super, Vol. 6, pp. 216, 220–1) of her judgement there: 'She abounded in their praise, and after the manner of Woollett – which made the manner of Woollett a lovable thing again' (ch. XXIV). The phrasing, with its echoes of religious solemnity, itself moves 'after the manner of Woollett' and presents us with the possibility of a reconciliation in Strether of his refined delicacy with his conscientious inheritance.

Might not a young American, less harsh than her elders, but true to their better self, help to achieve a coherence in Strether himself? Mamie particularly strikes a chord in Strether's heart when she protests that Jeanne de Vionnet ought not to be touched, ought not to be spoiled. That had been precisely Strether's own view before he knew of the arranged marriage. Mamie has, however, reached the same conclusion after having met Monsieur de Montbron. She had noticed that, whereas the fiancé was in love with Jeanne, Jeanne did not yet know if she was in love in return. So keen are Mamie's perceptions of these strangers that 'the momentary effect for Strether was that every one else, in all their affairs, seemed stupid'. This praise for the American girl is very high, and it is of course the very praise which Chad (and several others in so many words) heaps on Strether himself. It is Mamie's capacity for disinterested tenderness that endears her to Strether. She can accept his proposition that Jeanne is still 'probably in love with Chad' without knowing it and that she indicates that by complying with his wishes in the matter of her marriage. Mamie understands that such compliance on Jeanne's part suits everyone, including, as she admits, herself, since she is interested in Chad. She is also ready to assist Strether in 'ends of his own', ends which remain unspecified, but which doubtless involve his support of Madame de Vionnet. That, too, tends to free Chad, as she probably realises more clearly than Strether does. Strether is left admiring Mamie, although he is sure that she will be 'too fat, at thirty'. Lest this prediction should seem too cutting, we should perhaps remember Hamlet or look ahead to the admirable Rosanna Gaw of *The Ivory Tower*, also physically massive in her thirties. Mamie's presence in America, when Strether returns, at least cannot darken the atmosphere there.

Now, Mamie does seem well suited to Chad; her qualities of decisiveness and generosity seem the right ones to complement his. She is not Strether's choice for him; if she is Woollett's, it is, blindly, for the wrong reasons. The main problem is that he does not seem to be the novel's choice for her. *The Ambassadors* offers hardly any clues as to Chad's personal destiny. When Chad said he would 'like to see' Mamie, it was in a way which only brought out 'the facility of his attitude' (ch. XVII). It is an unpromising start, but Chad is not yet on the rebound. When Mamie arrives, he treats her privately like an old friend, suspecting that, like his sister, she hates him while he remains in France. Strether protests at this misreading, but Chad persists obtusely: 'She certainly doesn't like me.' He minds it because she is beautiful, adding: 'I'd like her if she'd like me. Really, really!' It is not really a matter of liking, but this is as far as the novel gets (ch. XXIX). It may seem probable that this misunderstanding can be cleared up in America. Little Bilham had assumed that Mamie would not want to take on Chad now that he had been 'spoiled' for her by another woman (ch. XXV), but . . . ? The avoidance of a topic in a James novel is the last thing to make it go away. Those two do have one thing in common, their enthusiasm for Strether. It is conceivable that their attachment to each other and to him might make a part of 'the great difference' to which he is to return in America and of which he will see what he 'can make' (ch. XXXVI). Meanwhile he is not likely to dwell on it while helping the two ladies who find him irresistible to bear up under his tactful valedictions. It is enough to know that, for all his talk of renunciation, Strether's positive work is never done.

THE AMBASSADORS AS COMEDY

James preferred to illustrate a mixed tragi-comic view of life in his fiction, but *The Ambassadors*, while not without sombre concerns like age, failure and loneliness, has all the makings of comedy, except perhaps one – the happy ending. It has a plot full of surprises and disconcerting discoveries. It has a leisured mood with people away from home freed from habitual restraints. It has a number of minor comic caricatures like Miss Barrace and Jim Pocock as well as a range of more gently satirised major characters, including Strether himself. It has, within the limits set by educated, early-twentieth-century propriety, an amusing variety of styles of speech, much of which is reflected in the choice of vocabulary attributed to Strether in his musings. The dialogue, most of which centres on matters of human character and morality, is frequently brilliantly witty, though also sometimes spoiled by an esoteric allusiveness and fragmentariness developed by James to avoid stating the obvious in communication. But it is in the running inner monologue of Strether, reported with very occasional brief interventions by the narrator, that the mastery of comic style is most evident in the work, as metaphors and comparisons are invented to bring out odd connections, and more solemn and intense bouts of reflective melancholy or aesthetic delight are rapidly succeeded by qualifying critical or realistically under-cutting comments. The somewhat undignified and minor nature of the main subject of the novel, the interest taken in the willingness of a spoiled young man to give up his French mistress, and the somewhat exaggeratedly sharp conflicts which blow up around it, leading to quarrels and tears, also suggest a comic scale. But *The Ambassadors* is not primarily corrective or burlesque in mode. The examination of cultural contrasts which it undertakes is serious without being prejudiced or bitter. The main focus, as I have argued in this chapter, is upon American civilisation, the area of inquiry which James had originally regarded as his main preoccupation and which, after an interval taken up with the drama and with stories of English High Society, he now re-sumes. Undoubtedly, in the consciousness of Strether, James was able to control his novel from the point of view of an untypical but highly signi-ficant and attractive American. Strether is a unique comic hero, fallible, fading, kindly, self-deprecating, and too old, really, to have a future in reversion that could convey any kind of uplift at the end of his European visit. His reluctance to gain anything for himself out of the episode, especially in the form of a second marriage based in Europe, is not in itself a sign of bewilderment, however. The return to America has to feel right; poignancy, cynicism and regret are all avoided. James liked his novels at their conclusions, at the very point of artistic perfection, to lead from art back to life, the relations of things which end nowhere. But from the point of view of a Jamesian novel the life into which it opens at the end must be unknown. Enough attention, nevertheless, is paid in *The Ambassadors* to young people who admire and like Strether for us to set aside any considerations of waste. Though not particularly weighted towards optimism, the novel raises one's curiosity about its characters' future in America. It ends with the past brought to the point of the present – 'Then there we are!' – and the future blank but to be played for. *The Ambassadors* was James's first novel of the new century, which, since it was to be the American century, it inaugurated very auspiciously.

CHAPTER 8

Critical Response to
The Ambassadors

IN JAMES'S DAY

In 1903, while *The Ambassadors* was actually being serialised in the *North American Review*, William Dean Howells contributed to that periodical a critical appreciation of 'Mr Henry James's later work' which gives us some idea of the range of critical receptions which the new novel could expect. Howells indicated that, though James's appeal was only to a minority readership, yet his reputation stood remarkably high at that period. Howells argued that both *The Awkward Age* and *The Wings of the Dove* were great novels, nothing less than incomparable and unique. He particularly praised in the latter the distilled 'New Yorkishness' of Milly Theale, who was a character 'most appreciable in that relief from the background which Europe gives all American character' (p. 128) and he liked the 'profound pathos' of the closing scenes of *The Awkward Age* (p. 137). At the same time he admitted that James had many detractors, partly because of the low moral tone of the English social world which he had exposed in his recent work and partly because of the much-discussed obscurity in his style, which was to be compared with Browning's, and often seemed to leave his characters' motivations to be divined by the readers. Howells even said that many of James's readers were in a state of 'hot insurrection against all that he says and is' (p. 125). James's reviewers, it is true, divide into those who condemn his indefiniteness and effeminacy and those who admire his subtlety and fineness. The paucity of dialogue in *The Wings of the Dove* had brought some baffled responses: 'His people never say anything outright' – the narrator smothers the plot with 'clouds of refined and enigmatical verbage' (Harriet W. Preston, 'The latest novels of Howells and James', 1903); or 'He makes his characters read each other's minds from clues that he keeps to himself', for 'with James analysis is the end in itself' (F. M. Colby, 'In darkest James', 1902). These reactions are collected in Roger Gard's *Henry James: The Critical Heritage* (1968). But James's moral impartiality in his handling of Kate Croy drew unstinted admiration from reviewers in the *Edinburgh* and the *Quarterly*: 'He tries seriously, strenuously, to produce the illusion of being, and he is well content to succeed' (*Edinburgh Review* (1903), p. 71) and James entangles our sympathies with the worldly as well as with the spiritual, pointed out Oliver Elton – nothing could be more wholly of the 'lay' life – James is 'trebly representative' of the sort of things 'our time' cares for (*Quarterly Review* (1903), pp. 369 and 379). The reviewer of *The Wings of the Dove* in *The Times Literary Supplement* (1902) was pleased, not worried, that James leaves 'the subject under discussion to the reader's intelligence without disconcerting appeals to his emotion'. *The Wings of the Dove* is an even denser and certainly a more sobering novel than *The Ambassadors*. Having assimilated the former, the contemporary critics could perhaps hardly be unprepared for the novel which James had actually written before it. *The Ambassadors* appeared in the shadow but also in the light of *The Dove*.

There was at once an intelligent review in *The Times Literary Supplement* (1903), again making the comparison with Browning (James was known to have been a friend and admirer of Browning): any inattention to detail on the reader's part would have the same effect on his understanding of *The Ambassadors* as it would on his understanding of *Bishop Blougram's Apology*. The difficulties in James are like those in Browning's poem, it is implied; due to the dense, indirect presentation of character and ideas. *The Ambassadors* is said to be 'all thesis'; everything in it contributes to the thesis, and 'Mr James thinks very hard indeed'. Complications in it are diagnosed as coming 'principally from the abrupt contact of New England and Parisian standards of feeling and behaviour'. The reviewer states the theme concisely and well, searching for the romantic critical key of organic unity and finding it. He notes also that *The Ambassadors* is 'largely composed of conversation' and suffers from an 'affected scorn of repetition' and an 'excess of allusiveness', but these are minor faults. It is notable that the perceptive early critics see James as seriously dealing with subjects for discussion in his novels and are not traduced by the indirectness of James's technique into affirmations of his indeterminacy or artistic nihilism. James is for them a late, subtle contributor to the Victorian debate.

Equally favourable was the notice by Frederick T. Cooper in the *Bookman* (1904), which defended James against the criticism that he was stating a clear story 'in a hopelessly involved manner'. On the contrary, James was 'giving as clear a statement as he can of a much befogged condition of facts'. It is life itself which is complex and allusively queer, and this is the tale that James has to tell. *The Ambassadors* is said to be easier reading than James's other recent works because he has 'a very definite central thought' in it, namely 'the influence of Europe, its older culture, its radically different standards, upon the American temperament'. Cooper calls *The Ambassadors* a 'study of the New England conscience, subjected to the hothouse atmosphere of the Parisian *Vie de Bohème*', though this definition scarcely touches on what Madame de Vionnet represents, it is interesting that the critic could conceive of the novel as a kind of 'study', as *Middlemarch* is also a 'study'. Cooper notes that the characters are 'refreshingly American' and that the 'curious and interesting readjustments' in the standards of Mr Strethers (*sic*) is the main point. It is a novel 'with all the tantalising vagueness of real life', he concludes. But the impressionism is not taken as invalidating the intellectual content of the work at all. It merely does justice to its subtlety.

Annie R. M. Logan, reviewing the novel in the *Nation* (1904), sees it as an elaborate and profound study of the different American and European 'outlook and attitude towards life'. The 'great thing' in it is the effect of Paris on the Ambassadors – 'the way Woollett standards of thought, conduct, even of abstract right and wrong, are, temporarily at least, infected and impaired'. Americans abroad occupy the scene virtually exclusively. She singles out chapter XXVII, when Sarah Pocock puts it to Strether straight, as the turning-point in the plot, leading to his belated understanding that he is 'inevitably and by the nature of things committed to Woollett'. Strether never could have adopted Maria's clever cynicism or Bilham's indifference. This interpretation may be too unequivocal, ignoring the role of Mamie Pocock, but Annie Logan gets the main idea of the work right. She even feels that the revelation at the Cheval Blanc is too explicit and Strether might have been left 'a solacing doubt' in 'the gray after years of Woollett'. Hers is the strongest 'American' interpretation of the novel possible.

The short notice in the *Athenaeum* (1903) lightly rebukes James for occasionally displaying too much 'verbal cleverness', but judges *The Ambassadors* to be 'altogether satisfying' as 'a study of life as it is lived in the world of fact by real Americans'. Maria Gostrey is mentioned as 'the lady whose thoughts fit rather loudly into their appropriate places', a character sympathetically illuminated by James's touch, as is Strether and Madame de Vionnet. This novel 'is indubitably good work'.

In the *Saturday Review* for 31 October 1903, James was praised for offering 'an intellectual amusement altogether enthralling', especially in unravelling the skein of the dialogue of *The Ambassadors*. Also the 'intricacies and subtleties of motive and character are twined so deftly, the ravelled web so trimly knit'. James is said to succeed 'in investing with amazing interest the slow change in the mental attitude of the ambassador, whose New England standards slowly fall before the larger, livelier standards of Europe'. This theme is called 'a thesis' on which James brings 'persistent ingenuity' to bear. The seriousness and difficulty of the work were not in doubt.

Apart from individual reviews and one enthusiastic and rather numerical, linguistic analysis of a passage from chapter IX ('Vernon Lee's (Violet Paget), 'The handling of words: Meredith, Henry James' (1910); see R. Gard, *Henry James: The Critical Heritage* (1968), pp. 480–7), comment on *The Ambassadors* during the remainder of James's lifetime tended to be subsumed in general essays on his works. Sydney Waterlow defended James as giving us real accounts of mental movements: he may be thought to be alluding to *The Ambassadors* in particular when he praised James's stylised dialogue as a polished mirror preserving the important 'substance of our mental life' ('The work of Mr Henry James' (1904), p. 240). Joseph Conrad in his 'Henry James: an appreciation' (1905) no doubt had Strether in mind, too, when he praised James as the historian of the 'fine conscience', which is 'troubled by the nice discrimination of shades of conduct' and, despite the 'sophism' of its mistakes, ultimately triumphs 'through an energetic act of renunciation'. Conrad notes wrily that such 'a solution by rejection must always present a certain apparent lack of finality', so that one remains with a 'sense of the life still going on'. His understanding of James's merits is penetrating, though generalised. On the other hand, W. C. Brownell (in 'Henry James', 1905) gave voice to a much cooler assessment of James's achievement, when he doubted if, 'to the majority of cultivated and intelligent readers', the difficulty of the later writing did not require 'an amount of effort disproportionate to the sense of assured reward' (p. 518). Brownell regretted that there were not more 'classic' scenes in the later works like the death of Ralph Touchett in *The Portrait of a Lady* and deplored 'the loss of integumental interest in the handling' in the later James. He welcomed the 'return to the cosmopolitan *motif* in *The Ambassadors*', but felt its development was encrusted and obscured with mannerisms (p. 516). James's art, Brownell argued, is a restricted one, which suggests but 'does not illustrate' culture, which scrutinises culture so much that it dispenses with its significance. This commonsensical, yet unpenetrating, critique of the novel is representative of the negative reaction of being put off by the style and has clearly been unhelpfully influential. There is a more particular accusation against James in M. Sturge Gretton's 'Mr Henry James and his prefaces' (1912), when he is said to create an atmosphere that is 'much more' (p. 73) than his individual characters – a point illustrated by what the reviewer considers an inconsistency in Madame de Vionnet's character: a sophisticated woman would not chaff and embarrass Strether as she does in Sarah Pocock's salon in chapter XXI. The nervousness there seems quite credible to me, but Gretton believes that 'our whole conception' of Madame de Vionnet requires the exclusion of such elements; she had earlier been 'so alluringly, so consummately' our heroine (p. 74). This is to overdo atmosphere utterly. It illustrates how frequently with *The Ambassadors* a general criticism breaks down when the example is carefully examined. But it is not usual for examples to be risked. Rebecca West's comments on *The Ambassadors* in her *Henry James* (1916), a contribution to the Writers of the Day series, suffer from lack of substantiation. She considers *The Ambassadors* untypical of its period in James's development since it lacks those great sprawling sentences which absorb the whole of his 'attention'. But she does not describe the kind of sentences it does contain. She considers the *donnée* of the novel to be 'trivial', lacking both dignity and significance. It is the artful display of the tale 'in the setting of lovely, clean, white Paris and green France, lifting her poplars into the serene strong light of the French sky' which ensures our sense of suspense (pp. 108–9). Such tributes, very remote from the text, are a form of faint praise. The novel is not really being taken seriously.

On the other hand, and more acutely, James's friend Morton Fullerton praised his refinement of the point-of-view technique in 'The art of Henry James' (1910, p. 395), likening his plastic treatment of a full consciousness like Strether's to the process of radioactivity, in which a myriad of unmeaning holes are transmuted into 'intelligible signs' (p. 408). More robust is the celebrated defence of James by Ezra Pound in the August 1918 number of the *Little Review*, in which he calls him splendidly 'the hater of tyranny', who was 'against all the sordid petty personal crushing pressure, the impinging of one personality on another; all of them in highest degree damn'd, loathsome and detestable' (p. 7 and note), a passage which is obviously applicable to Mrs Newsome and her daughter. Pound says he is 'tired of hearing pettiness talked about Henry James's style' and wants justice done to his 'striving to bring in America on the side of civilization': James had tried to make 'three nations intelligible one to another'. In his novels 'he showed race against race, immutable; the essential Americanness, or Englishness or Frenchness . . . "why" there is always misunderstanding, why men of different race are not the same'. James's great art was 'a struggle for communication', and communication 'is a recognition of differences, of the right of differences to exist, of interest in finding things different'. Few critics have got to the heart of James so clearly and emphatically as Pound in this tribute.

T. S. Eliot's memorial essay in the same number of the *Little Review* is a less happy affair. It denies that James was a literary critic and teases us about James's baffling escape from Ideas, while insisting that James's focus is on a 'situation, a relation, an atmosphere' rather than on characters and plot. These are tentative paradoxes, fruitful in suggestion, but liable to disperse interest into peripheral areas.

IN THE 1920s AND 1930s

During James's lifetime, critical appreciation of his work tended to be cautious out of personal respect, even awe, while attacks on him still had a careless, knockabout quality, which perversely suggest his greatness, like H. G. Wells's in his *Boon* (1915), where James is called 'the culmination of the Superficial type', a 'leviathan retrieving pebbles', and so on (see *Henry James and H. G. Wells: A Record*, ed. Leon Edel and Gordon N. Ray (1958), pp. 245–9). After his death, James rapidly seemed an old-fashioned, heavy-bound, prewar, sexually reticent writer, and his reputation temporarily declined. Pelham Edgar, while praising James's compositional mastery, complained that as readers we 'are impatient of so much perfection' and wish 'for some irruption of the incongruous'. In *The Ambassadors* James has imposed on himself 'a standard of composition too exacting and too unnecessarily high' ('Henry James and his method' (1918–19), pp. 230 and 235). Dorothy Bethurum, writing on 'Morality and Henry James' (1923), remarked that the prophecy made by a few of James's friends at the time of his death, that the American public would re-estimate his work favourably, had 'gone unfulfilled' (pp. 324–30). She countered Stuart P. Sherman's view, expressed in 'The aesthetic idealism of Henry James' (1917), that for James there were no moral questions, only aesthetic ones, by arguing that James's Americans, when face to face with Gallic culture, always keep their 'homely virtue' (p. 325): though Strether's prejudices are broken down by his contact with a different culture, his 'Puritan morality rises up' against the sexual irregularity of the relationship between Madame de Vionnet and Chad and against 'the lie necessary to cover it' (p. 328). Indeed, for Dorothy Bethurum, Strether's conduct and renunciation 'completely justify the Christian code of ethics' (p. 329), but hers is an old-fashioned verdict in the 1920s. The virtues she finds in *The Ambassadors* were more likely then to damn James further than to help his defence. Two main trends developed in the attempt to retrieve the position. James was treated, especially in America, as an academic classic who had to be explained historically. Also his work was assimilated to the category of Modernism and compared with that of Joyce and Proust. In this new critical enterprise *The Ambassadors* was much to the fore, being cited as a prime example of experiment in narrative.

The change in opinion can be detected in Joseph Warren Beach's *The Method of Henry James* (1918). He praises the slow process of change in the consciousness of Strether, whom he calls a 'broad, continuous figure'. He quotes from the Cheval Blanc scene to show that it is Strether's sensations that make it live and suggests that the novel as a whole gives us 'the entire focus of acclimatisation' of Strether. Throwing the whole weight of his interpretation on to narrative method, Beach then argues that the subject of *The Ambassadors* is, essentially, Paris. To drain the novel of its drama and surprises in this way and to replace them with a process of acclimatisation inevitably displaces its centre outwards from Strether to the scene. Beach finds the predominance of a 'special quality' of white in the picture of Paris conveyed, always bringing to mind 'the colour of Manet'. He assumes: 'The characters of Paris are spiritual . . . the spiritual atmosphere is one of intelligence tempered by imagination.' Beach believes that Strether, in allowing himself this Gallic pure luxury, takes on the tone of James himself, offering us 'fruits well ripened in the sun of his thought'. The gloss has settled here over the experience of France actually presented in the novel. In a later book, *The Twentieth-Century Novel: Studies in Technique* (1932), Beach actually compares James's subjective method in *The Ambassadors* to the 'amplifying' process in reproducing music (p. 228).

Percy Lubbock's treatment of *The Ambassadors* in *The Craft of Fiction* (1921), though much more precise in its arguments, shares some of Beach's presuppositions. He is out to defend James's narrative artistry. Seizing on Strether as James's fullest use of a dramatised consciousness, Lubbock plays down the American aspects of the novel and calls its subject 'purely pictorial'; it is the picture of an '*état d'âme*'. He claims that the theme of *The Ambassadors* is Strether's imaginative change of opinion in favour of 'the life of freedom' as represented by France; Strether 'sees an exquisite, bountiful world laid at a young man's feet', but he is too old to seize this world of freedom for himself (p.39). Lubbock's emphasis on the scene in Gloriani's garden (ch. XI) is too narrow. If *The Ambassadors* did purport to represent France as such a bountiful world, it would be open to the charge of superficiality and irrelevance. As a study of *fin de siècle* French wealth and art it is no match for Proust's works. Proust seems to lurk behind Lubbock's account of Strether's 'mind grown visible' and of the movements that 'flicker over' its surface. Lubbock's distinction as an analyst of fictional technique (he is especially good on James's unobtrusive control of dialogue) lent his general account of the novel considerable authority. When he says that 'the subject of the book would be unchanged if the story ended differently', since nothing in the scene has 'any value in itself', James criticism can be observed to be heading for its Modernist phase. The way is clear for relativity, the uncertainty factor and the stream of consciousness.

This last category is firmly applied to James's fiction by K. F. Gerould in 'Stream of consciousness' (1927), where James is said, quite wrongly, to have initiated this method in English fiction by recording

his characters' thoughts '*exactly as they go on in the mind*', using mental
rhythms and 'the syntax of solitary reflection', the 'almost unparsable
context' (p. 233). In the same year E. M. Forster in *Aspects of the Novel*
(1927) queried Lubbock's high estimate of *The Ambassadors*, by
arguing that its technical consistency was bought at the cost of lack of
number and variety in its characters and their attributes. Forster's
chatty tone covers a multitude of sins. He considers James's characters
to be incapable of carnality; they are 'exquisite deformities' with huge
heads and tiny legs. There are no stupid people in their world. He mis-
reads Mamie Pocock's character as 'second rate, deficient in sensitive-
ness, abounding in the wrong sort of worldliness' and categorises her as
a Henry James type of whom Mrs Gereth in *The Spoils of Poynton* (of all
people!) is another; suggesting that he has not read chapter XXIV at
all. He believes that 'Paris irradiates the book from end to end', being 'a
scale by which human sensibility can be measured'; Paris redeems
Strether by revealing itself as 'something finer' than anyone else can
imagine. Forster sees *The Ambassadors* as a work of rigid unity in the
shape of an hour-glass in which Strether and Chad 'change places' – an
idea which he makes no serious attempt to work out. To keep to this
pattern James, according to Forster, had to drop 'most of human life'
from the novel. *The Ambassadors* emerges as an uninteresting exercise
in aesthetic formalism. Edwin Muir took this idea over from Forster,
when he called the Jamesian novel 'a minor offshoot' of the tradition of
fiction, in his *The Structure of the Novel* (1928, p. 12), a work which
virtually ignores George Eliot, James and Conrad. On the other hand,
Forster does note that Strether is not just a passive observer, but one
who tries to influence the action and 'takes us along with him'. Forster
succeeds in toppling James from the position of novelist legislator to
which Lubbock had called him, but in so doing dents the reputation of
The Ambassadors rather badly. Undoubtedly, in attracting the attention
of Lubbock and Forster in this classic critical exchange, which is
basically concerned with narrative technique, *The Ambassadors* suffered
some distortion. The idea that it was mainly about France gained
ground.

Orlo Williams, in '*The Ambassadors*' (1928), continued the disparage-
ment. He stated that nobody read James any more, the First World
War having changed attitudes so much. Like Forster, Williams argues
that James avoids direct treatment of conflicting passions in the interest
of 'symmetry and harmonious unity of parts' (p. 50). James etherealises
life too much for the sake of art, stretching personal relations to 'a
tenuity of gossamer' (p. 62). Strether is even said to exhibit 'no
emotional reaction at all' to the scene at the Cheval Blanc: conversely,
he is culpable in that he lacks logic in exercising the claims of his
'fictional fancy' against the stronger Pocock claims of relationship and

interest. Williams assumes without question that any objection made against Strether is a point against the novel.

Carl H. Grabo, in *The Technique of the Novel* (1928, pp. 81–94), follows Lubbock in defending 'the deeper impression of realism' conveyed by the restricted point of view in *The Ambassadors*, but then complains that all the characters are 'too clever for life' (p. 87), especially Madame de Vionnet, who is subtle, intellectual and 'cast for no action' (p. 90). Grabo even maintains that we never share Strether's feelings deeply; we share only his thoughts, so fearful is James of passion.

James received rough treatment from another quarter when he was taken to task for abandoning his American roots. Van Wyck Brooks, in his very sarcastic *The Pilgrimage of Henry James* (1925), takes the nationalist view that expatriation ruined James's career. Settling in England lost James 'his instinctive judgement of men and things' (ch. 5), his 'firm knowledge of the phenomenal world, a living sense of objective reality' (ch. 7), which he had once had in the United States. The later novels are 'exhalations of intellectual vapour'. When he tried to return to his international theme in *The Ambassadors*, Brooks suggested, it had long since faded from his mind. What Brooks really regrets is that James did not belong to a simple pre-Arnoldian America like Hawthorne's. It can be said for this view that at least it permits a critical preference for the earlier works, up to *The Bostonians*, which are believed to have been written while James was in closer contact with his own people. Academic study of this earlier phase was strengthened by Cornelia P. Kelley's *The Early Development of Henry James* (1930), which drew attention to James's first forays into criticism. The most impressive essay in this field is, however, Stephen Spender's 'The school of experience in the early novels', contributed to the special James number of *Hound and Horn* in 1934, where the affinities between the early and late work are noted. The early and late novels both deal with Americans abroad and observe a social system in decay, as Spender rightly points out: also, *The Ambassadors* is a novel about a sexual subject; and Strether is an admirable character, not only talented and imaginative, but also anticipated to some extent in Rowland Mallet in *Roderick Hudson*. The Brooks view is countered from another angle by Philip Rahv in his 'The cult of experience in American writing' where, far from being thought un-American, *The Ambassadors* is seen as exploring the central *motif* of the national literature, the need to live fully, the claim of the private right to openness of experience. This lesson, which is said to be 'taught by James in *The Ambassadors*', links him to Whitman, Rahv unironically argues (pp. 413 and 415). And Whitman and James are presented exhilaratingly as 'the true initiators of the American line of modernity' (p. 415), which originates in a recoil from the inhibitions of Puritanism.

The defence of James was well under way in the 1930s. He was seen increasingly as a novelist of serious and intellectual interest. The 1934 *Hound and Horn* special issue contained, apart from the Stephen Spender article already referred to, R. P. Blackmur's study of 'The critical prefaces', also used to preface his *The Art of the Novel* (1934), which gave James's critical terminology a wide currency and presented him warmly as the novelist of 'the liberated intelligence', whose imaginative representation of life gave value and meaning to 'the contrasts and oppositions and processions of the society that confronted' him. Blackmur's long account of the preface to *The Ambassadors* notes James's points that chapters VII and XXIV are representational without being scenic and that Paris is 'a minor matter symbolising the world other than . . . Woollet [*sic*], Mass.' (p. 473). In the same issue Marianne Moore paid a tribute to 'Henry James as a characteristic American', stressing his idealistic good-nature and family feeling, and there also Edmund Wilson first published his important essay, 'The ambiguity of Henry James'. Wilson called James 'one of the coolest-headed of novelists' who presented the effect of sex and of industrialism 'with the most precise and scrupulous truth', yet at one remove. He discusses the possibly morbid psychology of the governess in 'The Turn of the Screw' and the narrator in *The Sacred Fount*, tracing the ambiguity in the presentation of such characters to the fact that James had been *déraciné* from his earliest years and was uncertain about his own timidity, primness, sense of superiority and caution, which he nevertheless exposed in his characters. In the later work 'the gas of the psychological atmosphere' (p. 402) expands and the central characters are seen dimly as missing out on emotional experience. Wilson almost leaves Strether out of the discussion. Yet, although Wilson notes that Strether is made sympathetic by James and that 'the Americans score morally off' the charming French lady in *The Ambassadors*, his psychological slant undoubtedly affected the critical view of Strether. Edna Kenton, whose essay 'Henry James to the ruminant reader: *The Turn of the Screw*' (1924) had influenced Edmund Wilson's idea of Jamesian ambiguity, concluded the *Hound and Horn* number with the first publication of the 1900 scenario of *The Ambassadors*.

A further testimony to James's importance came in Graham Greene's 'Henry James: the private universe' in D. Vershoyle's *The English Novelists* (1936). Greene contends that James was driven to write by 'a sense of evil religious in its intensity'. In this respect all of James's novels are 'of one moral piece'. His later work gives us the full truth about evil. His characters form the immoral background to the 'period of haphazard violence' which preceded the First World War. He was never exiled from the deep roots of knowledge of evil. James's studies of inhuman egotism, says Greene, and his pitying analyses of corruption place him beside Shakespeare. Although evil is not as prominent in

The Ambassadors as in several other James novels, there are traces of it in Sarah Pocock's behaviour and in Chad's. Greene's stern argument is valuable in showing again what to look for in James.

By way of contrast, the positive content of James's novels was stressed by Yvor Winters in his 'Henry James and the relation of morals to manners' (1937). Winters credits James with a powerful, but vulnerable, 'moral sense', which he projects in his novels as an American inheritance liable to weaken when it comes into contact with European manners (p. 483). He finds in Strether evidence of the continuance of the New England conscience beyond its early Calvinist and Unitarian phases: James's plots are almost wholly conceived in terms of ethical choice. Nevertheless, for Winters, James's moral sense is too delicate and intellectually unsupported. Winters considers it a fault in *The Ambassadors* that our attitude to Chad at the end of the novel is unresolved (p. 500), James not even judging the state of uncertainty: he is not sure to what extend Chad is a betrayer. He regards Maria Gostrey as one 'enriched' by European influence (p. 499). He believes somewhat naïvely that James was admirably serious in general, if at times his moral sense was doomed to be 'dissolved in air' (p. 490).

A more subtle understanding of James's art of evaluating life through fiction is to be found in L. C. Knights's essay 'Henry James and the trapped spectator' (1939), which is a brilliant synthesis of the critical discoveries about James which had been made in the 1930s and something more. Knights, accepting with qualifications Van Wyck Brooks's point that James's disconnection from America resulted in a disabling detachment, nevertheless notes the vitality of James's moral sense, the 'satiric verve' of the portrait of Sarah Pocock, the unholy righteousness and brutal goodness of his villains, and the thoroughly explored recesses of his egoists who use others. James's observers are the 'trapped spectators of life' (p. 605) who see this brutal truth too clearly for us to say they evade it. In the style the subjective alternates with the objectively critical or is presented simultaneously with it, thus combining pity with critical analysis of the spectator. The observers release indirectly 'a sense of life' which is an extension of the observing intelligence, even though they are withdrawn from life. Knights praises 'In the Cage' and 'The Beast in the Jungle' for producing this effect rather than *The Ambassadors*, where, he complains, there is more statement about Paris than 'achieved representation' of it (p. 614) and Strether may be too close to his creator, both trapped by 'the Genteel Tradition'. But James's sense of the isolated individual, divided from the public of common readers, aware of the general predicament of dishumanisation, makes him for Knights the first 'modern' novelist. Despite the conventionality of these later references to *The Ambassadors*, Knights's awareness of what the Jamesian irony can achieve by projecting 'the possible other case' makes his essay the outstanding piece of James criticism of this period.

LEAVIS AND AFTER

L. C. Knights, as a contributor to *Scrutiny*, acknowledged F. R. Leavis's views on James without dissent in the 'trapped spectator' essay. The main outline of Leavis's case on James was already evident from March 1937, when he contributed a review of Blackmur's *The Art of the Novel* to *Scrutiny* (vol. 5, pp. 398–417), entitled 'Henry James'. This review was incorporated into Leavis's longer third chapter of *The Great Tradition* (1948) with the same title. Leavis's achievement was to place James beside Jane Austen, George Eliot, Conrad and Lawrence in his tradition of excellence in fiction. To effect this end he adduced the quality of *The Europeans, Washington Square, The Portrait of a Lady, The Bostonians, The Awkward Age* and *What Maisie Knew*, as well as indicating the value of many parts of other novels and many tales. His critical strategy, however, involved him, as elsewhere, in dislodgement, and the object to be dislodged this time was *The Ambassadors*. It seemed to him 'to be not only *not* one of his great books, but to be a bad one', something like senility, but more interesting than senility, having gone wrong with James around the turn of the century (*The Great Tradition*, p. 126). James's tendency at that period was to lose 'his full sense of life and let his moral taste slip into abeyance' (*Scrutiny*, vol. 5, p. 405). Leavis seems unhappily close to Van Wyck Brooks. He also quotes Edmund Wilson from the essay in the *Hound and Horn* special issue on James on the inexplicitnesses of the later works as associated with loss of sureness in his moral touch; then Leavis questions if there is any irony at all in the presentation of the Ververs in *The Golden Bowl*. On this basis, the allegation of moral obtuseness, he mounts his attack on *The Ambassadors*; its subtlety of technique is 'not sufficiently controlled by a feeling for value and significance in living'. Has James asked himself what Paris symbolises?

> Is it anything adequately realized? If we are to take the elaboration of the theme in the spirit in which we are meant to take it, haven't we to take the symbol too much at the glamorous face-value it has for Strether? Isn't, that is, the energy of the 'doing' (and the energy demanded for reading) disproportionate to the issues – to any issues that are concretely held and presented? (*The Great Tradition*, p. 161)

This broadside has been pretty disastrous for the reputation of *The Ambassadors*. By assuming that the theme of the novel is the quality of life symbolised by Paris and missed by Strether, Leavis at best takes what is Strether's point of view at one stage in the plot for the whole truth; he trusts the teller, not the tale, and loses James's irony. The issues that are concretely held in *The Ambassadors*, surely, are those that come up between the various Americans. They have many attitudes to the glamour of living in Paris, and James deals with them with appropriately sensitive moral discrimination and a considerable feeling for the value in living, especially as regards Strether's own kind of living. One sees that Leavis's critical failure here is due to his having accepted the assumption of Lubbock and Forster that *The Ambassadors* centres on French glamour. He seems to think the novel not worth quotation even.

Attempts to counter Leavis's argument have tended to be handicapped by an initial acceptance of his chosen ground. Joseph Warren Beach, in his introduction to the 1954 reissue of his *The Method of Henry James*, for example, tries to represent James's Paris as 'the *Ville Lumière*, the place where ideas are everywhere in circulation' (p. xlviii), yet he cannot seriously mean philosophical, aesthetic or political ideas, can he? Joan Bennett considers Strether's experience of Paris to be emotional as well as intellectual; it involves 'those spontaneous joys that come from the contemplation of beauty, the culture of the mind and uncalculating love for a fellow-creature' ('The art of Henry James: *The Ambassadors*' (1956), p. 26). Such phrasing seems an apology for weakness in the novel, though Joan Bennett does note that Paris is later seen to contain 'cruelty, greed, and suffering'. 'Contain' rather begs the question of adequate presentation raised by Leavis, nor is it answered by Leon Edel's interpretation of the theme of the novel as '*seeing*', which requires the attentive reader to accept James's 'painter-sense, his brush-work, his devotion to picture and to scene' (Riverside Edition of *The Ambassadors* (1960), p. xvi). To challenge Leavis radically it is necessary to concentrate on the American element, not on Strether's impression of Paris, but on the reader's experience of Strether.

The number of critical essays on *The Ambassadors* since Leavis brought James to the fore again has been legion, surpassed, if at all, only by the totals of those on *The Portrait of a Lady* and 'The Turn of the Screw'. Several of the most interesting have been quoted and discussed already in this study (I will not reopen consideration of them at this point); altogether they touch on every conceivable aspect of the novel and reflect changing critical ideas over recent decades. A collection of *Twentieth-Century Interpretations of 'The Ambassadors'* (1969) was edited by Albert E. Stone. It included, apart from critical work already mentioned, a passage from F. O. Matthiessen's *Henry James: The Major Phase* (1944), in which the centre of vitality in the novel is placed in Madame de Vionnet's attractiveness both as an 'exquisite product cf tradition' and as a suffering individual (p. 40), and a contrasting passage from Maxwell Geismer's *Henry James and His Cult* (1964), where the portrait of Madame de Vionnet is called a 'technical "counter-screen"' designed to hide James's meaning that sex itself is disastrous and hideous (p. 288). A more fruitful critical debate emerges also in Stone's collection, that between Robert E. Garis and U. C. Knoepflmacher. Garis, in 'The two Lambert Strethers' (1961–2), had argued that Strether, far from increasing in moral awareness in Europe, is unexpectedly defeated in his attempt to fuse his conflicting feelings of admiration for and disgust with Madame de Vionnet by comparing her with Shakespeare's Cleopatra (pp. 305–16). Knoepflmacher argues that Strether's abstraction of Madame de Vionnet into Cleopatra is progressive, not a sudden reversal. He even argues that there is a resemblance between Strether and Shakespeare's Antony which converts Strether into 'a neutral figure of pathos' ('"O rare for Strether": *Antony and Cleopatra* and *The Ambassadors*' (1965), p. 343). Ludicrous though the idea of James's writing *The Ambassadors* with one eye on *Antony and Cleopatra* may be, there are certainly a few allusions to it; and the argument focuses attention on Strether's unreliable imagination and James's irony. Knoepflmacher has some illuminating asides on a critic like Leslie A. Fiedler who, simplistically, identifies James with Strether (*Love and Death in the American Novel* (1960), pp. 293–4).

Oscar Cargill in *The Novels of Henry James* (1961) provided a useful synopsis of critical and academic comment on *The Ambassadors* (pp. 302–37), especially of those who had written on its imagery. His own interpretation tends to be tentative, mainly through awareness of the faults of others. He mentions Quentin Anderson's allegorical version of *The Ambassadors* in *The American Henry James* (1957, pp. 208–31), but was too early for Brian Lee's refutation of it in his 'Henry James's "divine consensus"' (1962). Anderson's view of Strether as Mankind claiming Righteousness and as therefore doomed to divorce Appearance from Reality Lee replaces with one of him as a man who has lived through moral expansion but suffers from isolation; he feels 'these moral vibrations set up by collision with the world' (p. 12). Lee is one of a number of contemporary critics who stress Strether's closeness both to author and reader. He expands his account of *The Ambassadors* in his *The Novels of Henry James: A Study of Culture and Consciousness* (1978), arguing again that Strether comes to a sympathetic understanding of both the situation and himself. Lee inevitably finds the evidence of coarseness in Chad's character at the end of the novel a discrepancy: it cannot be reconciled 'with the general pattern of values', and is a 'major flaw' (pp. 97–8). Lee identifies too closely with Strether as the developing liberal to appreciate his discomfiture. John Goode argues in 'Character and Henry James' (1966) that '*The Ambassadors* is an intensely pessimistic novel because it portrays the destruction of the "liberal" personality' (p. 66). A more positive version of the liberal Strether is given by Brian Cox in *The Free Spirit* (1963); he sees him as one who heroically imposes 'an honest pattern on his behaviour', even if it involves 'a renunciation of vitality' (p. 58). Tony Tanner, in 'The watcher from the balcony: Henry James's *The Ambassadors*' (1966), suggests that the use of balconies has 'a profound iconographic significance', relating to James's interest in 'extensions of consciousness' (p. 43); Strether ends like an artist, 'somehow out of life, but full of a priceless vision'. If Cox and Tanner bring Strether close to the figure of the artist, Ronald Wallace brings him close to that of the fool who recognises that 'he is superbly and ridiculously human' in his innate limitations (*Henry James and the Comic Form* (1975), p. 158). Manfred Mackenzie, in *Communities of Honor and Love in Henry James* (1976), goes one stage further and brings Strether forward as 'a fully fledged divine fool' (p. 138). A still more recent interpreter, Nicola Bradbury, in her *Henry James: The Later Novels* (1979), has Strether as a mystic who achieves negative capability at a point like Eliot's 'still point' (pp. 69–71): he recoils to this vanishing-point from the exposure of 'Chad's baseness', his understanding being clearly fused 'with the omniscience of the narrator'. It was John E. Tilford, Jr, in 'James the old intruder' (1958), who had pointed out that an omniscient narrator was still an unfused presence in *The Ambassadors*. The moments when the point of view slips from Strether are more frequent than James the critic would suggest. Tilford treated these shifts in the point of view as though they were culpable inconsistencies on James's part, but it may be that they are significant pointers to the fact that the novel contains the subjective presentation of Strether without being confined to it. In this connection Sister M. Corona Sharp convincingly draws attention to the existence of an independent moral stand in the novel, provided by Maria Gostrey, a *ficelle* who lends herself 'to a characterization both demanding and self-sacrificing' (*The Confidante in Henry James* (1963), pp. 173–80). Focusing on the same character, however, Barbara Hardy argues that Maria is a functional character to whom James in the end gives *too much* life: the final renunciation of Maria by Strether only dissimulates her 'functional thinness', no previous view of their relationship having presented itself which would make the renunciation real (*The Appropriate Form* (1964), pp. 42–3).

Several critics have similarly stressed Strether's lack of male drive. For Philip Sicker, in *Love and the Quest for Identity in the Fiction of Henry James* (1980), Strether 'approaches the perfect condition of psychosexual androgyny' (p. 124). Richard Chase detected a softness at the centre in Strether's 'general lack of masculine reciprocation'

('James' *Ambassadors*' (1958), p. 136). Sallie Sears sees him as typically passive in a world dominated by aggressive American women and aggressive European men: she provides a fine analysis of his encounter with Gloriani (*The Negative Imagination* (1968), pp. 99–151). The evil glimpsed in Gloriani and associated with the past of Paris is also partly symbolised by Madame de Vionnet herself, according to J. A. Ward, who develops the insights of Graham Greene into this aspect of James, entitling his study *The Imagination of Disaster: Evil in the Fiction of Henry James* (1961). For D. W. Jefferson, however, these hints of wickedness have more the associations of Spenserian romance. The adventure and drollery of *The Ambassadors*, as Jefferson suggests in *Henry James and the Modern Reader* (1964), contribute to its effect as an American novel of manners in which 'the Americans draw out each other's Americanness': so Strether is odd and droll as well as timidly earnest. Jefferson's account of the novel's 'humour and ease' is, in my view, remarkably sensitive (pp. 188–201).

A number of recent studies of *The Ambassadors* centre on the visual appeal of its scenes. In *Henry James and the Visual Arts* (1970), Violet H. Winner argues that James draws from the art of painting the idea of the selection of significant relationships between details in landscape: in chapter XXX of *The Ambassadors* Strether's 'manner of seeing' changes from the intimate response to tranquil forms like Lambinet's to the description of 'an impressionist canvas' (p. 77), that is, from ruralism to impressionism. Charles R. Anderson also considers that throughout the novel James's descriptive language 'increasingly suggests the mode of the Impressionist painters' (*Person, Place, and Thing in Henry James's Novels* (1977), p. 239). Anderson actually adduces Monet's 'La Seine à Vétheuil' as a possible inspiration for chapters XXX and XXXI. H. Peter Stowell interprets the whole novel as an example of literary impressionism, a mode which requires the assertion of stability alongside the acknowledgement of flux (*Literary Impressionism, James and Chekhov* (1980), pp. 208–20).

Another theme of special interest to scholars has been the possible influence of French literature on *The Ambassadors*. In 1960, James W. Gargano discussed the similarities between Balzac's *Lewis Lambert* (1832), from which Strether gets his forenames, and James's novel, in '*The Ambassadors* and *Lewis Lambert*' (1960). Adeline R. Tintner considers other parallels with Balzac, his *Une Fille d'Eve* and 'Madame Firmiani', in essays in *English Language Notes* (1972) and *Comparative Literature* (1973), respectively. Philip Grover, in *Henry James and the French Novel* (1973), invokes the Goncourts, Flaubert and Daudet, concluding that '*The Ambassadors* is a subtle tribute to the living influence that French literature continued to be for James' (p. 175). David Gervais continues the general discussion in *Flaubert and Henry James* (1978).

Specialist articles of a curious nature which can be confidently recommended are R. W. Stallman's 'Time and the unnamed article in *The Ambassadors*' (1957), which claims to solve the problem of the object manufactured by the Newsome firm (it was alarm-clocks; E. M. Forster had suggested button-hooks), and a relevant piece by Patricia Evans, 'The meaning of the match image in James's *The Ambassadors*' (1955). D. J. Dooley's 'The hourglass pattern in *The Ambassadors*' (1968) and Albert O. Dunn's 'The articulation of time in *The Ambassadors*' (1972) are both intriguing essays. On linguistic points there are several essays of note; for instance, George Knox's 'James's rhetoric of "quotes"' (1956), Mary K. Michael's 'Henry James's use of the word *Wonderful* in *The Ambassadors*' (1960) and Marilyn L. Williamson's '"Almost wholly in French": the crisis in *The Ambassadors*' (1962). V. Kinoian wrote a study guide to *The Ambassadors* (1965). Robert L. Gale produced a study guide to *The Ambassadors* (1967) which is key-indexed.

The full amount of secondary material on the novel is listed most conveniently in three bibliographical works: Beatrice Ricks's *Henry James: A Bibliography of Secondary Works* (1975), Kristin P. McColgan's *Henry James, 1917–1959: A Reference Guide* (1979) and Dorothy M. Scura's longer *Henry James, 1960–1974: A Reference Guide* (1979).

BIBLIOGRAPHY

(1) TEXTS OF *THE AMBASSADORS*

'The Ambassadors', *North American Review*, vols 176 and 177 (January–December 1903), pp. 138–60, 297–320, 459–80, 634–56, 792–816, 945–68; 138–60, 297–320, 457–80, 615–40, 779–800 and 947–68.

The Ambassadors (London: Methuen, September 1903).

The Ambassadors (New York: Harper, November 1903).

The Ambassadors, The New York Edition of the Novels and Tales of Henry James (New York: Scribner, 1907–9), Vols 21–2.

The Ambassadors, The Novels and Stories of Henry James, ed. Percy Lubbock (London: Macmillan, 1921–3), Vols 32–3; Crown and Pocket editions.

The Ambassadors, ed. M. W. Sampson and J. C. Gerber (New York: Harper, 1930).

The Ambassadors, with an introduction by Frank Swinnerton, Everyman's Library (London: Dent, 1948).

The Ambassadors, Braille edition, 4 vols (Boston, Mass.: Howe, 1951).

The Ambassadors, ed. F. W. Dupee (New York: Rinehart, 1960).

The Ambassadors, ed. B. Evans (Greenwich, Conn.: Premier World Classics, 1960).

The Ambassadors, ed. Leon Edel (Boston, Mass.: Houghton Mifflin, 1960).

The Ambassadors, ed. R. W. Stallman (New York: New American Library, 1960).

The Ambassadors, with an introduction by O. Cargill (New York: Washington Square Press, 1963).

The Ambassadors, with a preface by L. Saalburg (New York: Heritage Press, 1963).

The Ambassadors, with an introduction by R. P. Blackmur (New York: Dell, 1964).

The Ambassadors, ed. S. P. Rosenbaum, Norton Critical Editions (New York: Norton, 1964).

The Ambassadors, with an introduction by N. H. Fisher (New York: Airmont, 1965).

The Ambassadors, with an introduction by A. Kazin (Toronto/New York: Bantam Books, 1969).

The Ambassadors, with an introduction by Leon Edel, The Bodley Head Henry James, Vol. 8 (London:Bodley Head, 1970).

The Ambassadors (Harmondsworth: Penguin, 1973).

(2) BIBLIOGRAPHICAL WORKS

Blanck, Jacob, 'Henry James', in *Bibliography of American Literature*, 5 vols (New Haven, Conn.: Yale University Press, 1955–69), Vol. 5, pp. 117–81.

Edel, Leon, and Laurence, Dan H., *A Bibliography of Henry James*, 3rd edn (Oxford: Clarendon Press, 1982).

McColgan, K. P., *Henry James, 1917–1959: A Reference Guide* (Boston, Mass.: Hall, 1979).

Phillips, Le Roy, *A Bibliography of the Writings of Henry James* (Boston, Mass.: Houghton Mifflin, 1906).

Ricks, B., *Henry James: A Bibliography of Secondary Works* (Metuchen, NJ: Scarecrow Press, 1975).

Scura, D. M., *Henry James, 1960–1974: A Reference Guide* (Boston, Mass.: Hall, 1979).

(3) AUTOBIOGRAPHY, BIOGRAPHY AND LETTERS, ETC.

Edel, Leon, *Henry James: The Untried Years, 1843–1870* (London: Hart-Davis, 1953).

Edel, Leon, *Henry James: The Conquest of London, 1870–1883* (London: Hart-Davis, 1962).

Edel, Leon, *Henry James: The Middle Years, 1884–1894* (London: Hart-Davis, 1963).

Edel, Leon, *Henry James: The Treacherous Years, 1895–1900* (London: Hart-Davis, 1969).

Edel, Leon, *Henry James: The Master, 1901–1916* (London: Hart-Davis, 1972).

Hasler, J., *Switzerland in the Life and Work of Henry James: The Clare Benedict Collection of Letters from Henry James* (Bern: Francke, 1966).

Hyde, H. Montgomery, *Henry James at Home* (London: Methuen, 1969).

James, Henry, *Henry James Letters*, ed. Leon Edel (London: Macmillan, 1975–   ). In progress; 3 vols so far issued.

James, Henry, *The Letters of Henry James*, ed. Percy Lubbock, 2 vols (London: Macmillan, 1920).

James, Henry, *The Middle Years* (London: Collins, 1917).

James, Henry, *The Notebooks of Henry James*, ed. F. O. Matthiessen and K. B. Murdock (New York: Oxford University Press, 1947).

James, Henry, *Notes of a Son and Brother* (London: Macmillan, 1914).

James, Henry, *Selected Letters of Henry James*, ed. Leon Edel (London: Hart-Davis, 1955).

James, Henry, *A Small Boy and Others* (London: Macmillan, 1913).

James, Henry, and Wells, H. G., *Henry James and H. G. Wells: A Record*, ed. Leon Edel and Gordon N. Ray (London: Hart-Davis, 1958).

Matthiessen, F. O., *The James Family* (New York: Knopf, 1947).

Nowell-Smith, S., *The Legend of the Master* (London: Constable, 1947).

(4) GENERAL STUDIES

Anderson, C. R., *Person, Place, and Thing in Henry James's Novels* (Durham, NC: Duke University Press, 1977).

Anderson, Q., *The American Henry James* (New Brunswick, NJ: Rutgers University Press, 1957).

Anderson, Q., 'Henry James and the New Jerusalem: of morality and style', *Kenyon Review*, vol. 8 (August 1946), pp. 515–66.

Auchinloss, L., *Reading Henry James* (Minneapolis, Minn.: Univeristy of Minneapolis Press, 1975).

Baker, E. A., 'Henry James', in *The History of the English Novel*, Vol. 9 (London: Witherby, 1938), pp. 243–87.

Banta, M., *Henry James and the Occult* (Bloomington, Ind.: Indiana University Press, 1972).

Bantock, G. H., 'Morals and civilisation in Henry James', *Cambridge Journal*, vol. 7 (December 1953), pp. 159–81.

Barzum, J., 'James the melodramatist', *Kenyon Review*, vol. 5 (Autumn 1943), pp. 508–21.

Beach, J. Warren, *The Method of Henry James* (New Haven, Conn.: Yale University Press, 1918; revised edn, Philadelphia, Pa: Saifer, 1954).

Beach, J. Warren, *The Twentieth-Century Novel: Studies in Technique* (New York: Century, 1932).

Beebe, M., *Ivory Towers and Sacred Founts* (New York: New York University Press, 1964).

Berland, A., *Culture and Conduct in the Novels of Henry James* (Cambridge: Cambridge University Press, 1981).

Bersani, L., 'The Jamesian lie', *Partisan Review*, vol. 36 (Winter 1969), pp. 53–79.

Bethurum, D., 'Morality and Henry James', *Sewanee Review*, vol. 31 (July 1923), pp. 324–30.

Blackmur, R. P., *The Art of the Novel: Critical Prefaces, by Henry James* (New York: Scribner, 1934).

Blackmur, R. P., 'The critical prefaces', *Hound and Horn*, vol. 7 (April–May 1934), pp. 444–77.

Bradbury, N., *Henry James: The Later Novels* (Oxford: Clarendon Press, 1979).

Brennan, J. G., 'Three novels of *depaysement*', *Comparative Literature*, vol. 22 (Summer 1970), pp. 223–36.

Brewster, D., and Burrell, A., *Dead Reckoning in Fiction* (London: Longmans, 1924).

Brooks, P., *The Melodramatic Imagination* (New Haven, Conn.: Yale University Press, 1976).

Brooks, Van Wyck, *The Pilgrimage of Henry James* (New York: Dutton, 1925).

Brown, E. K., *Rhythm in the Novel* (Toronto: University of Toronto Press, 1950).

Brownell, W. C., 'Henry James', *Atlantic Monthly*, vol. 95 (April 1905), pp. 496–519.

Buitenhuis, P., *The Grasping Imagination* (Toronto: University of Toronto Press, 1970).

Campos, C., *The View of France: From Arnold to Bloomsbury* (London: Oxford University Press, 1965).

Cargill, O., *The Novels of Henry James* (New York: Macmillan, 1961).

Cestre, C., 'La France dans l'œuvre de Henry James', *Revue Anglo-Américaine*, vol. 10 (October 1932), pp. 1–13 and 112–22.

Chatman, S., *The Later Style of Henry James* (Oxford: Blackwell, 1972).

Chernaik, J., 'Henry James as moralist: the case of the late novels', *Centennial Review*, vol. 16 (Spring 1972), pp. 105–21.

Clair, J. A., *The Ironic Dimension in the Fiction of Henry James* (Pittsburgh, Pa: Duquesne University Press, 1965).

Cohen, H. (ed.), *Landmarks of American Writing* (New York: Basic Books, 1969).

Colby, F. M., 'In darkest James', *Bookman*, vol. 16 (November 1902), pp. 259–60.

Conrad, Joseph, 'Henry James: an appreciation', *North American Review*, vol. 180 (January 1905), pp. 102–8.

Cook, D. A., 'James and Flaubert: the evolution of perception', *Comparative Literature*, vol. 25 (Fall 1973), pp. 289–307.

Cooper, F. T., 'The novelist's omniscience and some recent books', *Bookman*, vol. 18 (January 1904), pp. 530–7.

Cowley, M., 'The two Henry Jameses', *New Republic*, vol. 112 (5 February 1945), pp. 177–80.

Cox, C. B., *The Free Spirit* (London: Oxford University Press, 1963).

Cox, C. B., 'Henry James and stoicism', *Essays and Studies*, NS, vol. 8 (1955), pp. 76–88.

Cox, C. B., and Dyson, A. E. (eds), *The Twentieth Century Mind*, Vol. 1, *1900–1918* (London: Oxford University Press, 1972).

Crews, F. C., *The Tragedy of Manners* (New Haven, Conn.: Yale University Press, 1957).

Daugherty, S. B., *The Literary Criticism of Henry James* (Athens, Ohio: Ohio University Press, 1981).

Delbaere-Garant, J., *Henry James: The Vision of France* (Paris: Société d'Editions 'Les Belles Lettres', 1970).

Donadio, S., *Nietzsche, Henry James, and the Artistic Will* (London: Oxford University Press, 1978).

Donoghue, D., 'The American style of failure', *Sewanee Review*, vol. 82 (Summer 1974), pp. 407–32.

Dupee, F. W., *Henry James* (New York: Sloane, 1951).

Dupee, F. W. (ed.), *The Question of Henry James* (London: Allen Wingate, 1945).

Edgar, P., 'Henry James and his method', *Proceedings and Transactions of the Royal Society of Canada*, 3rd ser., vol. 12 (December 1918–March 1919), sect. 2, pp. 225–40.

Edgar, P., *Henry James: Man and Author* (Boston, Mass.: Houghton Mifflin, 1927).

Edel, Leon (ed.), *Henry James: A Collection of Critical Essays* (Englewood Cliffs, NJ: Prentice-Hall, 1963).

Edel, Leon, and Lind, I. D., introduction to *Parisian Sketches: Letters to the New York Tribune, 1875–1876* (New York: New York University Press, 1957).

Egan, M., *Henry James: The Ibsen Years* (London: Vision Press, 1972).

Eliot, T. S., 'In memory of Henry James', *Egoist*, vol. 5 (January 1918), pp. 1–2; *Little Review*, vol. 5 (August 1918), pp. 44–53.

Eliot, T. S., 'A prediction in regard to three English authors', *Vanity Fair* (New York), vol. 21 (February 1924), pp. 29 and 98.

Elton, O., 'The novels of Mr Henry James', *Quarterly Review*, vol. 198 (October 1903), pp. 358–79.

Fay, E. G., 'Henry James as a critic of French literature', *French American Review*, vol. 2 (September 1949). pp. 184–93.

Fiderer, G., 'Henry James's discriminated occasion', *Critique*, vol. 11 (1969), pp. 56–69.

Fogel, D. M., *Henry James and the Structure of the Romantic Imagination* (Baton Rouge, La: Louisiana State University Press, 1981).

Forster, E. M., *Aspects of the Novel* (London: Arnold, 1927).

Fox, H., *Henry James: A Critical Introduction* (Conesville, Ia: Westburg, 1968).

Fullerton, M., 'The art of Henry James', *Quarterly Review*, vol. 212 (April 1910), pp. 393–408.

Gale, R. L., *The Caught Image* (London: Oxford University Press, 1964).

Gard, R. (ed.), *Henry James: The Critical Heritage* (London: Routledge & Kegan Paul, 1968).

Garnier, M. R., *Henry James et la France* (Paris: Librairie Ancienne Honoré Champion, 1927).

Geismar, M., *Henry James and the Jacobites* (Boston, Mass.: Houghton Mifflin, 1963); published in Britain as *Henry James and His Cult* (London: Chatto & Windus, 1964).

Gerould, K. F., 'Stream of consciousness', *Saturday Review of Literature*, vol. 4 (22 October 1927), pp. 233–5.

Gervais, D., *Flaubert and Henry James* (London: Macmillan, 1978).

Goode, J. (ed.), *The Air of Reality: New Essays on Henry James* (London: Methuen, 1972).

Goode, J., '"Character" and Henry James', *New Left Review*, vol. 40 (November–December 1966), pp. 55–75.

Gordon, C., *How to Read a Novel* (New York: Viking, 1957).

Grabo, C. H., *The Technique of the Novel* (New York: Scribner, 1928).

Graham, K., *Henry James: The Drama of Fulfilment* (Oxford: Clarendon Press, 1975).

Grattan, C. H., *The Three Jameses: A Family of Minds* (New York: New York University Press, 1932).

Greene, Graham, 'Henry James – an aspect', in *Contemporary Essays: 1933*, ed. S. Norman (London: Mathews & Marrot, 1933), pp. 67–75.

Greene, Graham, 'Henry James: the private universe', in *The English Novelists*, ed. D. Verschoyle (London: Chatto & Windus, 1936), pp. 215–28.

Gretton, M. S., 'Mr Henry James and his prefaces', *Contemporary Review*, vol. 101 (January 1912), pp. 69–78.

Grover, P., *Henry James and the French Novel* (London: Elek, 1973).

Hardy, B., *The Appropriate Form* (London: Athlone Press, 1964).

Hocks, R. A., *Henry James and the Pragmatistic Thought* (Chapel Hill, NC: University of North Carolina Press, 1974).

Holder, A., 'On the structure of Henry James's metaphors', *English Studies*, vol. 41 (October 1960), pp. 289–97.

Holland, L. B., *The Expense of Vision* (London: Oxford University Press, 1964).

Howells, William Dean, 'Mr Henry James's later work', *North American Review*, vol. 176 (Janaury 1903), pp. 125–37.

Hutchinson, S., *Henry James: An American as Modernist* (London: Vision Press, 1982).

Isle, W., *Experiments in Form: Henry James's Novels, 1896–1901* (London: Oxford Univeristy Press, 1968).

'James's achievement', *Edinburgh Review*, vol. 197 (January 1903), pp. 59–85.

Jefferson, D. W., *Henry James* (Edinburgh: Oliver & Boyd, 1960).

Jefferson, D. W., *Henry James and the Modern Reader* (Edinburgh: Oliver & Boyd, 1964).

Jones-Evans, M., 'Henry James's year in France', *Horizon*, vol. 14 (July 1946), pp. 52–60.

Kappeler, S., *Writing and Reading in Henry James* (London: Macmillan, 1980).

Kelley, C. P., *The Early Development of Henry James* (Urbana, Ill.: University of Illinois Press, 1930).

Knights, L. C., 'Henry James and the trapped spectator', *Southern Review*, vol. 4 (Winter 1939), pp. 600–15.

Krook, D., *The Ordeal of Consciousness in Henry James* (Cambridge: Cambridge University Press, 1962).

Kubal, D. L., 'Henry James and the supreme value', *Arizona Quarterly*, vol. 22 (Summer 1966), pp. 101–14.

Leavis, F. R., *The Great Tradition* (London: Chatto & Windus, 1948).

Leavis, F. R., 'Henry James', *Scrutiny*, vol. 5 (March 1937), pp. 398–417.

Lebowitz, N., *The Imagination of Loving: Henry James's Legacy to the Novel* (Detroit, Mich.: Wayne State University Press, 1965).

Lee, B., 'Henry James's "divine consensus"', *Renaissance and Modern Studies*, vol. 6 (1962), pp. 5–24.

Lee, B., *The Novels of Henry James: A Study of Culture and Consciousness* (London: Arnold, 1978).

'Lee, Vernon' (Violet Paget), 'The handling of words: Meredith, Henry James', *English Review*, vol. 5 (June 1910), pp. 427–41.

Leyburn, E. D., *Strange Alloy: The Relation of Comedy to Tragedy in the Fiction of Henry James* (Chapel Hill, NC: University of North Carolina Press, 1968).

Liddell, R., *A Treatise on the Novel* (London: Cape, 1947).

Lodge, D., *Language of Fiction* (London: Routledge & Kegan Paul, 1966).

Long, R. E., *The Great Succession: Henry James and the Legacy of Hawthorne* (Pittsburgh, Pa: University of Pittsburgh Press, 1979).

Lubbock, Percy, *The Craft of Fiction* (London: Cape, 1921).

McCarthy, H. T., 'Henry James and the American aristocracy', *American Literary Realism*, vol. 4 (Winter 1971), pp. 61–71.

McCullough, B., *Representative English Novelists: Defoe to Conrad* (New York: Harper, 1947).

McElderry, B. R., Jr, *Henry James* (New York: Twayne, 1965).

Mackenzie, M., *Communities of Honor and Love in Henry James* (Cambridge, Mass.: Harvard University Press, 1976).

Marks, R., *James's Later Novels: An Interpretation* (New York: William–Frederick, 1960).

Martin, J., *Harvests of Change: American Literature, 1865–1914* (Englewood Cliffs, NJ: Prentice-Hall, 1967).

Matthiessen, F. O., *Henry James: The Major Phase* (New York: Oxford University Press, 1944).

Maugham, W. Somerset, *Ten Novels and Their Authors* (London: Heinemann, 1954).

Menikoff, B., 'Punctuation and point of view in the late style of Henry James', *Style*, vol. 4 (Winter 1970), pp. 29–47.

Menikoff, B., 'The subjective pronoun in the late style of Henry James', *English Studies*, vol. 52 (October 1971), pp. 436–41.

Miller, J. E., introduction to *Theory of Fiction: Henry James* (Lincoln, Neb.: Nebraska University Press, 1972).

Mizener, A., *Twelve Great American Novels* (New York: New American Library, 1967).

Mlikotin, A. M., *Genre of the 'International Novel' in the Works of Turgenev and Henry James* (Los Angeles, Calif.: University of Southern California Press, 1971).

Moore, Harry T., *Henry James and His World* (London: Thames & Hudson, 1974).

Moore, Marianne, 'Henry James as a characteristic American', *Hound and Horn*, vol. 7 (April–May 1934), pp. 363–72.

Mordell, A., introduction to *Literary Reviews and Essays by Henry James* (New York: Twayne, 1957).

Mulqueen, J. E.., 'Perfection of a pattern', *Arizona Quarterly*, vol. 27 (Summer 1971), pp. 133–42.

Nance, W. L., 'Eden, Oedipus, and rebirth in American fiction', *Arizona Quarterly*, vol. 31 (Spring 1975), pp. 353–65.

Nettels, E., *James and Conrad* (Athens, Ga: University of Georgia Press, 1977).

O'Neill, J. P., *Workable Design: Action and Situation in the Fiction of Henry James* (Port Washington, NY: Kennikat, 1973).

Perosa, S., *Henry James and the Experimental Novel* (Charlottesville, Va: Virginia University Press, 1978).

Pirie, G., *Henry James* (London: Evans, 1974).

Poirier, R., *A World Elsewhere* (New York: Oxford University Press, 1966).

Pound, Ezra, 'Henry James', *Egoist*, vol. 5 (Janaury 1918), pp. 2–3; *Little Review*, vol. 5 (August 1918), pp. 5–41 and 62–4.

Powers, L. H., *Henry James: An Introduction and Interpretation* (New York: Holt, Rinehart & Winston, 1970).

Powers, L. H., *Henry James's Major Novels: Essays in Criticism* (East Lansing, Mich.: Michigan State University Press, 1973).

Preston, H. W., 'The latest novels of Howells and James', *Atlantic Monthly*, vol. 91 (January 1903), pp. 77–82.

Purdy, S. B., 'Henry James and the *mot juste*', *Wisconsin Studies in Literature*, vol. 6 (1969), pp. 118–25.

Purdy, S. B., *The Hole in the Fabric* (Pittsburgh, Pa: University of Pittsburgh Press, 1977).

Putt, S. G., *A Reader's Guide to Henry James* (London: Thames & Hudson, 1966).

Rahv, P., 'The cult of experience in American writing', *Partisan Review*, vol. 7 (November–December 1940), pp. 412–24.

Raskin, J., 'Henry James and the French Revolution', *American Quarterly*, vol. 17 (Winter 1965), pp. 724–33.

Read, H. E., *Tenth Muse: Essays in Criticism* (London: Routledge & Kegan Paul, 1957).

Richardson, L., introduction to *Henry James: Representative Selections* (New York: American Book Company, 1941).

Rowe, J. C., *Henry Adams and Henry James: The Emergence of a Modern Consciousness* (Ithaca, NY: Cornell University Press, 1976).

Rubin, L., Jr, *The Teller in the Tale* (Seattle, Wash./London: University of Washington Press, 1967).

Russell, J., 'Henry James and the Leaning Tower', *New Stateman*, NS, vol. 25 (17 April 1943), p. 255.

Samuels, C.T., *The Ambiguity of Henry James* (Urbana, Ill.: University of Illinois Press, 1971).

Schneider, D. J., *The Crystal Cage: Adventures of the Imagination in the Fiction of Henry James* (Lawrence, Ka.: Regents Press, 1978).

Sears, S., *The Negative Imagination* (Ithaca, NY: Cornell University Press, 1968).

Segal, O., *The Lucid Reflector: The Observer in Henry James's Fiction* (New Haven, Conn./London: Yale University Press, 1969).

Sharp, M. C., *The Confidante in Henry James* (Notre Dame, Ind.: University of Notre Dame Press, 1963).

Sherman, S. P., 'The aesthetic idealism of Henry James', *Nation*, vol. 104 (4 April 1917), pp. 393–9.

Short, R. W., 'The sentence structure of Henry James', *American Literature*, vol. 18 (May 1946), pp. 71–88.

Sicker, P., *Love and the Quest for Identity in the Fiction of Henry James* (Princeton, NJ: Princeton University Press, 1980).

Slote, B. (ed.), *Literature and Society* (Lincoln, Neb.: University of Nebraska Press, 1964).

Spender, Stephen, 'The school of experience in the early novels', *Hound and Horn*, vol. 7 (April–May 1934), pp. 417–33.

Springer, M. D., *A Rhetoric of Literary Character: Some Women of Henry James* (Chicago, Ill.: University of Chicago Press, 1978).

Stallman, R. W., *The Houses that James Built* (East Lansing, Mich.: Michigan State University Press, 1961).

Stanzel, F., *Die Typischen Erzählsituationen im Roman* (Vienna: Braumüller, 1956); trans. J. P. Pusack as *Narrative Situations in the Novel* (Bloomington, Ind.: Indiana University Press, 1971).

Stewart, J. I. M., *Eight Modern Writers* (Oxford: Clarendon Press, 1963).

Stone, E., *The Battle and the Books* (Athens, Ohio: Ohio University Press, 1964).

Stowell, H. P., *Literary Impressionism, James and Chekhov* (Athens, Ga: University of Georgia Press, 1980).

Sweeney, J. L., introduction to *The Painter's Eye* (London: Hart-Davis, 1956).

Tanner, T. (ed.), *Henry James*, Modern Judgements series (London: Macmillan, 1968).

Taylor, G. O., *The Passages of Thought* (New York: Oxford University Press, 1969).

Tintner, A. R., 'Hyacinth at the play: the play within the play as a novelistic device in James', *Journal of Narrative Technique*, vol. 2 (September 1972), pp. 171–85.

Tomlinson, T. B., *The English Middle-Class Novel* (London: Macmillan, 1976).

Tuttleton, J. W., *The Novel of Manners in America* (Chapel Hill, NC: University of North Carolina Press, 1972).

Veeder, W., *Henry James: The Lessons of the Master* (Chicago, Ill.: University of Chicago Press, 1975).

Wagenknecht, E., *Eve and Henry James* (Norman, Okla.: University of Oklahoma Press, 1978).

Wagner, L. W., 'The dominance of heredity in the characterisations of Henry James', *South Dakota Review*, vol. 2 (Spring 1965), pp. 69–77.

Walcutt, C. C., *Man's Changing Mask* (Minneapolis, Minn.: University of Minneapolis Press, 1966).

Wallace, K., *Henry James and the Comic Form* (Ann Arbor, Mich.: University of Michigan Press, 1975).

Ward, J. A., *The Imagination of Disaster: Evil in the Fiction of Henry James* (Lincoln, Neb.: University of Nebraska Press, 1961).

Ward, J. A., *The Search for Form: Studies in the Structure of James's Fiction* (Chapel Hill, NC: University of North Carolina Press, 1967).

Warren, A., *The New England Conscience* (Ann Arbor, Mich.: University of Michigan Press, 1966).

Waterlow, S., 'The work of Mr Henry James', *Independent Review*, vol. 4 (November 1904), pp. 236–43.

Wegelin, C., *The Image of Europe in Henry James* (Dallas, Tex.: Southern Methodist University Press, 1958).

Weinstein, A., *Vision and Response in Modern Fiction* (Ithaca, NY: Cornell University Press, 1974).

Weinstein, P. M., *Henry James and the Requirements of the Imagination* (Cambridge, Mass.: Harvard University Press, 1971).

West, Rebecca, *Henry James* (London: Nisbet, 1916).

West, R. B., Jr, *The Writer in the Room: Selected Essays* (East Lansing, Mich.: Michigan State University Press, 1968).

Wilson, Edmund, 'The ambiguity of Henry James', *Hound and Horn*, vol. 7 (April–May 1934), pp. 385–406.

Winner, V. H., *Henry James and the Visual Arts* (Charlottesville, Va: University Press of Virginia, 1970).

Winters, Y., 'Henry James and the relation of morals to manners', *American Review*, vol. 9 (October 1937), pp. 482–503.

Wright, W. F., *The Madness of Art: A Study of Henry James* (Lincoln, Neb.: University of Nebraska Press, 1962).

Yeazell, R. B., *Language and Knowledge in the Late Novels of Henry James* (Chicago, Ill.: University of Chicago Press, 1976).

(5) SPECIAL STUDIES OF *THE AMBASSADORS*

Athenaeum, review of *The Ambassadors*, no. 3970, 28 November 1903, p. 714.

Auchinloss, L., '*The Ambassadors*', *Horizon*, vol. 15 (Summer 1973), pp. 118–19.

Bailey, N. J., 'Pragmatism in *The Ambassadors*', *Dalhousie Review*, vol. 53 (Spring 1973), pp. 143–8.

Bennett, J., 'The art of Henry James: *The Ambassadors*', *Chicago Review*, vol. 9 (Winter 1956), pp. 12–26.

Birch, B., 'Henry James: some bibliographical and textual matters', *The Library*, vol. 20 (June 1965), pp. 108–23.

Birch, B., 'Reply', *The Library*, vol. 21 (September 1966), pp. 250–2.

Bontly, T. J., 'The moral perspective of *The Ambassadors*', *Wisconsin Studies in Literature*, vol. 6 (1969), pp. 106–17.

Bookman, review of *The Ambassadors*, vol. 20 (1905), pp. 418–19.

Burde, E. J., '*The Ambassadors* and the double vision of Henry James', *Essays in Literature*, vol. 4 (1977), pp. 59–77.

Cargill, O., '*The Ambassadors*: a new view', *PMLA*, vol. 75 (September 1960), pp. 439–52.

Cecil, L. M., '"Virtuous attachment" in James's *The Ambassadors*', *American Quarterly*, vol. 19 (Winter 1967), pp. 719–24.

Chartier, R., 'The river and the whirlpool: water imagery in *The Ambassadors*', *Ball State University Forum*, vol. 12 (Spring 1971), pp. 70–5.

Chase, R., 'James' *Ambassadors*', in *Twelve Original Essays on Great American Novels*, ed. C. Shapiro (Detroit, Mich.: Wayne State University Press, 1958), pp. 124–47.

Cohen, S. B., '*The Ambassadors*: a comedy of musing and manners', *Studies in American Humor*, vol. 1 (October 1974), pp. 79–90.

Cosgrove, W., '"To see life reflected": seeing as living in *The Ambassadors*', *Henry James Review*, vol. 1 (1979–80), pp. 204–10.

Coursen, H. R., Jr, 'The mirror of allusion: *The Ambassadors*', *New England Quarterly*, vol. 34 (September 1961), pp. 382–4.

Cromwell, A. W., 'Innocent among the lions', *Vogue*, vol. 15 (November 1951), p. 158.

Deans, T. R., 'Henry James' *The Ambassadors*: the primal scene revisited', *American Imago*, vol. 29 (Fall 1972), pp. 233–56.

Dooley, D. J., 'The hourglass pattern in *The Ambassadors*', *New England Quarterly*, vol. 41 (June 1968), pp. 237–81.

Dort, B., 'Un roman de la connaissance: *Les Ambassadeurs* d'Henry James', *Cahiers du Sud*, vol. 38 (Summer 1951), pp. 329–33.

Dunn, A. O., 'The articulation of time in *The Ambassadors*', *Criticism*, vol. 14 (Spring 1972), pp. 137–50.

Durr, R. A., 'The night journey in *The Ambassadors*', *Philological Quarterly*, vol. 35 (January 1956), pp. 24–38.

Edel, Leon, 'A further note on "An error in *The Ambassadors*"', *American Literature*, vol. 23 (March 1951), pp. 128–30.

Edel, Leon, 'Henry James's revisions for *The Ambassadors*', *Notes and Queries*, NS, vol. 2 (January 1955), pp. 37–8.

Edel, Leon, 'A letter to the editors', *American Literature*, vol. 24 (November 1952), pp. 370–2.

Edel, Leon, 'The text of *The Ambassadors*', *Harvard Library Bulletin*, vol. 14 (Autumn 1960), pp. 453–60.

Edel, Leon, 'Time and *The Ambassadors*', *Modern Language Notes*, vol. 73 (March 1958), pp. 177–9.

Engstrøm, S., 'Epistemological and moral validity in Henry James's *The Ambassadors*', *Language and Literature*, vol. 1 (1971), pp. 50–65.

Engstrøm, S., 'Historical or moral validity, or two kinds of norms', *Language and Literature*, vol. 1 (1973), pp. 83–6.

Epifanio, S. J., Jr, 'James's *Ambassadors*: the trajectory of the climax', *Midwest Quarterly*, vol. 5 (Summer 1964), pp. 295–310.

Evans, P., 'The meaning of the match image in James's *The Ambassadors*', *Modern Language Notes*, vol. 70 (January 1955), pp. 36–7.

Finn, C. M., 'Commitment and identity in *The Ambassadors*', *Modern Language Review*, vol. 66 (July 1971), pp. 522–31.

Fletcher, P., 'The sense of society in *The Ambassadors*', *English Studes in Africa*, vol. 17 (September 1974), pp. 79–88.

Fogel, D. M., 'The Jamesian dialectic in *The Ambassadors*', *Southern Review*, NS, vol. 13 (July 1977), pp. 468–91.

Fox, H., Jr, 'Henry James and the antimonian (*sic*) James household', *Arizona Quarterly*, vol. 15 (Spring 1959), pp. 49–55.

Frederiksen, B. F., 'Moral or historical validity: Henry James, *The Ambassadors*', *Language and Literature*, vol. 1 (1972), pp. 58–66.

Gale, R. L., *Key-Indexed Study Guide to Henry James' 'The Ambassadors'* (Philadelphia, Pa: Bantam, 1967).

Gargano, J. W., '*The Ambassadors* and *Louis Lambert*', *Modern Language Notes*, vol. 75 (March 1960), pp. 211–13.

Garis, R. E., 'The two Lambert Strethers: a new reading of *The Ambassadors*', *Modern Fiction Studies*, vol. 7 (Winter 1961–2), pp. 305–16.

Gibson, W. M., 'Metaphor in the plot of *The Ambassadors*', *New England Quarterly*, vol. 24 (September 1951), pp. 291–305.

Greenstein, S. M., '*The Ambassadors*: the man of imagination encaged and provided for', *Studies in the Novel*, vol. 9 (1977), pp. 137–53.

Grigg, D., 'The novel in *John Gabriel Borkman*: Henry James's *The Ambassadors*', *Henry James Review*, vol. 1 (1979–80), pp. 211–18.

Hartsock, M. E., 'The dizzying crest: Strether as moral man', *Modern Language Quarterly*, vol. 26 (September 1965), pp. 414–25.

Higgins, J. A., 'The ambassadorial motif in *The Ambassadors*', *Journal of Narrative Technique*, vol. 8 (August 1978), pp. 165–75.

Hopkins, V., 'Gloriani and the tides of taste', *Nineteenth-Century Fiction*, vol. 18 (June 1963), pp. 65–71.

Hudspeth, R. N., 'The definition of innocence: James's *The Ambassadors*', *Texas Studies in Literature and Language*, vol. 6 (August 1964), pp. 354–60.

Humphreys, S. M., 'Henry James's revisions for *The Ambassadors*', *Notes and Queries*, NS, vol. 1 (September 1954), pp. 397–9.

Kamerbeek, J., Jr, 'Two golden nails: Henry James–Sainte-Beuve', *Revue de littérature comparée*, vol. 36 (July–September 1962), pp. 447–51.

Kaye, J. B., '*The Awkward Age*, *The Sacred Fount*, and *The Ambassadors*: another figure in the carpet', *Nineteenth-Century Fiction*, vol. 17 (March 1963), pp. 399–51.

Kenton, E. (ed.), '*The Ambassadors*: project of novel', *Hound and Horn*, vol. 7 (April–May 1934), pp. 541–62.

Kinoian, V., *Henry James's 'The Ambassadors'* (New York: Monarch, 1965).

Kirschke, J., 'Henry James's use of Impressionist painting techniques in *The Sacred Fount* and *The Ambassadors*', *Studies in the Twentieth Century*, vol. 13 (Spring 1974), pp. 83–116.

Knoepflmacher, U. C., '"O rare for Strether!" *Antony and Cleopatra* and *The Ambassadors*', *Nineteenth-Century Fiction*, vol. 19 (March 1965), pp. 333–44.

Knox, G., 'James's rhetoric of "quotes"', *College English*, vol. 17 (February 1956), pp. 293–7.

Logan, A. R. M., review of *The Ambassadors*, *Nation*, vol. 78 (4 February 1904), p. 95.

Lohmann, C. K., 'Jamesian irony and the American sense of mission', *Texas Studies in Literature and Language*, vol. 16 (Summer 1974), pp. 329–48.

Long, R. E., '*The Ambassadors* and the genteel tradition: James's corrections of Hawthorne and Howells', *New England Quarterly*, vol. 42 (March 1969), pp. 44–64.

McLean, R. C., 'The completed vision: a study of "Madame de Mauves" and *The Ambassadors*', *Modern Language Quarterly*, vol. 28 (December 1967), pp. 446–61.

Marks, S. P., 'A silent morality: non-verbal expression in *The Ambassadors*', *South Atlantic Bulletin*, vol. 39 (May 1974), pp. 102–6.

Maynard, R., 'The irony of Strether's enlightenment', *Lock Haven Review*, vol. 11 (1969), pp. 33–44.

Merrill, R., 'What Strether *sees*: the ending of *The Ambassadors*', *Bulletin of the Rocky Mountain Modern Language Association*, vol. 27 (June 1973), pp. 45–52.

Michael, M. K., 'Henry James's use of the word *Wonderful* in *The Ambassadors*', *Modern Language Notes*, vol. 75 (February 1960), pp. 114–17.

Nathan, M., '*Les Ambassadeurs* et les carnets de James', *Critique*, vol. 7 (June 1951), pp. 492–8.

Nettels, E., '*The Ambassadors* and the sense of the past', *Modern Language Quarterly*, vol. 31 (July 1970), pp. 220–35.

Outlook, review of *The Ambassadors*, vol. 75, p. 958, and vol. 78 pp. 112–13 (1903–4).

Poet-Lore, review of *The Ambassadors*, vol. 16 (Winter 1905), p. 94.

Quarterly Review, review of *The Ambassadors*, vol. 198 (October 1903), p. 358.

Reed, J. Q., '*The Ambassadors*: Henry James's method', *Midwest Quarterly*, vol. 4 (Autumn 1962), pp. 55–67.

Richards, Bernard, '*The Ambassadors* and *The Sacred Fount*: the artist *manqué*', in *The Air of Reality: New Essays on Henry James*, ed. J. Goode (London: Methuen, 1972), pp. 219–43.

Robinson, D., 'James and Emerson: the ethical context of *The Ambassadors*', *Studies in the Novel*, vol. 10 (1978), pp. 431–6.

Rose, S., 'Waymarsh's "sombre glow" and *Der Fliegende Holländer*', *American Literature*, vol. 45 (November 1973), pp. 438–41.

Rosenbaum, S. P., 'The editions of *The Ambassadors*', *The Library*, vol. 21 (September 1966), pp. 248–50.

Saturday Review, review of *The Ambassadors*, vol. 96 (31 October 1903), p. 551.

Schneider, D. J., 'The ironic imagery and symbolism of James's *The Ambassadors*', *Criticism*, vol. 9 (Spring 1967), pp. 174–96.

Shriber, M., 'Cognitive apparatus in *Daisy Miller*, *The Ambassadors*, and two works by Howells', *Language and Style*, vol. 2 (Summer 1969), pp. 207–25.

Shucard, A. R., 'Diplomacy in Henry James's *The Ambassadors*', *Arizona Quarterly*, vol. 29 (Summer 1973), pp. 123–9.

Sigaux, G., *'Les Ambassadeurs'*, *La Nef*, vols 71–2 (December 1950–January 1951), pp. 197–9.

Stallman, R. W., '"The sacred rage": the time-theme in *The Ambassadors*', *Modern Fiction Studies*, vol. 3 (Spring 1957), pp. 41–56.

Stallman, R. W., 'Time and Mrs Newsome's "blue message"', *Modern Language Notes*, vol. 76 (January 1961), pp. 20–3.

Stallman, R. W., 'Time and the unnamed article in *The Ambassadors*', *Modern Language Notes*, vol. 72 (January 1957), pp. 27–32.

Stein, A. F., 'Lambert Strether's circuitous journey: motifs of internalized quest and circularity in *The Ambassadors*', *Emerson Society Quarterly*, vol. 22 (1976), pp. 245–53.

Stein, W. B., *'The Ambassadors*: the crucifixion of sensibility', *College English*, vol. 17 (February 1956), pp. 289–92.

Stone, A. E. (ed.), *Twentieth-Century Interpretations of 'The Ambassadors'* (Englewood Cliffs, NJ: Prentice-Hall, 1969).

Tanner, T., 'The watcher from the balcony: Henry James's *The Ambassadors*', *Critical Quarterly*, vol. 8 (Spring 1966), pp. 35–52.

Terrie, H. L., Jr, 'The image of Chester in *The Ambassadors*', *English Studies*, vol. 46 (February 1965), pp. 46–50.

Thomas, W. B., 'The author's voice in *The Ambassadors*', *Journal of Narrative Technique*, vol. 1 (May 1971), pp. 108–21.

Thurber, J., Doren, Mark Van, and Bryson, L., *'The Ambassadors'*, *Invitation to Learning*, vol. 1 (Winter 1951), pp. 364–71.

Tilford, J. E., Jr, 'James the old intruder', *Modern Fiction Studies*, vol. 4 (Summer 1958), pp. 157–64.

The Times Literary Supplement, review of *The Ambassadors*, 16 October 1903, p. 296.

Tintner, A. R., 'Balzac's "Madame Firmiani" and James's *The Ambassadors*', *Comparative Literature*, vol. 25 (Spring 1973), pp. 128–35.

Tintner, A. R., 'Balzac's *Two Maries* and James's *The Ambassadors*', *English Language Notes*, vol. 9 (June 1972), pp. 284–7.

Tomlinson, T. B., 'An American strength: James's *The Ambassadors*', *Critical Review*, vol. 17 (1974), pp. 38–58.

Veeder, W., 'Strether and the transcendence of language', *Modern Philology*, vol. 69 (November 1971), pp. 116–32.

Wallace, R., 'Comic form in *The Ambassadors*', *Genre*, vol. 5 (March 1972), pp. 31–50.

Ward, J. A., *'The Ambassadors* as a conversion experience', *Southern Review*, NS, vol. 5 (Spring 1969), pp. 350–74.

Ward, J. A., *'The Ambassadors*: Strether's vision of evil', *Nineteenth-Century Fiction*, vol. 14 (June 1959), pp. 45–58.

Warner, J. M., '"In view of other matters": the religious dimensions of *The Ambassadors*', *Essays in Literature*, vol. 4 (1977), pp. 78–94.

Warren, A., 'The New England conscience, Henry James, and Ambassador Strether', *Minnesota Review*, vol. 2 (Winter 1962), pp. 149–61.

Watt, I., 'The first paragraph of *The Ambassadors*: an explication', *Essays in Criticism*, vol. 10 (July 1960), pp. 250–74.

Williams, O., *'The Ambassadors'*, *Criterion*, vol. 8 (September 1928), pp. 47–64.

Williamson, M. L., '"Almost wholly in French": the crisis in *The Ambassadors*', *Notes and Queries*, NS, vol. 9 (March 1962), pp. 106–7.

Wilt, J., 'A right issue from a tight place: Henry James and Maria Gostrey', *Journal of Narrative Technique*, vol. 6 (May 1976), pp. 77–91.

Wise, J. L., 'The floating world of Lambert Strether', *Arlington Quarterly*, vol. 2 (Summer 1969), pp. 80–110.

Wolf, H. R., 'The psychology and aesthetics of abandonment in *The Ambassadors*', *Literature and Psychology*, vol. 21 (1971), pp. 133–47.

Young, R. E., 'An error in *The Ambassadors*', *American Literature*, vol. 22 (November 1950), pp. 245–53.

Young, R. E., 'A final note on *The Ambassadors*', *American Literature*, vol. 23 (January 1952), pp. 487–90.

(6) RELATED WORKS (NON-FICTION)

Altick, R. D., *The Art of Literary Research* (New York: Norton, 1963).

Annuaire-Almanach du commerce de l'industrie (Paris: Didot-Bottin, 1899).

Arnold, Matthew, *The Complete Prose Works of Matthew Arnold*, ed. R. H. Super, 11 vols (Ann Arbor, Mich.: University of Michigan Press, 1960–76).

Asselineau, R., 'The French stream in American literature', *Yearbook of Comparative and General Literature*, vol. 17 (1968), pp. 29–39.

Bally, C., 'Le style indirect libre', *Germanisch-Romanische Monatschrift*, vol. 4 (1912), pp. 549–56 and 597–606.

Baedeker, K., *Paris nebst einigen Routen durch das Nördliche Frankreich*, 15th edn (Leipzig: Baedeker, 1900).

Bellringer, Alan W., '*The Sense of the Past*: the backward vision', *Forum for Modern Language Studies*, vol. 17 (July 1981), pp. 201–16.

Bellringer, Alan W., '*The Tragic Muse*: the objective centre', *Journal of American Studies*, vol. 4 (1970), pp. 77–89.

Bellringer, Alan W., '*The Wings of the Dove*: the main image', *Modern Language Review*, vol. 74 (Janaury 1979), pp. 12–25.

Berthoff, W., *The Ferment of Realism* (New York: Free Press, 1965).

Bewley, M., *The Complex Fate* (London: Chatto & Windus, 1952).

The Book of France (London: Macmillan, 1915).

Booth, W. C., *The Rhetoric of Fiction* (Chicago, Ill.: University of Chicago Press, 1961).

Bradbury, M., *The Expatriate Tradition in American Literature* (Durham: British Association for American Studies, 1982).

Bradbury, M., 'The expatriate tradition in American writing', *Yearbook of English Studies*, vol. 8 (1978), pp. 15–39.

Brooks, Van Wyck, *The World of Washington Irving* (London/New York: Dent, Dutton, 1945).

Crèvecœur, J. H. St J. de, *Letters from an American Farmer, 1782*, ed. A. E. Stone (Harmondsworth: Penguin, 1981).

Darwin, C., *On the Origin of Species* (London: Murray, 1859).

Downie, D., *The Paris Directory and Anglo-American Travellers' Guide* (Paris: Downie, 1896).

Eakin, P. J., *The New England Girl* (Athens, Ga: University of Georgia Press, 1976).

Fiedler, L. A., *Love and Death in the American Novel* (New York: Criterion, 1960).

Firebaugh, J. J., 'The Ververs', *Essays in Criticism*, vol. 4 (October 1954), pp. 400–10.

Ford, Ford Madox, *Memories and Impressions* (Harmondsworth: Penguin, 1979).

Franklin, Benjamin, *Benjamin Franklin, Autobiography, 1771–1789*, ed. D. Welland (Oxford: Clarendon Press, 1970).

Friedman, A., *The Turn of the Novel* (New York: Oxford University Press, 1966).

Glauser, L., *Die erlebte Rede im Englischen Roman des 19. Jahrhunderts* (Bern: Swiss Studies in English, 1948).

Gross, T. I., *The Heroic Ideal in American Literature* (London: Collier-Macmillan, 1971).

Gunn, G. B., *Henry James, Senior* (Chicago, Ill.: American Library Association, 1974).

Holder, A., *Three Voyagers in Search of Europe* (London: Oxford University Press, 1966).

James, Alice, *The Diary of Alice James*, ed. Leon Edel (London: Hart-Davis, 1965).

James, Henry, 'Anthony Trollope', *Century Magazine*, vol. 26 (July 1883), pp. 384–95.

James, Henry, *'Essays in Criticism'*, *North American Review*, vol. 101 (July 1865), pp. 206–13.

James, Henry, *Hawthorne* (London: Macmillan, 1879).

James, Henry, *A Little Tour in France* (Boston, Mass.: Osgood, 1884; reissued London: Heinemann, 1900).

James Henry, introduction to *Madame Bovary*, trans. W. G. Blaydes (London: Heinemann, 1902), pp. v–xliii.

James, Henry, 'Matthew Arnold', *English Illustrated Magazine* (January 1884), pp. 241–6.

James, Henry, *'Middlemarch'*, *Galaxy*, vol. 15 (March 1873), pp. 424–8.

James, Henry, 'The Minor French Novelists', *Galaxy*, vol. 21 (February 1876), pp. 219–33.

James, Henry, 'Mr Walt Whitman', *Nation*, vol. 1 (16 November 1865), pp. 625–6.

James, Henry, *Notes on Novelists* (London: Dent, 1914).

James, Henry, 'The Novels of George Eliot', *Atlantic Monthly*, vol. 18 (October 1866), pp. 479–92.

James, Henry, *Partial Portraits* (London/New York: Macmillan, 1888).

James, Henry, *Portraits of Places* (London: Macmillan, 1883).

James, Henry, *William Wetmore Storey and His Friends* (Edinburgh/London: Blackwood, 1903).

James, Henry, *Within the Rim* (London: Collins, 1919).

James, Henry, Sr, *The Literary Remains of Henry James*, ed. William James (Boston, Mass./New York: Osgood, 1884).

James, Henry, Sr, *Moralism and Christianity, or Man's Experience and Destiny* (New York: Redfield, 1850).

James, Henry, Sr, *The Nature of Evil* (New York: Appleton, 1855).

James, Henry, Sr, *The Secret of Swedenborg* (Boston, Mass.: Fields, Osgood, 1869).

James, Henry, Sr, *Society, the Redeemed Form of Man, and the Earnest of God's Omnipotence in Human Nature* (Boston, Mass.: Houghton, Osgood, 1879).

James, William, *The Meaning of Truth* (London: Longmans, 1909).

James, William, *A Pluralistic Universe* (London: Longmans, 1909).

James, William, *Pragmatism: A New Name for Some Old Ways of Thinking* (London: Longmans, 1907).

James, William, *The Varieties of Religious Experience* (London: Longmans, 1902).

Kenton, E., 'Henry James to the ruminant reader: *The Turn of the Screw*', *The Asts*, vol. 6 (November 1924), pp. 245–55.

Lease, B., *Anglo-American Encounters* (Cambridge: Cambridge University Press, 1981).

Leavis, F. R., *The Common Pursuit* (London: Chatto & Windus, 1952).

Leavis, Q. D., 'A note on literary indebtedness: Dickens, George Eliot, Henry James', *Hudson Review*, vol. 8 (Autumn 1955), pp. 423–8.

Lewes, G. H., 'The study of psychology', in his *Problems of Life and Mind*, vol. 3, no. 1 (London: Trübner, 1879).

Lips, M., *Le Style indirect libre* (Paris: Payot, 1926).

McMurray, W., 'Pragmatic realism in *The Bostonians*', *Nineteenth-Century Fiction*, vol. 16 (March 1962), pp. 339–44.

Martineau, Harriet, *Society in America* (New York and London: Saunders & Otley, 1837, 1839).

Muir, Edwin, *The Structure of the Novel* (London: Hogarth Press, 1928).

Nevins, A., *American Social History as Recorded by British Travellers* (London: Allen & Unwin, 1923).

Newman, J. H., *An Essay in Aid of a Grammar of Assent* (London: Burns, Oates, 1870).

Pascal, R., *The Dual Voice: Free Indirect Speech and Its Functioning in the Nineteenth-Century European Novel* (Manchester: Manchester University Press, 1977).

Pater, W. H., 'Poems by William Morris', *Westminster Review*, NS, vol. 34, (October 1868), pp. 300–12.

Pater, W. H., *Studies in the History of the Renaissance* (London: Macmillan, 1873); 2nd edn (under title *The Renaissance: Studies in Art and Poetry*) 1877; 3rd edn 1888.

Raleigh, J. H., *Matthew Arnold and American Culture* (Berkeley/Los Angeles, Calif.: University of California Press, 1957).

Rogers, R., *A Psychoanalytic Study of the Double in Literature* (Detroit, Mich.: Wayne State University Press, 1970).

Skard, S., *American Studies in Europe* (Philadelphia, Pa: University of Pennsylvania Press, 1958).

Spender, Stephen, *The Destructive Element* (London: Cape, 1935).

Tanner, T., *The Reign of Wonder* (Cambridge: Cambridge Univeristy Press, 1965).

Thoreau, H. D., *Walden* (Boston, Mass.: Ticknor & Fields, 1854).

The Times Literary Supplement, review of *The Wings of the Dove*, 5 September 1902, p. 263.

Tocqueville, A. Clérél de, *De la démocratie en Amérique* (Paris: Gosselin, 1835–40).

Trollope, Anthony, *North America* (London: Chapman & Hall, 1862).

Ullmann, S., *Style in the French Novel* (Cambridge: Cambridge University Press, 1957).

Wells, H. G., *Boon* (London: Fisher Unwin, 1915).

Wharton, Edith, *A Backward Glance* (New York: Appleton–Century, 1934).

Young, F. H., *The Philosophy of Henry James, Sr* (New York: Bookman, 1951).

INDEX